Romanian History

A Captivating Guide to the History of Romania and Vlad the Impaler

Free Bonus from Captivating History (Available for a Limited time)

Hi History Lovers!

Now you have a chance to join our exclusive history list so you can get your first history ebook for free as well as discounts and a potential to get more history books for free! Simply visit the link below to join.

Captivatinghistory.com/ebook

Also, make sure to follow us on Facebook, Twitter and Youtube by searching for Captivating History.

Contents

Part 1: History of Romania

A Captivating Guide to Romanian History, Including Events Such as the First Roman–Dacian War, Raids of Vlad III Dracula against the Ottoman Empire, the Great War, and World War 2

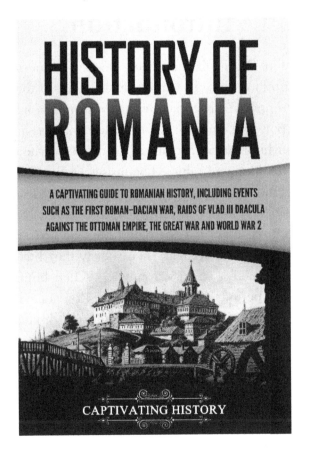

Introduction

The history of Romania has been deeply connected with its geographic position since its earliest times. It lies at the crossroads of not only important historical trading and migratory routes but also of very powerful empires. As such, Romania was influenced by the many neighbors it had, yet it managed to stay true to itself and preserve its tradition and values. The history of Romania starts with the first migrations of Homo sapiens who wandered on European soil. The evidence found in the caves around the Danube River suggests that it was there that the oldest humans first came to settle and mix with the Neanderthals. The society they built slowly but steadily transformed itself into a culture. When humans entered the Neolithic period, the territory of Romania found itself inhabited by various peoples who migrated from distant lands. The most important group was the Dacians, as modern Romanians see them as their ancestors. Although little evidence is left from the early Dacian period, the Greeks and Romans would soon start writing down the stories of these magnificent people with whom they traded or fought.

The first written sources about the Kingdom of Dacia mention King Burebista and the bravery of the Dacian people. As Roman influence spread, it was only the question of time when Dacia would fall. It occurred during the reign of Emperor Trajan, who warred against the most famous Dacian king, Decebal. Romans stayed in the territory of Romania until the 3rd century CE, and they even gave the name to the future country. It is believed that Roman settlers mixed with the native Dacians, bringing about the existence of the Romanian nation. But many years would pass before the people of the region gained a sense of ethnicity and of belonging to the same country. When the Roman Empire fell, three principalities emerged in the territory of modern-day Romania: Transylvania, Wallachia, and Moldavia. They each had rulers who either hated each other or worked together against a new enemy, the same enemy as Christian Europe—the Ottoman Empire. Following the siege and fall of Constantinople in 1453, the three principalities were a thorn in the sultan's eye. They managed to maintain their independence, pay tribute to the Ottomans, and plot against them with the great powers of Europe all at the same time. This period gave Romania a series of national heroes whose deeds against the invading Turks rightfully placed them in the history books of the world.

The Ottoman presence was deeply felt deep until the empire's fall in the 19th century. This was a period of national awakening for the Romanians, a period of revolution, and great changes shook the very foundations of Romanian politics and society. Nothing would ever be the same after Wallachia and Moldavia united under the rule of the first Romanian king, Carol I of the Hohenzollern-Sigmaringen family. The royal family would become a fundamental part of Romania's history, shaping its politics and social constructions. The constitutional monarchy of Romania ended in the mid-20th century after the country survived the horrors of the two world wars. Romania stepped in both world wars, intending to gain Transylvania, a region where Romanians represented the majority of the population but had no political or civil rights. Romania suffered immense losses of lives, endured occupation, and changed sides just to integrate Transylvania, Bessarabia, and Bukovina. But the price was perhaps too high, as at the end of

World War II, Romania was occupied by the Soviet communist regime and had to either adapt or disappear.

The new generation of Moscow-educated Romanians had to lead the country through communism. As part of the Eastern Bloc, Romania could not escape this fate, but it did try to preserve its independence. However, allowing one man, Nicolae Ceausescu, to gain all the power and rule as a dictator proved to be a mistake. Romania had to endure yet another period of hardship, one filled with a lack of civil freedoms, poverty, and isolation. For forty-five years, Romanians suffered in silence, waiting for the right time. And it was the people who finally found the strength to overthrow their dictator. Led by no one in particular, the common workers fought for the freedom of the nation and a better future. Like vultures, the ex-communist politicians were ready to pick up the pieces and construct their own Romania, one sunken in nepotism and corruption. Even though it had been constantly pulled down by a series of incompetent and corrupt politicians, Romania managed to stand on its feet again. The economy started recovering after the years of abuse by the communist regime, and with it came civil rights. The country started taking its first steps toward entering the European Union in the early 1990s, but it would take another seventeen years before it officially became a member. Romania is still pulled down under the weight of its turbulent past, but the future leaves all the cards open. With EU investments and widely adopted values, and with the generation born and raised after the 1990s who more fully embrace new ideas, this country's future looks very bright indeed.

Chapter 1 – The Beginning

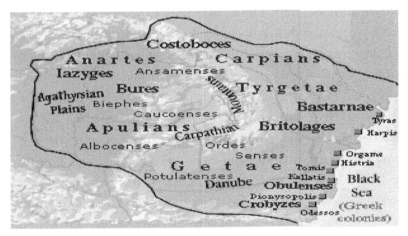

The Kingdom of Dacia during the rule of Burebista
(https://upload.wikimedia.org/wikipedia/commons/6/65/Dacia_82_BC.png)

The history of Romania begins with the Neolithic Age and the first settlements. The people gained control over the soil and learned how to grow their food, moving from a hunter-gatherer society to an agricultural one. This allowed various groups of people to grow enough in population to form permanent settlements. But the landscape of today's Romanian territory is very diverse, which allowed the people settled there to develop in more than just one way. The center of Romania is the Transylvanian Plateau, which is surrounded by the Carpathian Mountains from the west, south, and east. To the south, the mountains slope down through the hills and tablelands to the plains of the Danube Valley, reaching the mighty river of the Danube itself. Although the territory of Romania is vast and diverse, the regions are mutually connected through the tame mountain passes. The lowlands are connected by the Danube and other lesser-known rivers of the region. All of these regions, and above all, the Danube Valley, offered perfect conditions for settlement from the earliest days of human history. Thus, the caves occupying the slopes of the Carpathians were used as dwellings by the first humans.

In 2002, a cave was discovered in Romania, which was promptly named "Pestera cu Oase" (Cave of Bones). Inside, remains of modern humans were found, and they have been dated to about 37,800 years ago. Since they date so far back in history, it seems that this cave represents one of the first settlements of modern humans in all of Europe. The exciting results were discovered in 2015 when DNA analysis showed that at least 6 to 9 percent of the DNA extracted from the first remains found in the cave are of Neanderthal origin. Could this be the evidence we have been searching for to prove that the earliest modern humans mixed with the Neanderthals in Europe? Pestera cu Oase is still being researched, and it is no small task. The cave doesn't contain only human bones; in fact, the majority of the bones are of animal origin, primarily bears. It seems that the cave was a place of hibernation for bears and that the bones of humans ended up in it by accident.

During the Neolithic Revolution, men of the Romanian regions succeeded in ensuring their existence through the resources offered in nature and through the innovation of agriculture. The mountains were filled with rich forests and wildlife, as well as with different ores, such as copper, iron, and even tin. The hills were sunny and suitable for the growth of various types of cereals, as well as vineyards and fruit. The Danube was rich with fish, and it provided people with water for their fields, sustaining life itself. But when the region transitioned to the Bronze Age, its people saw constant invasions, as the Indo-European peoples moved to the continent. The moving tribes and peoples made a vital contribution to the development of the local cultures. These were the peoples that later inhabited all of Europe, and thus, the history of Romania, from its very beginning, belongs to early European history.

Although Romania can be observed as a whole, each region has slightly different aspects of society and culture. Therefore, Romania also must be observed in detail through its regions, which include Muntenia, Maramures, Dobruja, Moldavia, Banat, Bucovina, and Transylvania, among others. The regions developed separately, but through various cattle and trade paths and roads, they remained connected and influenced each other.

Numerous cultures developed in the territories of today's Romania during prehistory and early history, and to name them all would mean writing a book many times this length. But some aspects of these cultures were very similar to each other, not only between various Romanian regions but also between the neighboring countries of Bulgaria and Serbia. This is not that strange, as southeastern Europe was commonly influenced by early Mediterranean cultures. However, Romania's unique position allowed influence from Anatolia and the Near East to penetrate its regions. Romania was and still is a very large territory, and any influence that came from the outside took time to spread across the land. The cultures coming from the east influenced the regions on the banks of the Black Sea, while the Greeks and the cultures of the Adriatic Sea were strongly felt in the southern and western parts of the country.

The Dacians

The Greeks and Romans were the first to write the history of the Romanian territories. However, life was very abundant in the region even before their arrival. The written evidence of these times does not exist, so we must rely on archaeological findings and foreign records to learn about the people who inhabited the region.

Before Romans ruled the lands, it was inhabited by various Thracian peoples, with the most important ones being the Getae and the Dacians. They occupied the region between the Danube, Tisza, and Dniester Rivers, which corresponds to a large portion of what we today call Romania. The Getae and Dacians were two distinct peoples, but they were very much alike. In the past, some historians treated them as one group of people named the Getae-Dacians.

The Getae inhabited the regions of the Lower Danube Basin and had frequent contact with the Greek cities of the Black Sea. The Greeks came to the region as early as the 7th century BCE, and they founded cities on the shores of the Black Sea, intending to monopolize trade with the Near East. In fact, these Greek settlements are the reason why written evidence about the Thracians exists. Herodotus wrote his *Histories* around 430 BCE, and in it, he regularly refers to Dobruja (the modern name for the lower Danube region) and the Thracians who lived or traded there. The Dacians inhabited the lands of the Carpathian Basin. They occupied both sides of the southern Carpathian Mountains. The sources from the 1st century BCE mention that the Dacians spoke the same language as the Getae.

Both the Getae and Dacians were united into a powerful confederation under a ruler known as Burebista. Around 82 BCE, he became the king of the Getae-Dacians and strove to achieve his ambitions of expanding the territory. He immediately began forming an army, which he later used to conquer the territory of the middle Danube. In 55 BCE, he even conquered the Greek cities of the Black Sea, but this didn't stop the Greeks from trading. In fact, under Burebista, they were able to extend their trade to the inner regions of Dacia, away from the shores of the Black Sea. Burebista's capital city was Sarmizegetusa, deep in the present-day southwestern regions of Transylvania. The Greeks came there to trade, build, and teach.

During the reign of Emperor Augustus (r. 27 BCE-14 CE), Burebista came into contact with the Romans. Unfortunately, he was unwise and meddled in Roman ambitions. At the time, Roman legions were stationed in Thracian territories across the Danube, and the Dacian leader thought they were easy prey for raids. He wasn't as successful as he thought he would be, as the Romans were already known for their immense military skills and discipline. But this wasn't the first contact Burebista had with the Romans. He meddled in the power struggle of Rome's civil war (49-45 BCE), taking the side of Pompey, who went up against Caesar. Unlike Caesar, Pompey recognized Burebista's conquest of the Black Sea shores, so it was a natural decision to join Pompey in the war, which shook Rome and set the stage for the Roman Empire to rise. However, Caesar was victorious over Pompey, and modern historians believe he would have moved against Burebista next if he hadn't been assassinated in 44 BCE.

Burebista suffered a similar fate as Caesar. He was assassinated by disaffected nobles at about the same time Caesar himself. Without Burebista to push the Dacians into a confederation, his kingdom soon fell apart, with the tribal chiefs claiming their independence. The kingdom was split into five smaller ones, and their leaders repeatedly fought each other. When war didn't suit them, they tried to unite the kingdom of Burebista again. Until Decebal, none succeeded, and even Decebal, the most famous king of Dacia, never managed to reach the size of the first kingdom.

Between the rules of Burebista and Decebal, whose reign started in around 87 CE, Dacia is mentioned in Greek and Roman sources as a society divided into two main classes: the aristocracy and the commoners. All the kings, leaders, and clergy came from the aristocracy, while the commoners were simple people who provided labor and who paid taxes. The majority of the Dacian population lived in villages, where they worked the land and took care of sheep, pigs, goats, and different kinds of domestic animals. It seems the villages had the collective responsibility of paying taxes. Villagers were also responsible for providing the workforce for building projects and for the maintenance of already existing fortifications. Cities existed, for example, Sarmizegetusa, where urban life was well developed. The capital was a center where artists and traders gathered. It was also the seat of the royal administration, but each smaller kingdom had a city of its own that acted as a capital during the times of disunion. However, the size and the layout of other cities remain unknown, as very few have been found and explored.

The economy of Dacia was based on trade and agriculture. In fact, agriculture was the main source of income for the majority of Dacians. The main crops they grew were wheat, barley, and millet. Dacians were also herders, and some villages higher in the mountains were pastoral. Common domestic animals were pigs, sheep, and goats, although they did have horses, which were mainly kept as working animals. Next to agriculture and herding, the Dacians were miners. The Carpathian Mountains offered rich sources of copper, iron, gold, silver, and salt. By using these materials, artisans were able to craft various tools and develop ceramics, glass, masonry, and metallurgy. Dacians produced items for everyday use, as well as tools, armor, and weapons. The decorations they used on domestic products is a clear sign of Roman and Greek influence. But when it came to trade, Dacians mainly exported grain and other food products, as well as wood, salt, honey, and wax. The items they imported were mainly meant for the upper class, and these products included perfumes, lotions, luxury items, and jewelry. However, it seems that the Dacian trade was in the hands of foreign merchants.

By the reign of King Decebal (r. 87-106 CE), the Dacians had achieved the standard European levels of civilization, and it suited their needs well. They built around eighty fortresses (it is certain that more will be discovered in the future) and numerous religious sanctuaries, which suggest they had amazing architectural skills and solid knowledge of mathematics and engineering. The Dacians had a written language, but only a few inscriptions survived history. However, some Dacian words survived in Greek and Roman texts. It seems that Dacians also used the Greek and Latin alphabet, depending on their needs. The religion of the ancient Dacians is hard to identify, but Herodotus mentions that the Getae worshiped a deity named Zamolxis. The tradition says he was a priest and a student of Pythagoras. Once he finished his studies, he returned to his native lands to serve the supreme god Gebeleizis, with himself becoming a deity in the process. Gebeleizis is mostly known for his manifestations of thunder and lightning. He is often brought into connection with the Thracian god of storm and thunder, Zibelthiurdos. The story of Zamolxis continues to tell how he spread the idea of the immortality of the soul. There are even stories saying that the Getae and Dacians knew how to make themselves immortal. Nothing else can be said about the Dacian old religion with precision. It is fragmented and inconsistent, and describing the beliefs of these ancient peoples is a difficult task.

Celts in the North

While the Dacians occupied southern parts of Transylvania, during the 4th century BCE, the Celts arrived in the northwest. Transylvania is very rich for early Celtic archaeological sites, counting over 150. Each year, new ones are found, but the state lacks money for excessive research to be performed. The sites where Celtic necropolises have been discovered seem to be concentrated in the Upper Somes Basin and west of the Apuseni Mountains. These regions also contain some contemporary Dacian artifacts, indicating the connection between the two peoples. However, the nature of this connection remains hidden, as the items found are isolated cases, and there is no evidence of shared settlements or even settled regions.

The Celts arrived in the Transylvanian Basin in two waves. The first one was at the beginning of the 4th century BCE, and it was small in scale. The larger wave came later during the same century, and some historians consider it to be colonial by nature. First-century BCE Gallo-Roman historian Pompeius Trogus writes that the Celts were so numerous that some of them had to leave. While one part found their new homeland in the northern parts of Italy and eventually conquered Rome, others hurried eastward, crossing today's Czech Republic, Austria, Hungary, and finally settling in Pannonia and Transylvania.

The biggest foundations of Celtic cemeteries, containing over 150 individual graves, are in the Satu Mare and Bistrita-Nasaud Counties of modern-day Romania. The oldest Celtic cemetery in Romania is in Mures County, and it is also the second oldest in all of Europe. Weapons and armor were found in the graves, which suggest that an elite warrior class of Celts occupied Transylvania during the 4th century. They also prove that the Celts of this region often used the same burial sites for different individuals, reusing the grave spot multiple times. Some cemeteries contain both human remains and ashes. It seems the Celts often shifted from inhumation to cremation, but it remains unknown whether it was because of the influence of their neighbors, the Dacians, or if it was a pure coincidence.

The items found in the Celtic graves in Transylvania were typical for the La Tène culture of the period. This European Celtic culture developed during the Late Iron Age and is typical for the whole of Europe. In Transylvanian archaeological sites, La Tène pottery was found. However, it was wheel-thrown, which suggests that the arriving Celts mixed with the already existing culture of the locals. Nevertheless, the majority of the pottery was handmade, and it seems that the mixing of cultures was localized and never spread to fully engulf Transylvania. Only 11 percent of the Celtic graves discovered in Transylvania contained weapons. The weapons were ritually bent before burial. Some graves contained a sword, a spear, and a shield, but more often, they contained only a sword or a spear. This suggests the existence of a warrior hierarchy in the Celtic society, although more research needs to be done to reach a conclusion. One of the graves discovered in Piscolt (today's Satu

Mare County) contains remains of chariots, among many other artifacts. There was no weaponry in that particular grave; rather, only adornments, such as beads, brooches, and bracelets, were found, suggesting that this was a burial place for a noble female.

One of the most interesting findings in Transylvania is the grave of a "prince" from Ciumesti. It is unknown if the individual was a prince at all, but he was named this because of the richness and uniqueness of his gravesite. The main item of interest is an iron helmet with a large bronze raven on top. This type of helmet, known as the "helmet with the reinforced skullcap," is typical for the Celts who inhabited the eastern parts of Europe, but none of the other helmets have such an elaborate ornament on its top. The uniqueness of the helmet's design suggests that the individual who wore it was a very important person. Judging by the weapons found near it, this individual was a war chief of the entire area. It is believed he was buried together with his wife, as some objects typical for female burials were also found in the site.

The settlements of the Celts were mostly rural and were mainly found in Mures County and around Medias (a city in Sibiu County). The most important finding is in Moresti (today's Mures Country), which is of typical Celtic design. Celtic settlements had no fortifications, and all the buildings in the villages were shallow dugout huts containing no iron elements that would hold the wooden parts of the structure. In Transylvania and some parts of Pannonia, the Celts preferred less hilly terrain, and they built their settlements in close proximity to the rivers but far enough to avoid flooding. The main occupation of Transylvanian Celts seems to be animal husbandry, agriculture, hunting, and fishing.

For some reason, the Celtic layer of the archaeological excavation sites ends abruptly in Transylvania, which baffles scientists, as there seems to be no logical reason for it. The recent discoveries suggest the rise of a new culture, which was a mix of old Celtic and Thracian cultures. The burial sites of this period contain both typical Celtic weaponry as well as Thracian knives, pottery, and decorative items.

The Early Wars with the Romans

Decebal began his rule in 87 CE. Nothing is known of Decebal's youth, and the only sources that depict him are from the Romans, who saw him as an enemy. Thus, he is described as a ruthless, murderous individual with the ambition to endanger the integrity of the Roman Empire. It is possible that Decebal was mentioned in Roman sources even before he became king, as his predecessor, the lesser King Duras, organized a large raid into Moesia, which became a Roman province sometime in the early 1ˢᵗ century CE. Moesia extended from the Black Sea to Singidunum (modern-day Belgrade), which bordered the Dacian Kingdom. The sources mention that the leader of the Dacian army was one named "Diurpaneus," and modern scholars believe that was the early Roman version of Decebal's name. Later, it would transform into the more simple Decebalus. In this early raid, the Dacians managed to overthrow the governor of Moesia and take a large part of its territories. This was problematic enough for Roman Emperor Domitian to come and deal with them in person.

Domitian wasn't a skillful military leader, but he understood the importance of a professional approach to the problem. Even though he was present during these events, he let his trusted commander, Cornelius Fuscus, lead the expedition. Around 87 CE, Fuscus managed to push back the Dacians and stop their intrusions into Roman territory. Domitian returned to Rome with the news of victory, and he organized a celebration of a triumph. Seeing how easily the victory against the Dacian barbarians was won, Domitian decided to organize punitive raids across the Danube. Fuscus remained the leader of the Moesian legions, which means he was responsible for these new raids.

In the meantime, the Dacians had united under a single king, Decebal, who was a capable leader. He was able to mount a defense against the Roman attacks. Despite this, Fuscus still regarded them as simple barbarians, thinking they could be easily beaten. He never believed that the Dacians, even though they were united, could be a serious threat to the Roman army. Fuscus decided to ignore the unification of the Dacians and penetrate deeper into their territory to avenge the death of the previous governor of Moesia. Decebal proved his cunningness by drawing the Roman legions into an area where his soldiers were waiting to strike. The mountains and forests of Dacia were hostile terrain to the Romans, but Fiscus pushed his soldiers. In the end, the Roman commander died, together with his legion, which was annihilated. It is believed that the actual place of the ambush was in the gorge of the Bistra River, a tributary of the Timis.

Fuscus's replacement was Tettius Julianus, an experienced soldier from Dalmatia. Domitian appointed him with avenging Fuscus's death, but he didn't want to rush this time. He needed to make sure that the next military commander of Moesia would be disciplined and obedient. Julianus was a good choice, as he was known for his reputation as a disciplinarian. He successfully led an attack on Viminacium, from where he turned his legion toward the Danube. Passing the Iron Gates, the Danube's gorge between today's Serbia and Romania, he led his soldiers toward the Dacian capital, Sarmizegetusa. The Dacian royal city was defended by a fortified settlement named Tapae, where the first conflict occurred. The Dacians were defeated, but Decebal was warned of the marching Romans in time, and he was able to move his royal residence into the safety of the mountains. Nevertheless, Decebal lost many Dacian soldiers, so to inspire fear in the Romans, he cut down the woods, making fake soldiers out of the lumber, which he then dressed in armor. These makeshift soldiers were the protectors of his new residence. In Tapae, Domitian erected a monument with the engraved names of the soldiers who lost their lives in the battle. This monument survived, even though most of the names have been wiped clean from its surface by the passage of time. Scholars suspect it once held the names of around 3,800 Roman soldiers.

Domitian could have pushed forward and finished the conflict with the Dacians, but Rome was very turbulent. The Rhine border was under constant attacks, and some of Rome's northern provinces were organizing uprisings. The emperor had to put his focus on Germania, so he chose to leave Dacia for another time. He made peace with Decebal, promising him a yearly tribute to keep the peace. He also recognized the Dacian leader as the king and even sent him a royal diadem from Rome. Even though the peace was kept, Decebal never really hid his resentment toward Rome. He invited everyone who saw the empire as their enemy to his court, and he accepted the deserters of the Roman army. It is not clear if he planned to break the peace, but the evidence suggests so. Decebal tried to ally with the neighboring tribes, and although some of them refused, he made them promise they would not interfere in future conflicts between Dacia and Rome. Decebal also began inviting Greek engineers to his kingdom, who helped him build weapons and war machines. He recruited a large army and equipped it with the money he received as a tribute for peacekeeping. But even though he underwent all these preparations, Decebal wasn't the first to break the peace.

Chapter 2 – Dacia as Part of the Roman Empire

Scene of Decebal's suicide as depicted on Trajan's Column
(https://en.wikipedia.org/wiki/Decebalus#/media/File:Decebal_suicide.jpg)

In 98 CE, Trajan became the emperor of Rome. He refused to pay the tribute to Dacia that had been promised by Domitian. Instead, he decided to attack. It is possible that Decebal foresaw this behavior from Rome and that his preparation of the army wasn't intended as offensive but rather defensive. He understood well that Rome considered it insulting to have to pay tribute to other rulers. The Romans needed to clear their honor, and Dacia expected the attack. Trajan was lucky that Upper Moesia already had a garrison with a large army ready. This garrison later became the starting point of all Roman attacks on Dacia. The garrison housed two legions and fourteen auxiliary units. During the preparations for the First Dacian War, the number of units increased to twenty-one. Luckily, Domitian left the royal treasury back in Rome with a significant surplus. His successor, Nerva, never got the chance to use this money, so Trajan was well set when he decided to move against the Dacians.

The First Dacian War started in 101, with the Roman legions marching deep into Dacian territory, burning villages down. The army Decebal had gathered during his years of preparations proved successful at launching an attack against the invading Romans, but it was not sufficient to completely stop their conquest. After some lost battles, Trajan decided to use the Danube and move his army downstream to Oescus, an ancient town in what is today Bulgaria. There, he regrouped his forces and set on a march for Sarmizegetusa. The Second Battle of Tapae, which took place in 101, was a decisive battle between the Dacians and the Romans. Trajan managed to capture all the Dacian fortifications, engines, and arms. He even captured the sister of King Decebal. Realizing he was defeated, the Dacian king agreed to humiliating terms. He was to move his people from the parts of Dacia that had been captured by the Romans, treat Rome's enemies as Dacia's enemies, and stop sheltering Roman deserters. The Dacians waged guerilla warfare until 102, but it became evident they couldn't achieve anything without a strong leader like Decebal.

Although Trajan defeated Decebal, he didn't destroy him. The Dacian king used the next three years to collect a new army, and soon, he started disobeying the peace treaty with the Romans. He formed new alliances with his neighbors and started new conflicts. He even dared to annex the territory of the Iazyges (an ancient Sarmatian tribe), which lay west and north of Sarmizegetusa. That prompted the Roman Senate to declare Decebal an enemy of the Roman Empire. The Second Dacian War started in 105 when Decebal attacked a newly conquered Roman territory. Although the name of this territory remains a mystery, historians believe it was somewhere in the Banat region. Trajan was surprised by the Dacian attack, and after seeing the initial success, Decebal decided to continue harassing the Roman garrisons in the area with guerilla attacks. During one such attack, Decebal captured a Roman military commander named Pompeius Longinus. He planned to use him against Trajan or at least as a bargaining chip, but the Roman commander drank poison to avoid being used against his own empire.

When Trajan arrived in Moesia, he sent smaller forces across the Danube to raid and pillage Dacian settlements. These tactics were completely different from the ones used in the First Dacian War. This time around, the Roman emperor was trying to buy time to build a bridge over the mighty river to transfer a large army across it. Once the bridge was done, there was no stopping the Roman legions. They kept pushing forward, and by the summer of 106, they had besieged Sarmizegetusa. The Dacians successfully repelled the first Roman assault on their capital. However, the legions started cutting the water supply from the city, forcing their enemy to surrender. Once their victory was complete, the Romans leveled the Dacian capital to the ground. Decebal and his convoy managed to escape the city before its fall, but they soon realized it would be impossible for them to escape. Instead, Decebalus, King of the Dacians, committed suicide. He didn't want to be captured by the hated Romans, who were known for torturing their political and war prisoners.

Due to his victory in the Second Dacian War, Trajan decided to annex Dacia, and some of its territories became part of Moesia Inferior (Lower Moesia). The Romans claim they found Decebal's treasure, and while it is true that Rome profited immensely by conquering Dacia, there is no evidence of any kind of kingly treasure. Contemporary Roman writers claim that the amount of gold and silver captured during the wars with Dacia didn't only pay for the war losses; it also financed extensive building projects within the whole empire. The Dacian treasure was used to build new roads, which led to the territory of today's Oltenia and Wallachia. The Romans had a policy of inhabiting their newly conquered regions with their own people. But the Kingdom of Dacia was a vast territory, and Trajan decided to inhabit it not only with Romans but also with other peoples of the Roman Empire, such as Celts from Transylvania, Greeks who wished to restore their monopoly on the Black Sea trade, and Thracians. The evolution of the Dacian society ended, and with it, the Dacian civilization was gone. The Dacians were one of the few peoples who were completely absorbed into the Roman world, absorbed to the point where it's impossible to differentiate them from Romans. But they also brought change to the Roman world with their influence.

Even before the final victory in Dacia, Trajan organized its territories as a newly added province of Rome, with the capital in Ulpia Traiana Sarmizegetusa, forty kilometers (25 miles) from the old Dacian capital of Sarmizegetusa. By August 106, he had organized its civil and military administration, defined its boundaries, and organized its defenses. He even specified how many taxes should be collected from the Dacians and what percentage of said taxes would be sent directly to the royal treasury in Rome. Trajan stayed in Dacia to personally observe the execution of his plans. The boundaries of the newly acquired province became the new boundaries of the Roman Empire. It stretched from today's Oltenia to the east of the river Olt. The southern boundary was the Danube itself, while Banat and most of Transylvania presented its western and northern borders. The territory from the Olt River to the Danube Delta became part of Moesia Inferior, which also included parts of present-day Moldavia.

The new boundaries of the Roman Empire remained stable until 271, when the provincial administration was withdrawn. But even before that, there were numerous changes in the administration of the province. A notable one occurred during the reign of Emperor Hadrian (r. 117–138 CE). He divided the single province of Dacia into three smaller ones. In the north was Dacia Porolissensis, while the south occupied Dacia Inferior. The largest one was in the center, and it was called Dacia Superior. Hadrian divided Dacia so the defenses of its borders with the Iazyges and other tribes could improve. In 168, Roman Emperor Marcus Aurelius (r. 161–180) wished to centralize the administration of Hadrian's provinces of Dacia. He put them all under a single governor, whose capital was in Apulum (modern-day Alba Iulia). From this point on, Dacia remained a unified territory until the end of Roman rule.

Under Roman Rule

After Trajan's conquest, Dacia went through rigorous Romanization. During its 165 years of Roman rule, Dacia became a part of the complex structure that was the Roman Empire. It wasn't only the administration that changed. Its judicial system and the laws of the country also changed. In addition, the different peoples who were brought to permanently occupy Dacia had to think of a language of communication between themselves. Since the merchants and political leaders of the province used Latin, it was the only natural choice for widespread communication. The ethnicity of the province probably changed the most, as the various migrants diversified Dacia's demography. But the diversity could be seen on the social levels too. The highest of the society were the governors, military commanders, and wealthy merchants and businessmen. The next level were various artisans, soldiers, shop owners, and veterans of the empire's wars. The next on the social ladder were farmers and laborers, and rock bottom was the slaves.

The Dacians still formed a majority of the population, but they retreated to the countryside to live as farmers and to cultivate the land. But even in these backward villages, Dacians constantly communicated with the major urban centers. This was due to the wide network of roads, which was built for faster transportation of the legions, supplies, and merchandise. Rural Dacians were a part of the Roman economy, even if they tried to keep away from the empire's influence. It was of no use, though; if they wanted to survive, they had to give in and deal with the provincial administration of Rome. To transition from the Dacian to the Roman system, the people had to adapt some of their habits. They had to accept Latin as their official language, and to make the transition even easier, they also adopted the Roman belief system. With the diversity of the peoples who came to inhabit the new province came the diversity of religion. Christianity was on the rise in the Roman Empire, even though Christians were being persecuted. But in Dacia, the people refused to convert to the new religion because they wanted to avoid persecution.

During the first century of Roman rule, Romania experienced prosperity and general peace, although crises would occur occasionally. The period between Emperor Hadrian (117–138) and Marcus Aurelius (161–180) was the most peaceful for the region. But during the reign of Septimius Severus (r. 193–211), the barbarian tribes started attacking. With these attacks came insecurity in the Dacian province, and because of that, the economy started to decline. During the 3rd century CE, the Roman Empire was in the midst of a crisis. The emperor's authority was constantly challenged, which meant the integrity of the whole empire was challenged as well. These turbulent times were felt even in the faraway province of Dacia. At the end of the 3rd century, the Dacians were forced to abandon their northeastern territories due to the constant attacks by the Goths and Carpi. Rome was still dealing with its own internal crisis and was unable to send help. The people were left to defend themselves, but at the time, the Dacians were mostly villagers, not warriors. Those who served in the Roman legions were in faraway lands. In around 271, Emperor Aurelian (r. 270-275) moved the military and civilian administration south of the Danube, as it was being pressured by the constant attacks from the north. The Danube served as a new defensive border.

The same year, Aurelian officially abandoned the province of Dacia and made a new one in Moesia named Dacia Aureliana. With this move, the old lands of the Dacians were left exposed to the Goths. The sudden withdrawal of the Roman administration brought a decline to Dacia. The Roman influence in the province slowly died between the 4th and the 6th century. There was little to no contact with the empire, which lay just south of the Danube. The effect of the Roman withdrawal from the province of Dacia was mostly felt in the cities. The decline of urban life occurred strikingly fast, and it probably shocked even contemporary visitors, such as the traders from across the Black Sea. Even the ex-capitals of Sarmizegetusa and Apulum became ruralized, and they shrank in size as people followed the withdrawal of the Romans. The economy was affected as well. Since there was no more need for the extensive production of food and other goods, it was changed to suit local needs. The villages became the centers of society and the economy. Everything assumed more modest dimensions, from buildings to agriculture, from production to social gatherings.

Constantine the Great (r. 306-337) was the only Roman emperor who tried to integrate at least some parts of old Dacia back into the Roman Empire. However, the integration was very limited, as he was only interested in the cities on the bank of the Danube. Dierna, Sucidava, and Drobeta became Roman cities, and the Roman urban way of life continued there until the 7th century. Transylvania, on the other hand, completely lost contact with the empire. There, by the 6th century, Roman rural and urban lives, as well as Roman traditions, were forever lost.

Even after the Romans left Dacia, the territory continued to attract migratory peoples. The population of Dacia was so diverse that modern scholars simply call them "Daco-Romans." The ethnicity was lost, as various tribes and migratory peoples came to settle and mix with the locals. Because of this ethnic diversity, it is quite impossible to pinpoint the emergence of modern Romanians. The Goths came first from the Baltic regions. They didn't stay for long, but during the 4th century, they settled between the southern Carpathians and the Danube. By 332, they were the auxiliaries of the Romans. But even the Goths got pushed outside of the territory of Dacia when the Huns arrived in around 376. The Goths moved south of the Danube, while the Huns inhabited former Dacia. By 420, they occupied the territories north of the Danube Delta (today's Moldavia and Wallachia), as well as Oltenia in the west. The Hunnic Empire grew, with Pannonia becoming its center in 454. They were soon defeated by the united Germanic tribes. With the Huns being pushed back, one of the Germanic tribes, the Gepids, settled in what is today Transylvania. The quick change of the settlers of the region continued, and by 567, the Avars replaced the Gepids. In what forms modern-day Romania, the Avars created a multi-ethnic khaganate consisting of Gepids, Slavs, and a local Romanized population. As the khaganate grew, it encompassed the area between the Black Sea and the Alps.

During the 6th century, the migration of Slavs left a deep impact on the Daco-Romans. They moved from the north, reaching the eastern Carpathians, from where they turned toward Wallachia and later to Transylvania. During the early 7th century, the Slavic tribes continued their migration, crossing the Danube in the south and moving into the Balkans. The Slavs were already well established between the Danube and the Balkan Mountains when the Bulgars, a Turkic people, first came into the region. They were mostly influenced by the numerous Slavs who inhabited the region, and by the end of the 10th century, they became the modern Bulgars. Their leader, Tzar Boris I (r. 852–889), accepted Christianity and expanded the territory of Bulgaria, which absorbed most of the lands of modern Romania. The Avar khaganate collapsed once it was pressured by the attacks of Charlemagne, which allowed the Bulgarians to take some of its lands. With this move came renewed Slavic influence on the Daco-Romans, but those Slavs who remained a part of the previous Avar khaganate were assimilated by the Daco-Romans.

It was during these turbulent times of Bulgarian rule that Christianity finally penetrated the lands inhabited by the Daco-Romans. Sadly, the evidence of it remains sparse. The first archaeological evidence of Christianity in old Dacia comes from the 4th century. But at those times, the Christians came as colonists and legionaries, and they never managed to impose their religion on the local people. It was the expansion of the Bulgarian Empire during the 9th century that brought the official Christian Church to the old Dacian lands. Christians started inhabiting the lands north of the Danube and across the Carpathians, bringing their faith with them. They established the Byzantine-Slavic rites in Romania, and the old Slavic language was the first official language of the Church. To this day, some of the Slavic words, which describe the worship and everything church-related, are a part of the modern Romanian language. This connection of the Daco-Romans with the Slavs became crucial for the Romanian decision to turn to the East.

Chapter 3 – Romania, A Bridge between the East and the West

Transylvania, Wallachia, and Moldavia during the Middle Ages
(https://en.wikipedia.org/wiki/Romania_in_the_Middle_Ages#/media/File:Mihai_1600.png)

At the end of the 9th century, the Hungarians arrived in the territory of central Europe. This was a crucial moment for the further development of Romania because almost immediately, they started expanding their land possessions into Transylvania. The Bulgarian

Empire collapsed when Tsar Simeon died in 927, as there were no further obstacles to Hungarian expansion. When they migrated to the east and south of modern-day Romania, they encountered already-formed Romano-Slavic political entities, but they had no trouble bringing them under their control. The anonymous chronicle of Hungarian King Béla II (r. 1131–1141) described these political entities as duchies. The first one was called Menumorut, and it encompassed the territories between the Tisza, Mures, and Somes Rivers (approximately today's Bihor County). The second duchy was Glad, consisting of territories encompassed by the Tisza, Mures, and Danube, as well as by the Carpathian Mountains in the south. This territory today represents the Banat. The third duchy was Gely, and its territories were east of Bihor, in the intra-Carpathian region. The first Hungarians who came to Transylvania were led by tribal leaders. In the beginning, during the late 9th century, they organized their political entities, which grew into a principality during the 10th century. This principality was independent of the Kingdom of Hungary until the 11th century. It was King Stephen I (r. c. 997–1038) of Hungary who, in 1002, annexed Transylvania to his kingdom in the northwest. Nevertheless, Transylvania managed to preserve its autonomy even as a part of Hungary.

Two more peoples influenced the history of the old Dacian region. The first one was the Szeklers, a group of people whose origins remain a mystery. It is believed they are related to modern-day Hungarians and that they followed them westward during their migrations from the Ural Mountains. The other possibility is that the Szeklers came later, around the 10th century, and joined their relatives, the Hungarians, in the Pannonian Plain in present-day Hungary. They came to Transylvania in the 12th century and chose the eastern Carpathians as their settlement. More Szeklers came in the 13th century, but instead of occupying other parts of Transylvania, they chose to join their brothers in the already-established Szekler region in the east. The other group of settlers that came to Transylvania was from the lands between the Elbe River in the east and the Rhine River to the west. They were partially Germans. According to contemporary writers, they were called Flandrensi, Saxony, and Theutoni. Their migration started in the 12ᵗʰ century and lasted until the end of the 13ᵗʰ century. By then, they were all referred to as Saxons. In 1224, King Andrew II of Hungary (r. 1205-1235) issued a charter by which a large portion of land was given to these people, and they were given full autonomy in exchange for annual taxes and military service. The Saxons settled mainly in the south of Transylvania, in modern-day Sibiu County, where Saxon cultural elements can still be observed. Their presence is evident in some old family names, which are clearly of Germanic origin.

During the 14ᵗʰ century, Transylvania remained a part of the Kingdom of Hungary, but its three nationalities—the Hungarians, the Szeklers, and the Saxons—remained largely autonomous from each other. The destiny of Transylvania was completely different from the parts of Romania to the south and east of the Carpathians, the principalities known as Wallachia and Moldavia. While Romanians in the south were the main populace, in the north, they were treated as a minority. The Hungarians and their relatives, the Szeklers, were the nobility of medieval society, while Romanians mostly inhabited the rural parts of Transylvania. In Wallachia and Moldavia, the rulers were uncertain if they should lead their countries on the Western political models or the Eastern. But their territories were in the way of the Ottoman conquest, and soon, Ottoman influence would completely turn them to the East. Byzantine Christianity also played a large role in the choice of the ruling model. Romanians remained Orthodox Christians, which they inherited from the Slavic influence of the Bulgarians, and Catholicism and Protestantism never really penetrated the regions of Wallachia and Moldavia. Eastern Orthodoxy played a significant role in the establishment of the national identity of Romanians, but that doesn't mean that all the connections with the West were cut.

The higher classes of Romanians were always aware of their Roman heritage, but the shift in their political aspirations would come much later in the 17th century. Until then, the territories of present-day Romania were influenced by the East. The Ottoman conquest meant a shift of trade toward the East, which meant, as one might expect, a shift in culture and society.

Romanian Foundations

By the 13th century, the territories east and south of the Carpathian Mountains were already going through the process of state formation. The kings of Hungary claimed suzerainty over these territories too, calling them the *cnezate*, a small regional assembly of territories ruled by a *cnez*. Soon, these *cnezates* started uniting in principalities, and by the end of the 13th century, Wallachia rose into existence as a separate political entity. Some of the medieval sources refer to Wallachia as *Ţara Românească*, the Romanian Land. It was ruled by a prince (*Mare Voievod*), and in the early 14th century, it gained complete independence from Hungary. Prince Basarab I (r. c. 1310-c. 1352) fought and defeated the Hungarians at the Battle of Posada in 1330. But the defeat wasn't permanent, as even the successors of the Wallachian prince and the Hungarian king continued the conflict. However, it was confined to the territory that linked Hungary with the Danube Delta and the Black Sea.

Basarab's successor, Nicolae Alexandru (Nicholas Alexander; r. c. 1352-1364), proclaimed himself Domn Autocrat (Prince Autocrat). This title made it possible for him to rule with unprecedented powers, which he needed to reinforce his position. He founded the Metropolitanate of Ungro-Vlachia, a dependency of the Patriarchate of Constantinople. Wallachia finally got the institutions that were considered the norm for a medieval independent state, such as an authoritarian secular ruler and the dominant Church. The king of Hungary could not impose himself as a ruler of Wallachia without starting a war. Also, other religions could not establish themselves as official state religions. Nicolae

Alexandru did not only secure the independence of Romania, as he also turned it forever to Eastern Orthodoxy, setting the direction in which future Romania would evolve.

His successor, Prince Vladislav I (r. 1364–1377), on the other hand, accepted the sovereignty of Hungarian King Louis I (r. 1342–1382) in turn for the fiefdom of the territories of Fagaras and Severin, located within Transylvania. He also granted the merchants of Brasov a free passage to the Black Sea. However, Vladislav resisted Hungarian Catholic influence and preserved Eastern Orthodoxy as the official religion of his lands. He worked on strengthening the relationship with Constantinople, and he founded a second metropolitanate in 137, this time in Oltenia. He also founded the monastery of Cutlumuz in 1369, located on Mount Athos in modern-day Greece.

Just like Wallachia, the principality of Moldavia came to be, and it was located in the northeast of modern Romania. Two local rulers in Moldavia defied the king of Hungary's efforts to impose his dominion over the lands. A revolt started in 1359, and by its end, Moldavia was an autonomous principality ruled by Dragos. He was a military leader from what is today Maramures County, north of Transylvania. His countryman, Bogdan, started a second revolt in 1364, and he won independence for the region. Just like the princes of Wallachia, the Moldavian rulers sought to consolidate their positions with the help of foreign powers. But unlike Wallachia, Moldavia turned to the Catholic West rather than to the Eastern Orthodox Byzantine Empire. Latcu of Moldavia (r. c. 1367–c. 1374) asked Rome for help, and Pope Urban V named him the voivode of Moldavia. He also permitted him to start a bishopric in the capital of Moldavia, Siret (Suceava County). In the early 1370s, Holy Roman Emperor Charles IV recognized Moldavia as an independent duchy, but it seems that at the end of his life, Latcu submitted to King Louis I of Hungary. It seems that the Hungarian king attacked Moldavia or was preparing an attack when Latcu chose to submit. But at this point, these theories are only speculations, as there is no concrete evidence to support them. Some scholars even go so far as to speculate that it wasn't Latcu who accepted the supremacy of Hungary but rather his father and predecessor, Bogdan I. Latcu died probably in 1374, and he was succeeded by his brother, Petru (Peter) II of Moldavia.

Prince Petru (r. c. 1374–1391) abandoned his predecessor's Catholicism and turned to Constantinople. In 1386, he opened a metropolitanate in his capital, which had been moved to the city of Suceava. He also turned his diplomacy toward Poland, and in 1387, Moldavia became a Polish fiefdom. The famous Neamț Citadel was built during the rule of Prince Petru II, but it remains a mystery if he was the one who ordered its construction. This citadel would later play a crucial role in Moldavia's defense against the Ottomans. Nevertheless, the ruins of the citadel are opened to visitors today, and a large medieval festival is held there annually. Petru's nephew, Roman I (r. 1391–1394), succeeded Petru, and he ensured the principality's independence. Although he ruled for only two years, he managed to expand the borders of Moldavia to the shores of the Black Sea. He also took the lands between the Carpathians and the river Dniester in the north (today in Ukraine). Unlike his predecessor, Roman I didn't maintain good relations with the Polish king. In fact, in 1393, he joined forces with the ruler of Podolia (a region in modern-day Ukraine) against Poland. However, he was defeated and forced to abdicate the throne.

At this point in the medieval history of Romania, both Wallachia and Moldavia were independent. What set their rulers apart from the rest of the nobility and landowners was their wisdom to keep close to the Church. By maintaining good relations with the Patriarchate of Constantinople, both Wallachian and Moldavian rulers were anointed by the Orthodox Church. This meant they were chosen by God to lead the people and rule in the autocratic style of the Byzantine emperors. However, these rulers wouldn't be able to achieve so much without the wealth that came from the lands they owned. Once the prince became an autocrat, he gained the power to take lands that had not been under his direct control. He would then grant these lands to the *boieri* (boyars), the nobles, and the clergy in return for their loyalty. The autocrat was also the supreme commander of the military forces, both the "small army," which was made up of higher social classes obliged to perform military service, and the "large army," which was made up of all the able-bodied men in the country. As the head of the army, the autocrat was able to collect taxes, with which the costs of military campaigns would be covered.

The dominant social class was the boyars. They could be involved in the country's politics and serve the military. At first, they were called *cnez*, and they were the local clan leaders. But when the prince took control of the whole principality, their authority had to be confirmed by him. But not every *cnez* turned into a boyar. The prince rewarded loyalty, and those who were out of his favor were reduced to the status of a free peasant. Other classes were able to become a boyar through land grants and loyalty shown to their prince. They could also be appointed into the high offices if they were educated and able to lead the principality's administration. In time, a distinct difference between the greater and lesser boyars was made, which was based on the size of their land possessions or the importance of the services they performed for the prince.

The largest part of society was made up of peasants. Even here, there was a division between the free peasants and those who lost their liberty and their land. Depending on the region, the free peasants were called *Moşneni* (Wallachia) or *Răzeşi* (Moldavia). These terms are preserved in modern Romanian as names of distinct villages in their respective regions. The majority of the peasants were not free. They were obliged to pay tithes or perform laborious duties for the higher classes. The village communities, no matter if they were free or dependent, had a form of self-government through the election of a council known as the *Oameni buni şi bătrâni* ("good and old men").

Even though the prince ruled as an autocrat, that doesn't mean he had no political enemies. The prince and the boyars often engaged in a power struggle, both political or economic. The boyars enjoyed some of the administrative and judicial privileges, but they strived to decentralize the prince's grasp on the whole country. The prince was always able to counter the boyars by using his own vast lands and giving them to those who remained loyal. Of around 3,000 villages in Wallachia, only 313 were in the hands of the boyars, which enjoyed immunity. The rest was considered to be the personal possession of the prince, and as such, they were obliged to pay princely taxes. Even though the prince and the boyars clashed because of their political interests, for most of the time, they cooperated to ensure the prosperity of their lands. However, they often cooperated just so they could exploit the peasants more efficiently.

The Ottomans

Just as the two principalities of Romania—Wallachia and Moldavia—took form, they found themselves in the way of the Ottoman conquest. In 1389, the Ottoman Empire defeated the Serbian army at the Battle of Kosovo. This victory opened the way toward the rest of eastern Europe. The Ottomans advanced toward the Danube, and in 1393, they captured the capital of the Bulgarian Empire, Tarnovo. Prince Mircea the Elder (r. 1386-1418), still believed to be the greatest ruler of Wallachia, gave his best to keep the enemy at bay by using both the military and diplomacy. Unlike the enemy, Wallachia was a Christian domain, and Mircea asked the Western powers for help. During his rule, the Wallachian territories expanded to their fullest potential, as he gained large parts of Dobruja, Severin, and the Timok Valley. He was the grandfather of the most famous Romanian figure in both history and fiction, Vlad Țepeș (the Dracula).

Mircea experienced his first engagement with the Ottomans in 1394 when he took Dobruja. Sultan Bayezid I (1389–1402) took advantage of Mircea's absence and invaded Wallachia. The two rulers finally met at the Battle of Rovine, which Mircea won, preserving the independence of his country. There is no evidence to suggest he paid the *haradj*, a tribute Ottomans usually demanded to keep the peace. Under renewed attacks, the Wallachian prince was forced to retreat to Hungary, where he joined an alliance with the French and Hungarians. In 1396, as a part of the alliance, Mircea marched his army to Nicopolis, where the anti-Ottoman crusade took place. However, the Crusaders were crushed by Bayezid's forces. The Wallachian ruler retreated in time and suffered no losses. Instead, he took his army back to his own country, where he found his throne occupied by Prince Vlad the Usurper. After the Ottomans had forced Mircea to Hungary, they installed Vlad as their puppet ruler. He ruled for only three years, and during that time, he led an exclusively pro-Ottoman policy.

But even though Vlad I of Wallachia was a pro-Ottoman and a usurper, he was a very strong ruler. Backed by his new allies, he was able to crush the Hungarian invasion, whose purpose was to return Wallachia to Christianity. After the defeat, the Hungarian king thought Wallachia would be lost forever, but in truth, Vlad never strayed from Christianity. Instead, he confirmed it through his relationship with Stephen I of Moldavia and through the diplomatic missions in Poland. In 1397, Mircea defeated Vlad I the Usurper and took back Wallachia. With the help of the Hungarians, Mircea was able to stop two more Ottoman military expeditions, one in 1397 and the other in 1400. Three years later, Sultan Bayezid I died in captivity after the Battle of Ankara, creating a power vacuum in the empire. It took more than ten years for the Turks to stabilize their leadership, doing so when Mehmed I took the throne in 1413. During those ten years, Mircea gave his support to both Ottoman throne pretenders, Musa and Mehmed, in hopes he would gain some favorable terms for coexistence.

However, before helping Musa take the throne of the European part of the Ottoman Empire in 1411, he took Dobruja back for Wallachia. He then supported Musa's endeavors to overthrow Sultan Suleyman and rise to the throne as the co-ruler of the Ottoman Empire, together with his brother Mehmed, who controlled Anatolia.

But Musa's reign was short. In 1413, he was killed by Mehmed. In 1417, Mehmed decided to attack Wallachia. Mircea was already old by this time and unable to defend his lands from yet another invasion. Instead, he signed a treaty with the Ottomans and agreed to pay an annual tribute of 3,000 gold pieces. However, he made Mehmed promise he would not attempt to turn Wallachia into an Ottoman province. Years of peace followed, but they proved to be nothing more than the calm before the storm. By 1431, Sultan Murad II (r. 1421-1444, 1446-1451) had turned Wallachia into a vassal state, which forced Wallachia to not only pay the yearly tribute but to also send military help whenever the sultan called. The princes were also obliged to send sons of the boyars as hostages in Constantinople.

Moldavia was farther away from the main Ottoman operations in the region, and because of this, it didn't suffer attacks, at least at first. The Moldavian princes managed to keep the Ottomans at bay until the first half of the 16th century. However, this doesn't mean there were no conflicts. The first encounter between Moldavia and the Ottoman Turks occurred in 1420. The Turkish army besieged the Black Sea port of Cetatea Alba ("White Citadel"), but they couldn't capture it. To secure the peace, the Moldavian princes sent "gifts" to the sultans. Although these gifts could be seen as *haradj*, the Turks themselves referred to them as *peşkeş*, the presents. But in 1456, Sultan Mehmed II demanded *haradj* from Prince Petru Aron of Moldavia (r. 1451-1452, 1454-1455, 1455-1457) to finance his campaign against Hungary. Prince Petru agreed to pay it to preserve the independence of Moldavia.

When one of the greatest Moldavian princes, Stephen the Great (1457-1504), succeeded the throne, he realized his immediate neighbors intended to expand their territory. To the south, it was the Ottomans; to the west, it was Hungary; and to the north, it was Poland. All of them wanted direct control over the Moldavian territories because of their position on the Black Sea. By gaining these territories, they would also gain full control of the Black Sea trade routes. To keep the independence of his own country, Stephen had to learn how to juggle between his three neighbors. To the Ottomans, he paid tribute when he saw he could gain something out of it. To King Casimir IV of Poland, he paid homage to admit his sovereignty only when it was wise to do so. When Stephen had no other options, he would pick up his weapons and fight. The first opportunity for war came when the Hungarian king, Matthias Corvinus (r. 1458-1490), invaded Moldavia in 1467. At the Battle of Baia, Stephen of Moldavia managed to defeat the Hungarian king and drive him out of his lands. This was also the last large-scale attempt of the Hungarian kings to impose their authority over Moldavia.

In 1475, Stephen had to pick up arms yet again and fight the Ottomans at the Battle of Vaslui. He managed to win this battle too, and after it, he constantly attempted to ally with the Western Christian powers in vain. Pope Sixtus IV awarded him the title "Defender of Christ," but he was unable to win against the Ottomans. While on his deathbed, he advised his son and successor, Bogdan III, to remain on good terms with the Turks. He was well aware that alone, he wouldn't be able to fight them off and preserve Moldavian independence. Bogdan III and his successors managed to maintain the independence of Moldavia until 1538 when Sultan Suleiman I (r. 1520-1566) brought it under his control. To secure Moldavian allegiance to the Ottoman Empire, Suleiman disposed of its prince, Petru Aron, and placed a puppet ruler on the throne named Stephen Lacusta.

Both principalities, Wallachia and Moldavia, changed their judicial systems to more comfortably fit into the Ottoman sphere of influence. The main changes came in the 15th and 16th centuries, and they were instigated by Ottoman pragmatism and legal theory, but they also had to conform to the political and social conditions of Moldavia and Wallachia, as well as to the international circumstances of medieval Europe. The Ottomans observed the Islamic law of nations, and according to it, the principalities occupied the intermediate zone between the domain of war (*dar al-Harb*) and the domain of Islam (*dar al-Islam*). That meant that the territories were subject to the Muslim ruler and Islamic law, even though its people practiced their own religion, one that was not Islam. By the 16th century, the principalities were no longer an intermediate zone, but they hadn't become fully Islamic lands either. Some contemporary and modern historians call them the domain of peace (*dar al-Sulh*). But others insisted that Wallachia and Moldavia belonged to the domain of armistice (*dar al-muvada'a*) or the domain of protection and tribute (*dar al-dhimma*). This classification was accepted by the Hanafi school of law, which was predominant in the Ottoman Empire at the time.

The two principalities shared the protection of the sultan, and in this way, the relations between them became tighter. Wallachia and Moldavia escaped being incorporated into the Ottoman political system, which was the fate of Bulgaria and Serbia. The principalities had almost full internal autonomy, which meant the sultans recognized the prince's and boyars' right to rule. They also never meddled in the internal politics of the regions and prevented other Muslim individuals from influencing the political life of these two vassal states. Boyars elected the prince, but the sultan was the only one who was able to approve the choice and present the new prince with the insignia of his office. Because Wallachia and Moldavia enjoyed such autonomy, the social, cultural, political, and religious lives of the principalities didn't change. But when it came to foreign affairs, the sultan would take matters into his own hands.

He prohibited the princes of Wallachia and Moldavia from creating any diplomatic relationships with foreign powers, and the defense of the principalities against foreign attacks was solely his duty.

Wallachia and Moldavia were under the Ottoman sphere of influence, but unlike Serbia and Bulgaria, which were south of the Danube, they were never really occupied or turned into one of the empire's provinces. The question is, what was so special about these principalities that their destiny was completely different from the rest of the Christian world conquered by the Ottoman Empire? The answer lies in the fact that the principalities continued to grow their relationship with the empire, forcing the Turks to restrain themselves. During the 14th and 15th centuries, Wallachia and Moldavia were simply not worth the bother, as the sultans' main assault was planned to happen in the west. At first, it was enough to prevent the principalities from joining the anti-Ottoman coalitions. Also, the princes and the boyars seemed to cooperate very well, giving the sultans nothing to worry about. Another reason for Turkish restraint comes from an economic point of view. The principalities filled the royal treasury with sufficient riches, and they provided food to Constantinople, as well as arms, food, and animals to the Ottoman army. If there were major changes in the administration of the principalities, the sultan would risk local Ottoman governors rising to power. Everything worked well, or so it seemed on the surface.

In reality, neither the princes nor the sultans respected the relationship between the principalities and the empire. The first administrative and bureaucratic troubles rose during the early 16th century, and the sultan started taking a more active role in the rule of Wallachia and Moldavia. Soon, the princes were reduced to the position of an imperial official, and the sultan was able to manipulate them and treat them as he saw fit. Suleiman I wrote a letter to King Sigismund I of Poland in 1531, and in it, he refers to the principalities as his slaves and tributaries. He claimed he had the power to dispose of Wallachia and Moldavia since they were his property, just like Serbia was. It is no wonder his successors, who ruled at the end of the 16th century, treated the principalities as conquered lands. They even called them provinces (*vilayet*). The princes were aware that their status had diminished and that they were only the custodians of their lands, so they started complaining about Turkish oppression. By the end of the 16th century, the sultan was the one who appointed the prince directly, although the boyars were still allowed to vote for the candidates. While they were free, the princes of Wallachia and Moldavia ruled as anointed rulers by the will of God. But now, they were aware their position was nothing more than the sultan's will.

Culture of Medieval Romania

Romanian culture between the early 12th to late 16th centuries was quite different from the one typical for western Europe. It was dominated by the aesthetic and religious ideals of the Byzantine Orthodoxy, which was typical for the countries in southeastern Europe. However, Romania never drew directly from the Byzantine Empire, even though some medieval Byzantine novels were popular, such as *Barlaam and Josaphat* or *Alexandria*. The majority of cultural influence came from neighboring Bulgaria and, to a lesser extent, from Serbia. The attachment of Romania to their Eastern neighbors is probably best seen in the persistence of the Slavic language. To be precise, the Middle Bulgarian language was used for writing until the mid-17th century. But in the 14th century, Slavic was introduced as the liturgical language of the Church and of the princes, chancellors, and other high-ranking state officials. This language secured the ties of Romania and the Byzantine Church, and it provided Romania with the means of transmitting sacred and secular ideas.

The Slavic language of the medieval period was ranked on the same level as Greek, Hebrew, and Latin because the Eastern Orthodox Church recognized it as an official language of the religion. Greek Saints Cyril and Methodius undertook an enormous task of making Christianity appeal more to the masses. To do this, they had to introduce literacy to the people and translate church liturgies so that the people could understand them. They worked and lived surrounded by the Slavic peoples, and they are still celebrated as saints who brought literacy to Bulgaria, Macedonia, Serbia, Ukraine, Russia, Slovakia, and the Czech Republic. Although they had no direct influence on Romanian literacy, their work influenced the acceptance of the Slavic language as the official language of the Church. Its acceptance in the official use of secular matters only proves the prestige of the language. However, the Slavic language was never spoken by the masses. And because of that, it was never used by anyone else except state officials, boyars, scholars, and some clergy. Most of the Romanian Orthodox clergy could not use the Slavic language outside of learned liturgies. The common people prayed in Romanian, and they created a rich folk literature in their native language. Folk literature was the main aspect of their culture until the 18th century, when literacy spread through the masses.

Monasteries were not only places of worship and learning but also cultural centers. The transcription of Slavic religious documents was a tradition during the 15th and 16th centuries, during which time monks worked on preserving the ancient texts. More than a thousand manuscripts written in Middle Bulgarian have been preserved. Romanian monks also preserved some Serbian texts and contributed greatly to the preservation of the Serbo-Byzantine tradition of eastern Europe. The princes of Wallachia and Moldavia were patrons of these transcriptions. Since their roles as the leaders of the country diminished during the Ottoman rule, they became aware that to preserve the Orthodox cultural identity, they had to contribute to it. Some of them were more than patrons and indulged in writing their own documents in the Slavic language, but the greatest contribution they brought was through building new churches and monasteries. Stephen the Great took his role seriously as God's champion on Earth, and he built beautiful monasteries throughout Moldavia, in which some of the most beautiful texts are still kept. Monks would embellish the copied manuscript with works of art. The decorative details, which are often found on the margins of the text, were the creative expressions of those who did the copying. Sometimes, they don't even represent the message that was conveyed through the text but rather are unique to the monk's imagination. These texts weren't reserved only for the clergy. They were read by the princes and the boyars, and with them, they would exit the walls of places for prayer and enter secular society. The illustrations of mythological creatures and the drawings on the margins of the religious texts soon became an integral part of the literature of higher social classes.

Among the most famous texts of purely Romanian origins are the chronicles of three Moldavian churchmen. Although they wrote in Slavic, they let the Romanian language influence their writing, and they created something now referred to as Slavo-Romanian. The first among them was the bishop of Roman, Macarie, who wrote a history of Moldavia from the reign of Stephen the Great until Petru Rares, who ruled until 1546. Eftimie was the second. He was an abbot in the monastery of Capriana, and he described Moldavia's history from 1541 to 1554. The third one, Azarie, who was the abbot of the Golia Monastery in Iasi, wrote about Moldavia between 1551 to 1574. All three were heavily influenced by the earlier written chronicles of the Byzantine scholars, but that was the normality at the time. These Moldavian churchmen didn't write the history of a nation; instead, they wrote chronologies of Moldavia as part of the larger history of the Orthodox community. Their texts were the last to be written in the Slavic language in Moldavia. From the 17th century onward, the Romanian language came into widespread use, even in the Church. In Wallachia, chronicle writing followed a similar path, but those texts largely didn't survive.

The princes also wrote. Since they were secular leaders, they wrote about secular matters. Prince Neagoe Basarab of Wallachia

(r. 1512–1521) wrote what is today considered a masterpiece of medieval Romanian literature. His work, *The advice of Neagoe Basarab to his Son, Teodosie,* was meant to be a comprehensive guide on how to rule. It was dedicated to his presumed son and successor to help him rule justly and successfully. The text of Neagoe Basarab is complex, as it is a textbook on governing techniques, an introduction to diplomacy, philosophy about religious morality, and a codebook of knighthood and bravery all in one. It is dominated by the Christian worldview of medieval Romania, in which a prince ruled by the will of God. But it also warned the ruler that his reign should be just and merciful as such is the will of God.

But during the late 16th and early 17th centuries, new social classes emerged. Lesser boyars, wealthy merchants, and rich citizens all needed a common language to conduct their businesses and convey messages between themselves and the rulers, as well as with the clergy and God. Romanian started pushing out Slavic as the official state and Church language. Since they were influenced by the political views of central Europe of the 16th century, where the Protestant Reformation occurred, Romanian people saw fit to include their language in all aspects of their lives. But this influence of the Protestants from the West meant so much more for the Romanian culture. It started turning from the Byzantine world of the East to the Roman world of the West. Even today, Romania stands like a cultural bridge, connecting its Eastern tradition with Western worldviews and ideas. The first literary works written in Romanian were secular. The Church resisted introducing the vernacular language until the late 17th century. Even then, it only used Romanian for public and practical works. Slavic continued to be the main language of hagiography and chronicles written by the clergy. The first liturgy book translated to Romanian came out in 1679, and this year is taken as the official date of the Romanian language entering the Church. In 1688, in Bucharest, the first Bible in the Romanian language was translated and published.

In Transylvania, where the nobility was Hungarian, medieval culture had a different path. Transylvania turned to Rome, not the Byzantine Empire. After the Reformation, the Saxons turned to Lutheranism and established the earliest Romanian press in Sibiu. Almost immediately, they started publishing in the Romanian language because they intended to convert the Romanian population of Transylvania to their faith. In 1544, the Lutherans of Sibiu printed the first book in Romanian, a Lutheran catechism. Ten years later, the Gospel was published in the Romanian language, but it also had a Slavic translation so it could appeal to all levels of society. The second printing press in Transylvania was set up in Brasov in order to promote using Romanian in the churches. However, the Lutherans weren't in charge of this press. Instead, it was the main base of the Calvinists, who also wanted to convert Romanians to their faith. But other than establishing a southern Transylvanian and northern Wallachian dialect as the standard form of the written language, they didn't achieve much, as Romanians mostly stayed true to Orthodoxy.

Chapter 4 – Three Great Rulers

Many controversies and prejudices surround Romanian rulers and figures, but to understand them, one has to learn the story of conquest, shifting allegiances, betrayal, and imprisonment. The greatness of historic individuals cannot be measured through the prism of the modern age. To fully understand the actions and motivations of Vlad Tepes, Stephen the Great, and Michael the Brave, we have to understand that Romania was positioned between the Ottoman Empire and Europe, between the traditional East and the modern West. Just as the world was torn between the great powers, so were the rulers of Romania, as it was the land of the crossroads, a land under Ottoman suzerainty that was willing to endorse European ideals.

Vlad Tepes (the Impaler)

Vlad Tepes
(https://ro.wikipedia.org/wiki/Vlad_%C8%9Aepe%C8%99#/media/
Fi%C8%99ier:Vlad_Tepes_002.jpg)

Vlad Tepes is one of the most controversial figures in world history. Modern scholars often portray him as a ruthless murderer who enjoyed impaling innocent and guilty people for the sake of his own entertainment. This image of the Wallachian prince even entered the fictional stories of modern writers, for he served as the inspiration for the famous Count Dracula, which was written in the 19th century by Bram Stoker. But Vlad Tepes was just a mortal, raised in a world divided between two powerful enemies: the European monarchies and the Ottoman Empire. As a son of Vlad II Dracul, he was born into the royal family. His father, although an illegitimate son of Prince Mircea I of Wallachia, became the successor to the throne after the death of his older half-brother. It was Vlad II who lent his surname to his more famous son, Vlad III Tepes (or Vlad III the Impaler). In 1408, the Holy Roman emperor founded a knight's society called the Order of the Dragon with the purpose of gathering all the European rulers and nobles willing to fight the Ottoman Empire. On February 8th, 1431, Vlad II became a first-class member of the Order of the Dragon, and because of this, he became popularly known as Vlad Dracul. In old Romanian, the term "dracul" meant dragon, but its modern meaning has changed into "devil." Because of this, Vlad Tepes was often called "Dracula" or "Draculea," meaning "of the Dragon" or "the Son of the Dragon."

In the same year, King Sigismund of the Romans recognized Vlad II Dracul as the rightful ruler of Wallachia, but he offered no help in dethroning Vlad's cousin, Dan II, who ruled the region. Vlad II settled in the Saxon town of Sighisoara in Transylvania for the next several years, and it is believed that Vlad Tepes was born here. However, nothing is known of the young Vlad's mother, but some theories suggest she was a Moldavian princess. Most contemporary scholars agree Vlad's mother should simply be designated as the unknown first wife of Vlad II. Vlad's father managed to take Wallachia in 1436 after his older half-brother, Alexander Aldea, died of illness.

Vlad Tepes had two brothers, the older Mircea and the younger Radu. When their father assumed the throne of Wallachia, the whole family moved to the city of Targoviste. In 1442, Vlad II paid a visit to the voivode of Transylvania, John Hunyadi, who persuaded the Wallachian prince to resist the Ottomans and join him in defending Transylvania from an Ottoman invasion. But Wallachia was under Ottoman suzerainty, and when Sultan Murad II learned of Vlad's disobedience, he called Vlad to Gallipoli. Vlad knew it would be a diplomatic scandal if he refused to obey the sultan, so he agreed to travel to the Ottoman capital, but he took his sons, Vlad III and Radu, with him. At first, Sultan Murad had them all imprisoned, but by the end of the year, he agreed to release the Wallachian prince. After all, he needed an obedient monarch to administer the principality. To ensure his loyalty, Murad II kept his sons in the fortress of Dogrugoz, in today's Turkey. Recently, archaeologists believe they have discovered a cell in which Vlad and Radu were kept. At the time of their imprisonment, Vlad was only twelve years old, so it is difficult to believe he spent all his time in a cell. More than likely, Vlad and his brother received a proper education in Turkey, and they were trained as warriors. Nevertheless, it was here in Turkey that Vlad first witnessed impaling as a method of torture. It was a method he himself would adopt and use later in life.

Some accounts mention that Vlad was often tortured during his years as a Turkish captive, and many historians cite this as the main reason for his hatred toward the Ottomans. Nevertheless, his family back in Wallachia had an even worse fate. The local boyars rebelled against Vlad II and had him killed in the swamps of Balteni in 1447. His eldest son, Mircea, was also captured and tortured. It is believed he was blinded and buried alive as punishment for his father's sins. Shortly after Sultan Murad heard the news of the Wallachian princely family, he released Vlad III. But Vlad couldn't assume his father's throne yet because John Hunyadi had invaded Wallachia and installed Vladislav II, the son of Dan II, as its new prince.

The first opportunity to take back Wallachia presented itself in 1448 when Vladislav left the principality and accompanied John Hunyadi to the Second Battle of Kosovo, where they fought the Ottomans. Sultan Murad II gave Vlad a small army with which he took Wallachia for himself and ruled it for a couple of months. However, when Vladislav came back from the war in December of the same year, Vlad had no army of his own to oppose his cousin. Instead, he chose to flee to the territories of the Ottoman Empire and wait for a better opportunity. Soon, Vlad decided to pay a visit to Moldavia, where he met with his father's brother-in-law, Prince

Bogdan II. It is uncertain what he did until 1451 when Bogdan was dethroned and his son, Stephen the Great, went to Transylvania to ask Hunyadi for help. Vlad traveled with the future Moldavian ruler, and over the next few years, he managed to gain Hunyadi's support. In 1456, the Transylvanian voivode lent his army to Vlad to take Wallachia. During this invasion, Vladislav II died, and Vlad became the voivode with the support of John Hunyadi. As payment for Hunyadi's support, Vlad promised he would guard the Transylvanian border from the Ottomans. To succeed in this new task, he wrote a letter to the boyars of Brasov, asking for their assistance and promising he would also protect them from the Ottomans.

During the early years of Vlad's second rule, he mounted an act of revenge against those boyars who had participated in his father's and brother's murder. The historical accounts claim he killed thousands of people in his rage, whether they were proven to be guilty or were just suspicious. But it seems that revenge wasn't the only drive behind these killings. Vlad would seize land, money, and other properties of the boyars he killed and gifted them to his supporters. He wasn't only punishing the culprits of his family's murder; he was also buying the loyalty and support of the people around him. To keep peace with the Ottomans, he sent a yearly gift to the sultan, a tribute both Wallachia and Moldavia had to pay to avoid Ottoman annexation. But it was this tribute that got him accused of being disloyal to Hungary and his deal with Hunyadi. When John Hunyadi died, his son, Ladislaus Hunyadi, wrote a letter to the boyars of Brasov, ordering them to take action against Vlad. He planned to remove Vlad from the Wallachian throne and install Dan III, the brother of Vladislav II, in his place. However, Ladislaus didn't succeed in his intentions because he was executed by the Hungarian king in 1457.

With the execution came an internal power struggle within Hungary, as Ladislaus's wife and her brother, Michael Szilagyi, led a rebellion against the Hungarian Crown. Vlad took this opportunity to raid some of the Transylvanian villages near Brasov and Sibiu, as well as to help his friend and possibly his cousin, Stephen the Great, to take over Moldavia. Vlad's moves against the Transylvanian Saxons signified his support to the Szilagyi family, as the Saxons remained loyal to the Hungarian king.

It was actually Vlad's actions during this conflict that started the stories of his ruthlessness. However, there is no other evidence of Vlad's bloody reign, and the Saxon stories and their legitimacy cannot be confirmed. Nevertheless, they claim Vlad took prisoners from the Saxon villages and towns and had them moved to Wallachia, where he would impale them just so he could enjoy watching them scream. These claims of Vlad's bloodthirst were later used against him when Matthias Corvinus (r. 1458–1490), the younger brother of Ladislaus Hunyadi, became the king of Hungary and started supporting Dan III as the rightful ruler of Wallachia. In 1460, Vlad defeated Dan III and punished all the inhabitants of Wallachia and Transylvania who had supported his enemy. It is said that on one occasion, he captured all the citizens of Brasov's suburbs and impaled them, whether they were men, women, or children.

The bloodthirst of Vlad Dracula is probably best seen in his wars against the Ottomans. One of the Janissary soldiers, Konstantin Mihailovic, wrote a memoir in which he mentions that the Wallachian ruler used impaling as a method of torture during his campaign. He also claims Vlad had a habit of cutting off the noses of Ottoman soldiers to send to the Hungarian king as a sign of a successful fight. It is not known when exactly Vlad decided to renounce the Turkish suzerainty of Wallachia, but historical records mention that he failed to pay tribute to the sultan for three consecutive years. It is also unknown when he launched his first attack on the Ottoman Empire, but in his letter to Matthias

Corvinus, which was written in 1462, he stated that he killed more than 23,000 Turkish and Bulgarian soldiers during his campaign across the Danube. In the same letter, Vlad claims he launched an attack so he could defend the Christian world, and he asked Corvinus to send the Hungarian army to his aid. When Mehmed II (r. 1444-1446, 1451-1481) learned of Vlad's invasion, he first responded by inviting him to Constantinople. Although this seems like a nice diplomatic gesture, the sultan actually planned on tricking Vlad and imprisoning him and then installing his younger brother, Radu, as the prince of Wallachia. Vlad learned of the sultan's plans, and he captured and killed his messengers. Angered, Mehmed raised a huge army, numbering around 150,000 soldiers, which he planned to use to conquer Wallachia for Radu.

The Turkish army landed at Braila, a town in eastern Romania, where Vlad planned to meet them. However, after seeing that he was outnumbered, the voivode of Wallachia decided to retreat to his capital in Targoviste. On his way back, he burned all the resources the Ottoman army could have used, making it difficult for the Ottomans to move across Wallachia. The sultan personally accompanied his army, and Vlad plotted to capture or kill him, as this would cause the Ottoman army to panic and help him to expel the invaders from Wallachia. But during the attack on the sultan's camp, his soldiers wrongly attacked the tent of the grand vizier, and the opportunity was missed. Vlad and his men managed to escape the Ottoman camp without being discovered, but Mehmed led his army straight to Targoviste the next morning. Upon entering the city, the sultan saw a discouraging scene. According to Turkish accounts, around 20,000 impaled people were scattered across an otherwise abandoned city. Greek historian Laonikos Chalkokondyles wrote that the sultan wasn't just appalled by the scene; he was impressed. He also mentions that the sultan changed his mind about Vlad and said that a person who was capable of governing a country and who did such deeds was a very worthy ruler. The sultan decided to abandon his invasion of Wallachia and moved his army back to Braila. However, the Ottoman records mention that the army was suffering from poor health and starvation, and that was the real reason for the Ottoman retreat.

While the main part of the sultan's army left, Radu stayed behind with a small detachment. During the next few months, the brothers met in two battles, and both times, Vlad defeated Radu. Nevertheless, the Wallachians, who were tired of the constant warfare, chose to join Radu rather than Vlad, and the voivode was forced to hide in the Carpathian Mountains for some time before deciding to appeal to Matthias Corvinus for help. In 1462, the Hungarian king came personally to Transylvania to negotiate with Vlad. He was indeed willing to help him regain the throne of Wallachia, but Corvinus refused to help Vlad pursue his conflict with the Ottomans. Unable to reach an agreement, Corvinus accused Vlad of conspiring with the sultan and had him imprisoned. As evidence, the Hungarian king forged three letters in which Vlad allegedly promised the Ottomans his allegiance in the future invasion of Hungary if they recognized him as the legitimate ruler of Wallachia. The majority of modern historians agree that these letters were forged due to the poor wording and bad Latin, which are not in accordance with other letters from Vlad. It is believed that the Saxons, who still held a grudge against Vlad, were involved in the forging.

Not much is known of Vlad's fourteen years of imprisonment, but according to Slavic sources, he was released by the Hungarian king once he turned to Catholicism. However, the Moldavian sources claim that Stephen the Great asked Matthias Corvinus to reinstall Vlad on the Wallachian throne, as he needed an ally against the sultan, and Vlad had previously proved his hatred for the Ottomans. In 1475, Corvinus recognized Vlad as the rightful ruler of Wallachia, but he did so only in words. He was unwilling to provide him with an army to regain his principality. Instead of going to Wallachia, Vlad decided to stay in the Hungarian city of Pecs. Matthias Corvinus used Vlad as the commander of the army, which, together with Serbian Despot Vuk Grgurevic Brankovic, took Bosnian Srebrenica. The two commanders bonded, and when Vlad went to Moldavia to help Stephen the Great fight the Ottomans at Neamț Citadel, Vuk was there with his army.

In 1476, Matthias Corvinus and Stephen the Great planned to invade Wallachia and remove Prince Basarab Laiota, who had climbed onto the throne with the support of the Ottoman sultan. While the Hungarian forces fought for Targoviste, Vlad and Stephen joined forces and occupied Bucharest. On November 16th, Basarab Laiota escaped the city, seeking refuge with the sultan. Vlad Dracula was officially crowned as the prince of Wallachia for the third and last time that December. A month later, Basarab came back to Wallachia with the Ottoman army behind him. In the fighting that ensued, Vlad lost his life. Some contemporary historians claim that his body was butchered, that his whole army was massacred, and that his head was sent to Sultan Mehmed II in Constantinople.

Stephen the Great

(https://en.wikipedia.org/wiki/Stephen_the_Great#/media/
File:Tablou_votiv_Manastirea_Dobrovat_1503.jpg)

Stephen III of Moldavia, better known as Stephen the Great, is Romania's most celebrated ruler. He ruled the principality of Moldavia from 1457 until 1504, but he began overseeing the administration of the principality much earlier, during the reign of his father Bogdan II. The charters dating from the rule of Bogdan II mention Stephen as the voivode, which could only mean that his father designated him early on as his co-ruler and heir apparent. Nothing much is known about the early years of this great ruler except that he had five siblings and that his mother may have been related to the ruling family of Wallachia. This would make him a cousin of Vlad Tepes, and the possibility is high because the two were contemporary rulers and friends who often worked together.

Bogdan II was killed by his brother, Petru (Peter) III Aron, who attacked Moldavia in 1451 and took it for himself. Stephen was forced to seek refuge at the court of John Hunyadi, who was, at the time, the regent governor of Hungary. The two already shared an alliance since it was Hunyadi who had helped Bogdan take the throne of Moldavia after the death of who is thought to be his father, Alexander the Good, in 1432. When John Hunyadi sent Vlad Tepes to take Wallachia, Stephen went with him, but it is unknown if he played a role in the campaign or if he visited his friend and supposed cousin after he became the ruler of Wallachia. Nevertheless, the two joined forces, and in the spring of 1457, they wrestled Moldavia from the hands of Stephen's uncle, Petru Aron, forcing him to seek refuge in Poland. The sole rulership of Stephen the Great began then.

The first task Stephen faced was consolidating his power. He made sure he was crowned as a prince by the Orthodox Church, which gave him not only legitimacy but also holiness. Therefore, he ruled by the grace of God. However, his uncle in Poland still represented a threat to his throne, so as early as 1458, Stephen attacked King Casimir IV of Poland, forcing him to sign a treaty in 1459 that favored Stephen. According to the treaty, Casimir was not to allow Petru Aron to return to Moldavia under any circumstance. After the Polish king made this promise, Stephen's uncle lost his military support, without which he had no hope of seizing Moldavia again. He chose to settle in Transylvania, which was, at the time, Hungarian territory, although not for long. In 1462, Stephen attacked part of Transylvania where Petru was staying, forcing him to run to Budapest, where he was accepted in the court of King Matthias Corvinus. Grateful for Casimir's compliance, Stephen promised him he would help Poland fend off the attacks of the Tatars whenever Casimir needed it. He promised the Transylvanians who helped him locate his uncle that he would defend their Three Nations from the Hungarians' wrath.

Although Moldavia was an autonomous principality, it was still under the suzerainty of the Ottoman Empire, and Stephen decided not to agitate the Turks. He regularly paid the yearly tribute or a gift to the sultan to keep the peace. He even acted against the unification of the Orthodox and Catholic Churches in Moldavia by expelling the Franciscans (a Catholic religious group created in the 13th century by Saint Francis of Assisi), as they were the ones advocating for unification and a crusade against the Ottomans. Stephen's allegiance to Sultan Mehmed II is visible in the fact that he attacked Wallachia in 1462 while his friend and supposed cousin, Vlad Dracula, was waging his war against the Ottomans. If one is to trust the written sources that date decades later, Stephen invaded Wallachia by order of the sultan, who also led his army to Wallachia later that same year. Those same sources claim that Vlad was forced to defend himself from both the Moldavian army and the Turkish one.

Stephen took the opportunity of the Ottoman invasion of Wallachia to take the Chilia fortress located on the Daube Delta in Bessarabia, which was under Hungarian rule at the time. Even though Stephen had the support of the Ottoman soldiers, he was unsuccessful in taking this strategically important fortress and port, as it was guarded by the Hungarians and Vlad Dracula. Not only did the Moldavian prince miss the opportunity to regain this valuable possession, but he was also severely wounded during the attack. By some accounts, he sustained a wound to his left foot, while other sources mention his left calf. Whatever it was, the wound certainly bothered him to the end of his life, as it never properly healed. In the end, the wound, combined with gout, would be the cause of his death. Stephen finally managed to take the Chilia fortress in 1465 after bombarding it for two days. But the Wallachian ruler at the time, Radu the Fair, Vlad's brother, also laid claim on Chilia. Since he was an Ottoman vassal, Stephen created tensions with Hungary, Wallachia, and the Ottoman Empire.

The loss of the Chilia fortress, as well as Stephen's promise to defend the Three Nations of Transylvania against the Hungarians, led Matthias Corvinus to the decision that the time was ripe to invade Moldavia. He did so in late 1467, and he managed to take the cities of Roman, Baia, Bacau, and Targu Neamt. In the Battle of Baia on December 15th, 1467, Stephen managed to defeat Matthias Corvinus, although the Hungarian chroniclers claim the victory belonged to their king. The truth is while both rulers proclaimed victory, Matthias Corvinus was actually forced to retreat because he sustained wounds during the battle. One source claims that to avoid being captured, Matthias called some of the Moldavian boyars who had previously sworn allegiance to him due to their private wishes to get rid of Stephen.

Between 1468 and 1470, Stephen raided Transylvania, probably encouraged by the defeat he had inflicted on the Hungarian king. Agitated by these raids, the Szeklers gathered around Petru Aron and helped him invade Moldavia. But it seems that Stephen was well aware of his uncle's intentions, for he prepared a defense in advance. During the conflict, he managed to capture his uncle and had him executed, but the exact year is lost. Modern historians believe it could have happened anytime between the Battle of Baia in 1467 and the events in 1470, which was when he started negotiating peace with the Hungarians. The year 1469 is most commonly taken as the year of Petru Aron's death.

Stephen III was named "the Great" long after his death, as the people of Romania finally realized his efforts to preserve the integrity and autonomy of Moldavia. He became a national hero because he went against Ottoman rulers who tried to impose their will on the principality. He couldn't allow the annexation of Moldavia, as that was how Serbia and Bulgaria lost their independence. It is not known when Stephen had a change of heart regarding the Ottomans, as up until 1470, he paid a yearly tribute and provided the empire with his army whenever he was called. But in around 1470, the Ottomans wanted Stephen to abandon his ambitions to hold the Chilia fortress and port. Stephen wasn't ready to defy them openly, but it is believed that he stopped paying tribute. It is also possible that the Moldavian ruler had built good relations with the sultan of Aq Qoyunlu (in modern-day Anatolia) and that the two rulers plotted against the Ottomans together. While Mehmed II warred against Aq Qoyunlu, Stephen took the opportunity and removed Muslim-converted Radu the Fair from the Wallachian throne and install his protégé, Basarab III Laiota. After a short battle in 1473, Basarab and Stephen took Bucharest, but before the year ended, Radu was back on the Wallachian throne due to the fast reaction of the Ottomans. Basarab wouldn't take Wallachia until 1475. Stephen once more helped him onto the throne, this time successfully.

That same year, Mehmed II gathered his forces and sent them to invade Moldavia. His intention wasn't only to avenge Radu the Fair but also to, once and for all, end the question of the principality and join it to his vast empire. Together with Radu's Wallachian supporters, more than 120,000 Ottoman soldiers rushed to Moldavia. But Stephen became allies with the Hungarians and the Polish, and together, they inflicted what was probably the heaviest defeat for the Ottoman army on European grounds. For the next three years, the Turks who lingered in Moldavia were ruthlessly killed, and finally, the remaining Turkish people agreed to leave. Stephen rightfully asked the European rulers for further help against the Ottomans, but none of them responded. Pope Sixtus IV proclaimed him the "Christ Athlete" (the defender of the Christian faith), as he single-handedly guarded the entrance to the Christian world, but Stephen was unable to move the kings of Europe to send their army or resources to Moldavia. Having no other choice, Stephen was forced to approach Mehmed II with offerings of peace. Basarab III Laiota, who Stephen had helped claim the Wallachian throne, sided with the

Ottomans during their invasion of Moldavia. For this, he had to be removed. Stephen then remembered his old friend, Vlad Dracul. At that moment, Vlad was in a Hungarian dungeon, and the Moldavian prince persuaded King Matthias Corvinus to release him. Although Corvinus agreed to let Vlad go, he refused to support his claim to Wallachia.

The peace with the Ottomans didn't last long. In 1476, Sultan Mehmed launched yet another invasion of Moldavia. This time, Stephen's fate was different, but he did manage to persuade the Tatars, who were on the sultan's side, to defect and fight for him. Nevertheless, Stephen suffered a defeat at Razboieni and was forced to run to Poland to save his life. Luck was on Stephen's side, as illness spread among the Ottoman soldiers, causing the sultan to leave Moldavia. But before coming back home, Stephen decided to plead again with Matthias Corvinus, and this time, he won his support to invade Wallachia. In 1476, Vlad and Stephen rode their armies to Wallachia and expelled Basarab Laiota for good. Unfortunately for Vlad, when the Ottomans came back to Wallachia, Stephen was already long gone, leaving Vlad to be massacred. Stephen couldn't allow the return of Basarab, and in 1477, he led yet another army to the neighboring principality and successfully installed Basarab IV the Young on the throne.

Mehmed II ordered a third invasion of Moldavia in 1481, but in the spring of that year, he died of illness, and the conflict for the succession of the Ottoman throne began. Although the Moldavian invasion was halted, the peace only lasted for a short time. The new sultan, Bayezid II, continued what his father had started, and a new invasion was launched in 1483. Since Bayezid had signed a peace treaty with Hungary that same year, and since the treaty extended to some of the Moldavian territories, the new sultan satisfied himself with only conquering the ports of Chilia and Cetatea Alba. Moldavia lost control over the Black Sea trading routes, and Stephen was forced to pay homage to Bayezid and offer his allegiance. The Ottoman sultan had no interest in annexing

Moldavia at this point, but its prince had to start paying a yearly tribute again. Matthias Corvinus knew Stephen's temper, and he was afraid that the prince would take the loss of the seaports personally and seek to retake them. The king of Hungary was unwilling to start yet another war with the Turks, especially at this crucial time, as he had his own war to wage in the west. Therefore, Corvinus ceded some Transylvanian territory to Stephen as compensation for the lost ports. These territories included two fortresses, Cetatea de Balta and Ciceu, but Stephen never really gave up on the idea of regaining the lost fortresses on the Black Sea.

The opportunity presented itself in 1485 during the Polish-Ottoman War. When the Ottomans took these fortresses, it put them in charge of both the Danube and Dnieper Delta, which directly threatened Poland. The war between the two nations ensued, and Stephen chose to pledge his allegiance to Casimir IV of Poland instead of Bayezid. With Polish support, Stephen managed to expel the Ottomans from some parts of Moldavia, but he wasn't able to regain Chilia and Cetatea Alba. In fact, he barely survived the conflict and was defeated so thoroughly that he had to sign a peace treaty and pay tribute to the sultan.

The last years of Stephen the Great were marred by the conflict with Poland. When Casimir IV died in 1492, his son, John I Albert, succeeded him. Unlike his father, John decided to recognize Ottoman rule in Chilia and Cetatea Alba, which broke the treaty between Casimir and Stephen from 1485, as the Polish king had promised he would not recognize the Ottoman rule over the Black Sea fortresses without Stephen's permission. John Albert's action greatly offended the Moldavian prince, who, in turn, approached Ivan III of Moscow (better known as Ivan the Great) and helped him coordinate attacks on Polish and Lithuanian territories. In the meantime, Hungary and Poland wanted to launch a crusade against the Ottomans, and Stephen planned to join them because his disdain for the sultan was still great. During the conference held in Levoca, Slovakia, in 1494, between King Ladislaus of Hungary (who succeeded Matthias Corvinus) and other European powers interested in the crusade, it became apparent that John Albert planned to overthrow Stephen from the throne of Moldavia and install his son, Sigismund, in his place. This only worsened the relations between Hungary and Poland, and the crusade never happened.

Nevertheless, John Albert still planned to attack the Ottomans, and he wanted to take Chilia and Cetatea Alba, thus gaining the suzerainty over the Black Sea trade routes for Poland. Stephen was suspicious of this, as he thought that John Albert hadn't completely abandoned his idea of Polish suzerainty over the whole of Moldavia. He warned Bayezid II and asked for his help in defending the fortresses. On September 24th, 1497, the Polish army laid siege at Suceava, revealing that John Albert still intended to overthrow Stephen. However, the Teutonic Knights, who had promised to help John, never arrived. Stephen managed to secure the help of 12,000 Hungarian soldiers sent by Ladislaus and around 600 Ottoman Janissaries sent by the sultan. By the end of October, the Polish were expelled from Moldavia, and Stephen even led several raids in their territory.

In around 1500, Stephen's health started deteriorating rapidly. The old leg wound never really healed because he developed gout. He was in tremendous pain, and some witnesses claim that during the last battles he ever participated in, Stephen was pulled on sleds. His son, Bogdan, slowly started taking over the princely duties, and he negotiated the peace with Poland in 1499, which ended their claims of sovereignty over Moldavia. The next year, Stephen stopped paying tribute to the sultan again because he wanted to join the war between the empire and Venice. His delegation to Venice was supposed to negotiate Moldavia's participation in the war, and it was also tasked with bringing him a doctor. Previously, Stephen had been treated by various medical professionals, ranging from Polish, Tartar, Ottoman, Hungarian, and Genoese, but none of them was capable of curing him. They only made the pain bearable enough for the old prince to lead his country and enjoy warring against his many enemies. Even though he was sick and at the end of his strength, Stephen launched his last attempt to regain Chilia and Cetatea Alba in 1502, but he failed. He then chose to follow the Hungarian example and make peace with the Ottomans. In 1503, he started paying them a yearly tribute, and in July 1504, while he was on his deathbed, he forced his son Bogdan to promise to continue paying tribute once he took the throne of Moldavia. It was as if Stephen finally realized that keeping the peace was far more beneficial than constantly warring. As long as Moldavia wasn't under direct threat, it was wiser to remain in the background of the play between the great forces.

Michael the Brave
(https://en.wikipedia.org/wiki/Michael_the_Brave#/media/
File:Misu_Popp_-_Mihai_Viteazul.jpg)

The third individual celebrated as a national hero of Romania is Mihai Viteazul (Michael the Brave), and he is famous for uniting the three principalities that make up modern-day Romania: Wallachia, Moldavia, and Transylvania. Although he was a noble, Michael wasn't born into a princely family. It is unknown who exactly his father was, but to legitimize his rule, he came up with the idea that he belonged to the Patrascu family. Some historians believe this bond is real and that he was an illegitimate son of Prince Patrascu cel Bun (Patrascu the Good). He also claimed his mother was Theodora Kantakouzene, who was the direct descendant of Byzantine Emperor John VI Kantakouzenos, but this connection cannot be confirmed either. Nothing is known of Michael's childhood except that he was probably born in 1558. In 1588, he was proclaimed Ban of Mehedinti, and his steep climb on the political scene of Wallachia began.

In the same year, Michael became the *stolnic* of Mihnea II Turcitul (r. 1577-1583, 1585-1591), Prince of Wallachia. This title meant Michael belonged to the rank of the boyars. It was a position similar to a seneschal, but it was limited to supervising a ruler's table, food supplies, and organizing feasts. Michael had the task of personally serving the prince on special occasions such as holidays, but he would also taste the food before serving it to make sure it wasn't poisoned. During the rule of Prince Alexandru III cel Rau (Alexander the Bad; r. 1592-1593), he was promoted to the position of Ban of Craiova. But before giving him the title, Alexandru forced Michael to swear he was not a descendant of a prince, which he obliged. Nevertheless, the two ended their relations on bad terms, and Michael was forced to flee Wallachia. In 1593, he paid a visit to Constantinople, where he started convincing the sultan to elevate him to the position of prince of Wallachia. He had the support of the patriarch of Constantinople, Jeremias II; his cousin, Andronikos Kantakouzenos; and a British ambassador to the Ottoman Empire, Edward Barton. Michael became the prince of Wallachia on October 11th, 1593, after being elevated to the position by Sultan Murad III (r. 1574-1595).

But as soon as Michael became the prince, he turned against Murad III. The very next year, he joined the Christian alliance, which had been founded to combat the Ottomans, and he launched his first campaign against them without his new allies. Michael managed to conquer some of the territories along the Danube, including some important fortresses such as Silistra and Braila. He took advantage of the fact that his neighbor, Aaron the Tyrant, who ruled Moldavia, was fighting the Turks at this time.

Michael went deeper into Ottoman territory and took Chilia, Nicopolis, and even faraway Adrianople, a city near the Turkish border with Greece and Bulgaria. But while Michael was busy fighting in distant lands, the Wallachian boyars took the opportunity to make a deal with the Transylvanian ruler, Sigismund Bathory. The Treaty of Alba Iulia, signed in 1595, gave the boyars a unique opportunity to get involved in politics, as they had the right to form a council of twelve, which would share executive and legislative powers with the prince. Of course, the boyars had to think of their safety, and the treaty contained a few notes that protected the lives and property of boyars in case the prince charged them with treason. Michael didn't want this treaty, but he understood its importance to keep the internal peace of Wallachia. He never openly acted against the Treaty of Alba Iulia, but he did try to avoid consulting the council as much as he could.

During this time, Michael managed to free Wallachia from Ottoman suzerainty, although it was only briefly. He joined forces with Sigismund Bathory, and in August 1595, he fought at the Battle of Calugareni. He won, but his army was so weakened that he had to retreat and wait for support. Sigismund sent 40,000 men, and the Wallachian prince used them to inflict the final blow to the Turkish army and free both Targoviste and Bucharest, which had been conquered earlier that year. Michael continued his actions against the Ottomans during 1596, but that year, Wallachia endured the Tatars' attacks, and Bucharest and Buzau were destroyed. There was nothing Michael could do while the Tatars raided. He could only rebuild the cities and wait for a better opportunity. Michael continued his efforts against the Ottomans, this time acquiring the financial help of Holy Roman Emperor Rudolf II. He fought well into 1599 but was then forced to sign a peace because he had spent all of his resources. He also had no help from his neighbors, and none of them agreed to send their armies.

The year 1598 was a very turbulent one, as Sigismund Bathory resigned as the prince of Transylvania in favor of his cousin, Cardinal Andrew Bathory. The new Transylvanian prince disliked Michael, and he demanded that the Wallachian prince abandon his throne. Hearing this, Michael decided to lead his army to Transylvania and occupy it rather than sit at home and wait for Andrew to move first. But Michael was not alone; he had the support of the Transylvanian Szeklers, who shared no love for the new ruler. Together, they fought against Andrew Bathory in the Battle of Selimbar on October 18th, 1599, and they were victorious. Andrew was killed after the battle while leading his army into a retreat. Michael honored his dead enemy by granting him a princely funeral at the Catholic cathedral in Alba Iulia. After the funeral, the Transylvanian nobles elected Michael as the new prince of Transylvania, and he was formally handed the keys of the principality's capital, Alba Iulia. But even though he was now the ruler of Transylvania, he was well aware that he was still a subject of the Holy Roman emperor. Therefore, he demanded the Transylvanian nobles to first swear an oath to the emperor and then to him. Michael was Romanian by ethnicity, but oddly enough, he didn't grant any new freedoms to the Romanians in Transylvania. Instead, he continued the traditional rule of the "Union of the Three Nations." Perhaps because he was aware that if he gave political power to ethnic Romanians, who were mainly a peasant class in Transylvania, his rule would never last. Michael employed some of the Saxons, Hungarians, and Szeklers in the administration of Wallachia, relying on their skills as experienced nobles and politicians.

Andrew Bathory didn't get the idea of forcing Michael to abdicate the Wallachian throne on his own. Indeed, he was persuaded to do so by the ruler of Moldavia, Prince Ieremia Movila, who wanted Wallachia for his brother Simion. In fact, since 1595, Simion called himself the voivode of Wallachia, but he never effectively ruled the principality. Michael planned to deal with the Movila brothers, but for the time being, he satisfied himself with keeping a close eye on Moldavia. However, in 1600, a Polish envoy came to Brasov. They offered Michael the Moldavian throne sometime in the future in exchange for recognition of the Polish king as his sovereign. Michael accepted, and he even persuaded them to make the princely title hereditary so that Wallachia, Transylvania, and Moldavia would stay in the hands of his family. Michael knew he needed to deal with Ieremia Movila first, and on April 14th, 1600, he launched an attack on Moldavia without Polish approval. By May 6th, he occupied Iasi, the capital of Moldavia, forcing Ieremia to flee. He sought refuge in the Polish Khotyn Fortress, but when his soldiers deserted him, he escaped and took refuge at the Polish military camp. Michael became the ruler of Moldavia, showing everyone he was capable of taking what he wanted without outside help. However, ruling Transylvania, Wallachia, and Moldavia meant upsetting the power balance in the region, and the first to rise as his opponents were the Hungarians of Transylvania. In the Battle of Miraslau, they managed to defeat Michael's army and force the prince to abandon Transylvania.

Luck turned against Michael, for Ieremia made a new deal with Poland, managing to persuade the king to send his army to regain Moldavia. Michael was defeated on several fronts and had to abandon the Moldavian throne. The Polish army continued to pursue him, taking parts of Wallachia in the process. They then installed Ieremia's brother, Simion, as its ruler. Only Oltenia remained loyal to Michael. In 1601, Michael asked Holy Emperor Rudolf II for assistance in his last stand. Since Sigismund Bathory had come back with Ottoman support to take over Transylvania, Rudolf hurried to give his support to Michael to keep the principality within his empire's domain. While Michael was preparing to enter Transylvania with his army, his son, Nicolae Patrascu, defeated Simion and drove him out of Wallachia. At the Battle of Guruslau, fought on August 3rd, 1601, Michael and General Giorgio Basta of the Habsburg Empire defeated

Sigismund Bathory and his rebelling Hungarian nobles. However, General Basta, despite being an ally of the Wallachian prince, sought to take Transylvania for himself, and he plotted the assassination of Michael the Brave. Basta gained the approval of the Holy Roman emperor and personally assassinated Michael on August 9th, 1601, ending all hopes that Transylvania, Wallachia, and Moldavia would be united under the rule of one man any time soon.

Chapter 5 – Romania in the 17th and 18th Centuries

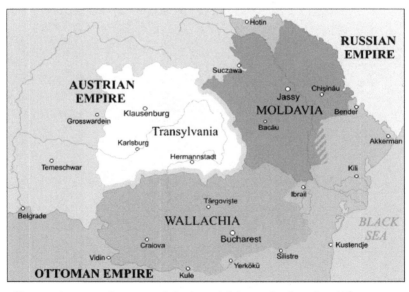

Romanian provinces and their neighbors during the 17th century
(https://en.wikipedia.org/wiki/Early_Modern_Romania#/media/
File:Rom1793-1812.png)

At the end of the 16th century, the greatest threat to the Ottoman rule came from Michael the Brave of Wallachia. As soon as he came to power in Wallachia, he set his politics around the idea of freeing his country from Ottoman rule. At the same time, Pope

Clement VIII planned an anti-Ottoman crusade together with Holy Roman Emperor Rudolf II and King Philip II of Spain. Michael, together with the princes of Moldavia and Transylvania, joined this anti-Ottoman alliance, which was named the Holy League. In 1594, Michael raised a revolt against the Ottomans, and in only one year, he managed to drive the Turks back south of Danube. Unfortunately, the Holy League's leaders had different ambitions, and the allegiances soon became vague. Michael's unification of Wallachia, Transylvania, and Moldavia was short-lived, and in 1601, he was assassinated, even though he had the unconditional support of the Holy Roman emperor. His efforts to unite Romania continued to inspire the nation during the 17th and 18th centuries, and it would shape Romanian patriotism and nationalism of the 19th and 20th centuries.

In 1606, the Treaty of Zsitvatorok was signed, and with it, the war between the Habsburg and Ottoman Empires ended. The sultans took the opportunity of peace and relative order within their domain to claim Wallachia and Moldavia once again. However, the old way by which the Ottomans ruled the principalities had to change. Michael the Brave had proved the effectiveness of choosing a new prince ever so often, so the Ottoman sultans needed new methods by which the principalities would be governed, something that would be effective over a longer period of time. The autonomy of Wallachia and Moldavia remained official, so the Ottomans had to find a way to undermine it. And they did so by introducing the upper-class Greeks and Levantines into the principalities in the 17th and 18th centuries. They were brought in so they could dilute the solidarity of the prince and the boyars. Without solidarity, the principalities wouldn't be able to resist the rule of the sultans. The migration of this new upper class seemed to be enough, as the princes started enjoying fewer constraints than their predecessors. The Ottomans continued gaining from the economic systems of Wallachia and Moldavia, but they also restricted themselves from interfering in the internal matters of the principalities. Even the presence of the Turkish military was lessened and was mostly concentrated along the shores of the Danube.

Besides the addition of the Greeks and the Levantines, the social structure of the principalities remained the same as before. The boyars, especially those of higher ranks, predominated the economies of the principalities, and they strived to gain even better positions in the political sphere through the installment of a nobility regime. They demanded that some offices be restricted to higher-ranking boyars, which would prohibit others from elevating themselves. However, the boyars were not united, and the division between the high-ranking and low-ranking boyars was often exploited by the prince, who wanted to keep them in check. Peasants still represented the most numerous social class, but during the 17th century, they suffered the deterioration of their legal status and their quality of life. The Ottomans demanded high taxes, while the boyars demanded a free labor force. Many free peasants lost their possessions, and their lands were seized by either the prince or the boyars. Nobody defended the commoners, not even the Church. The middle class existed, but it was too small to have any influence on political or economic life. Peasants were simply abandoned by all to try and survive the best they could.

Much of the 17th century was dominated by the conflict between the princes and the boyars in both Wallachia and Moldavia. The princes wanted a strong monarchy modeled on the absolutist states of Europe. The boyars wanted to be included in the political realm, and they wanted to limit the monarchy. But the main challenge for both the boyars and the princes was the new aristocracy coming from Greece and the Levant. They used their money and influence to buy land and titles in Wallachia and Moldavia. This allowed them to rise to the status of boyars and get involved in the internal politics of the principalities. Native boyars were united against the newcomers, and they thought the Ottoman royal court was directly responsible for their establishment. Sometimes, they were able to persuade the prince to act and do something about the newcomers. In 1631, Prince Leon Tomsa of Wallachia issued a charter by which he ordered all Greeks who had not been naturalized to leave the principality. Even though the charter was a victory for the boyars, it did little to diminish Greek influence on internal politics. In Moldavia, Prince Miron Barnovschi (r. 1626-1629) issued a similar act during his reign, but it focused more on economic problems. The native boyars were exempted from taxes on their lands, while the Greek and Levantine boyars had to pay increased taxes. He hoped this would be enough to make them leave Moldavia.

During the mid-17th century, two different rulers consolidated their power. In Wallachia, it was Matei Basarab (r. 1632-1654), and in Moldavia, it was Vasile Lupu (r. 1634-1653). However, they used different means to achieve this. Matei Basarab worked with the boyars of Wallachia. He understood their hatred of the Greeks, and to win their support, he included them in the governance of the country. He started gathering them in the Assembly of the Estates to discuss the internal politics of Wallachia. In contrast, Vasile Lupu was an authoritarian ruler. He allied with the Greeks against the native boyars and allowed them to buy local villages and collect taxes in his name. Both of these princes were able to consolidate their power because, at the time, the Ottoman grasp over their principalities had loosened. The 17th century was a period of change for the external territories of the empire, and with it came changes in how the sultans controlled the principalities of Wallachia and Moldavia. First, they allowed boyars to choose their princes completely on their own, and they allowed the princes to oversee the foreign politics of their principalities. This meant that Wallachia and Moldavia were free to establish foreign relations how they saw fit. Toward the end of the century, the Ottomans were at war with the Habsburgs, and they intended to make the principalities a buffer zone between them and their enemy.

The war between the Ottoman and Habsburg Empires started with the siege of Vienna in 1683 and ended with the Treaty of Karlowitz in 1699. The Habsburgs were victorious, and the treaty included the cession of Ottoman territories in Europe (Transylvania included). Thus, the principalities turned to a new source of influence: western Europe. But a third player entered the scene, for Russia, the Habsburgs' ally, turned its attention toward the principalities too. Emperor Peter the Great of Russia (r. 1682–1725) involved himself in the region, and he used their shared faith to cast his sphere of influence onto the principalities.

The princes of Wallachia and Moldavia weren't blind to the events that were happening around them. They knew the defeat of the Ottomans was a perfect opportunity to gain independence. However, they had to be cautious because they were aware of Austrian and Russian ambitions for the region. In Wallachia, Prince Serban Cantacuzino (r. 1678–1688) made an alliance with Austria, hoping that good relations would ensure not only their separation from the Ottoman Empire but also complete independence. He knew very well that Austria sought to expand its territory south of the Carpathians, and to counter that, he also reached out to Russia. Serban died before he could conclude the treaty with either side, but his efforts were continued by his successor, Constantin Brancoveanu (r. 1688–1714). To ensure his position on the throne of Wallachia, Constantin turned toward the Ottomans, as they managed to persuade him that the sultan alone could guarantee the independence of the principality. However, he continued negotiations with Austria and Russia, hoping to gain a better deal from the European powers. In the end, he saw Russia as the most reliable ally, as one that would be able to protect the territorial integrity and complete independence of Wallachia.

The Moldavian princes had the same ambitions as the ones in Wallachia. In 1711, Prince Dimitrie Cantemir (r. 1710–1711) signed an alliance with Peter the Great of Russia, who recognized Moldavia as an independent and sovereign state. Dimitrie also made Moldavia a hereditary monarchy so that the title of prince would stay in the Cantemir family. Although the boyars lost their power to elect the prince, Dimitrie still needed the support of the boyars, so he made sure to keep the Moldavian nobility as a privileged social class. During the Russo-Ottoman War, Peter the Great's army lost the battle at the Pruth River in 1711. Both the Wallachian and Moldavian princes were forced to stop their negotiations with the Austrians and Russians. Afraid of the sultan's wrath, Cantemir escaped to Russia. Brancoveanu chose to stay, and in 1714, he was executed by Sultan Ahmed III, but not before he witnessed the beheadings of his four sons. Because he declined to renounce Christianity moments before his death, he was sanctified in the Eastern Orthodox Church. With his death and the flight of Cantemir to Russia, the Ottomans resumed their direct intervention in the governments of Wallachia and Moldavia.

The Phanariots

To prevent Russian and Austrian influence on the principalities, the sultans decided to choose the princes of Wallachia and Moldavia from a community that had served their cause in the past: the wealthy Greeks from the Phanar (modern-day Fener) district of Constantinople. The Phanariot regime began in 1711 in Moldavia and in 1716 in Wallachia. The Greek families of the Phanar ruled the principalities until 1821. Although the principalities remained autonomous, the Ottomans continued to profit from them. Their demands for taxes constantly rose, and the supplies sent to Constantinople included food, cattle, textiles, and raw materials. Luckily, the provinces managed to produce enough to both supply the Ottoman Empire and to export their merchandise to other countries in the East and West. However, there were periods when supplies grew short, causing the sultan to suspend all exports on short notice. Aside from paying taxes, Ottoman merchants had the privilege of buying produced goods from the principalities at significantly lower prices.

The candidates for the Wallachian and Moldavian courts had to pay into the sultan's treasury, and they also had to bribe other state officials to gain their goodwill and support. The expenses were enormous, and only the wealthiest among them were able to afford to become a prince. Sultans changed princes often because it was a good business practice and an excellent way to fill their pockets. Between 1730 and 1768, Wallachia saw eighteen princes while Moldavia had around seventeen. Unfortunately, this resulted in an administration crash, although some form of government continuity was preserved, as the sultan chose to switch the places of the princes of Moldavia and Wallachia. Constantin Mavrocordat, for example, ruled Wallachia six times and Moldavia four times. Although the Phanariot princes were often abused and manipulated by the Ottomans, they managed to display high qualities and achieve solid accomplishments, given the period and political scene. Constantin Mavrocordat carried out a series of reforms in both principalities, and he did it in the manner of the period's enlightened monarchs of central Europe. He rationalized the government administration, thus creating a monarchy suitable for the privileged classes. He wanted to expand the power of the government and regulate landholdings. With it, he would also regulate the relationship between the boyars and the peasants by demanding fair pay for the producers. In 1746, he abolished serfdom in Wallachia, which brought stability to agriculture. He did the same in Moldavia in 1749. His reforms were approved by the Ottoman sultan, who hoped to gain increased production in the provinces as well as continuous peace.

Culture and Society during the 17th Century

The 17th century brought various foreign influences to the principalities, and writers and intellectuals quickly adopted them and moved away from the medieval traditions. Although some aspects of tradition remained visible in the Romanian culture, most influences came from the West. This foreign influence created an identity crisis, and it further deepened the division between the clergy and the intellectuals. The creativity of the Romanian people was severely influenced by the political and economic situation of the principalities, which brought about the secularization of culture. It was no longer closely related to the Church, and individual creators started appearing, influenced by the great minds of Western civilization. Monasteries were no longer centers where culture bloomed, as they were not seen as the means of bringing God closer to the people. The Romanian people learned how to look to themselves and find inspiration in earthly delights. The Romanian language became the predominant language of this new secularized culture, but the Church language (Slavic) was often used as well. During the 17th century, the Slavic language was pushed out of the religious rites, and the Romanian language took its place. It penetrated all aspects of religion, and soon, the lesser clergy didn't even bother to learn Slavic. However, the Slavic language still lingers in Romania, especially when it comes to religious life. Some Slavic words are still in use today to describe the holiness of church rites.

Even though intellectuals turned to this Western influence willingly, the traditional ways had their defenders. Wallachia and Moldavia were still under Ottoman rule, and in order not to lose their Christian identity, the pan-Orthodox consciousness was kept alive. The secular and religious leaders were aware of its importance in preserving the Christian spirit in the communities dominated by the Islamic Ottomans. The princes of Wallachia and Moldavia were in a unique situation. Of all the southeastern European countries, they were the only ones to possess some level of independence. Serbia and Bulgaria were transformed into Turkish provinces, leaving the Romanian principalities as the only successors of the Byzantine heritage. The princes were aware of their situation in the Orthodox community, and they invested generously in Orthodox churches and monasteries, not only in their principalities but also in Constantinople, Jerusalem, and on Mount Athos.

The second half of the 17th century saw the revival of the traditional ways and an attempt to bring the Slavic language back to the Church. But besides defending tradition, many intellectuals remained open to the influence of the modern era, thus creating a bridge between the Romanian past and future. Two individuals who best represent this duality of tradition and modern thought are Udriste Nasturel, a high-ranking boyar and an intellectual from Wallachia, and Varlaam of Moldavia, who was born to a free peasant family. While Nasturel strived to bring back the Slavic language to Romanian Orthodoxy, Varlaam recognized the importance of keeping the Romanian language in the Church, as it would bring God closer to the common people. Even though Nasturel was a traditionalist, he remained open to the ideas of humanism and the Renaissance that came from the West. But it was Varlaam's work that not only brought the people closer to the Church but also created the first spark of Romanian patriotic spirit. He worked tirelessly on translating the book of sermons from Slavic to Romanian so everyone could read it. He also wrote a response to the Transylvanian Calvinists' work, "Calvinist Catechism," to prevent Romanians from joining this sect.

Romanian culture remained free of Ottoman bonds. In neighboring Ottoman provinces, the expression of Slavic culture was forbidden and was practiced in secrecy. But in Wallachia and Moldavia, people were culturally free. The Slavs were the intermediates of the Western influence, as it came through the trade routes of Poland and Ukraine. The Latin culture of the West was already transformed by humanism, and this trend then moved on to Orthodoxy. Moldavian historian Miron Costin and Moldavian poet Dosoftei were strongly influenced by Polish humanism and the literary works of the baroque epoch. They attended Polish schools when they were young, and there, they realized the importance of rediscovering the classical past of the nation. They came back to Moldavia, bringing those humanist ideas with them. Moldavian princes didn't see this Western influence as a threat to Orthodox tradition. Instead, they regarded it as a means of strengthening the relationship with the Ottoman-free West.

Another strong cultural influence on the principalities came from Greece. Because their country was under direct Ottoman rule, many Greek scholars and clergy escaped the uncertainty of life in their home country and settled in the provinces of Wallachia and Moldavia. During the 17th century, Greek became the third main language spoken among the upper classes and educated civilians. The ethnic and cultural divisions between the Romanians and Greeks were also diminished by the fact that the two countries were united in their efforts to fight not only Islam but also Catholic influences. By the second half of the 17th century, Greek, alongside Romanian, became the official language of the Church and intellectual elite. Although it became the most important trade language in the East, Greek never managed to replace the Romanian language when it came to literature and history.

In Transylvania

During the 18th century, Transylvania went through a change that influenced its Romanian inhabitants. Since the Habsburg victory against the Ottomans in 1699, the principality belonged to the Austro-Hungarian Empire and, therefore, to the Habsburg dynasty. As a result, Romanians found themselves involved in the political currents of central Europe. Habsburg rulers brought efficiency and reason to the administration of Transylvania, and they inspired the people to take on the spirit of entrepreneurship. They also brought technical, economic, and intellectual innovations to Transylvania so it could develop into something similar to the great European powers. All these changes proved to be a challenge to the Romanians, who had been brought up in the Eastern way of life, with Eastern ideas and worldviews. Suddenly, they found themselves on the path of modernization, and they realized they had much catching up to do.

The Eastern mentality of the people inhabiting Transylvania slowed down the progress set out by the Habsburg dynasty. To succeed, the Habsburgs had to cancel the autonomies for which various groups of people had fought. The Hungarians, Saxons, and Szeklers had formed a Union of the Three Nations in 1438, but over time, the Union grew to be much more. Social class mattered, and to enjoy the privileges monopolized by the Union, one had to belong to the Hungarian nobility, the Saxon patriciate, or the upper class of the Szeklers. Romanians, who composed at least half the population of Transylvania during the 18th century, were not a part of the Union and were excluded from enjoying the privileges, along with the Hungarian, Saxon, and Szekler peasants.

The Church also played an important role in monopolizing political privileges. The Catholics, Calvinists, Protestants, and Lutherans made a deal that if an individual belonged to any other faith, they would be ostracized. Thus, Romanians, who belonged to Orthodox Christianity, could not be a part of the Transylvanian upper classes. Some cities were even closed to Romanians, and they were prohibited not only from settling in them but also from entering them at all. The Romanian Orthodox Church was allowed to exist, and it was tolerated by the Union of the Three Nations, but it had to endure the constant pressure of the Calvinist princes, who wanted to convert the Romanians. When the Orthodox clergy stood against the Calvinist conversion, they were imprisoned or executed. To protect the Church from the Calvinists, the Habsburgs pressed the Orthodox Church to step into a union with Rome. However, the Habsburgs had their own reasons to create this unlikely alliance with the Orthodox Church. To successfully rule Transylvania, they had to bring down the dominion of the Three Nations. Since Romanians were the outsiders in Transylvanian political and social life, they were the natural choice for an ally.

The union between the Roman Catholic and Romanian Orthodox Church would give the Habsburgs the means of holding together multiethnic principalities, such as Transylvania. In 1701, the Roman Catholic primate of Hungary and the Romanian Orthodox bishop started negotiating the union, and the result was the Act of Union. Under its terms, the Orthodox clergy of Romania recognized the pope as the head of the Christian Church. They accepted the usage of unleavened bread in communion, and they acknowledged the existence of purgatory and the procession of the Holy Spirit from the Father and the Son. These were the main points in which Catholicism and Orthodoxy differed. By accepting these terms, the Romanian Orthodox Church came one step closer to Roman Catholicism. However, the canon law, rituals, and practices of the Orthodox Church remained unchanged, and the Orthodox clergy was still allowed to marry. In return, the Orthodox clergy gained the rights and privileges of the upper classes. With their influence over the large, rural society, the Habsburgs gained an ally who would influence the masses to serve the imperial cause.

The Church union opened the way for Western cultural and intellectual influences in Transylvania. The Romanian Orthodox clergy now had the right to send their representatives for higher education in Rome, Vienna, or any other Roman Catholic lyceum in Europe. However, in Vienna, the imperial throne and the representatives of the Roman Catholic Church regarded Romanian Orthodoxy as dead; they thought of the Church union as the birth of a new Greek Catholicism. Nevertheless, the intellectuals who studied under this new Romanian Church saw the opportunity to bring forth the idea of a nation. They were aware of the Roman origins of their people, and the Church union gave them the means to act as the bridge between their Roman heritage and the Eastern tradition. For Romanians, who had spent centuries influenced by Eastern doctrine, the Church union felt like a return home, a return to their origins. It was only natural for the Romanian masses to accept this transition from East to West with ease. However, the sense of Eastern cultural and religious heritage remained strong, and the Romanian Orthodox Church would never go so far as to become entirely Catholic.

Although the Romanian clergy and intellectuals accepted the union peacefully, the wider masses, the peasants, in particular, presented a problem. They considered Orthodoxy not only a part of their heritage but also a part of their ethnic identity. At first, the new Greek Catholic clergy refused to even preach the union to peasants, as they feared violent reactions. The majority of Romanian people didn't even know that they accepted the union because there was no one to tell them. It was only in 1744, when a Serbian Orthodox monk named Visarion Sarai came to "spread the truth of Orthodoxy," that Romanians became aware of the union. As predicted, the reaction was violent, and many villages rose up to demand the return to their original faith. The uprisings were quickly quelled once authorities arrested Visarion. However, violence broke out again in 1759 when a Romanian monk, Sofronie of Cioara, started calling for true Orthodoxy. He preached against the union with the Catholics, and he shunned those families who accepted the union. Empress Maria Theresa was forced to restore the Orthodox Church in Transylvania that same year to stop the spreading violence.

The 18th century brought all three principalities—Wallachia, Moldavia, and Transylvania—to the threshold of the modern world. Politics, the economy, and the intellectual elite were all drawn toward European ideas and modern behaviors. But it turned out that tradition was an integral part of the Romanian identity. Without it, the nation couldn't move forward. The only possible thing Romanians could do was make a truce between their Eastern heritage and their desire for Western innovation and progress.

Chapter 6 – The Birth of a Nation

Tudor Vladimirescu
(https://en.wikipedia.org/wiki/Tudor_Vladimirescu#/media/
File:Tudor_Vladimirescu.jpg)

Between the late 18th century and the first half of the 19th century, the three principalities that were to become Romania went through fundamental changes. Wallachia, Moldavia, and Transylvania were ruled by enlightened princes, and its politics were influenced heavily by the "reforming" boyars and, in the middle of the 19th century, by the revolutionary ideas of the intellectuals. But when it came to international relations, Russia emerged as the main opponent to the Ottoman rule in the principalities of Wallachia and Moldavia. Still, the main change came from the people within the principalities. The educated Romanians started changing their minds about who they were and what their relationship with Europe should be like. Slowly but certainly, the Eastern influence of the Ottoman Empire began to disappear, and Western ideas poured in to fill the gaps. The late 18th century saw the printing of *Carte de rugaciuni*, a little book of prayer printed in Latin instead of Cyrillic. However, it grew to be more than just a little prayer book. It turned into a statement of ethnic distinctiveness and a confirmation of the bonds between Romania in the East and the rest of Europe in the West.

Travel between the principalities and central and western Europe grew steadily. The people who came to the Romanian territories brought new and innovative ideas, and their influence slowly shifted the consciousness of the upper social classes from the heritage of the East to the modern world of the West. However, the peasants remained stubborn in their traditional worldviews, and the divide between the cities and the villages grew to be more than just social. During the early 19th century, the difference became spiritual and material. The modernization of the cities was quickly accepted, but in the rural part of the principalities, it was effectively rejected.

The internal development of the principalities was also heavily influenced by their international status. Due to the Ottoman Empire's weakened grasp, other great powers sought to control the area. The Romanian political elite sought to gain complete independence, and they were ready to use the rivalries between the European powers to achieve their goals. But there was still a question to be answered. If the principalities achieved autonomy and eventually independence, where would their future lie? In the East or the West? Romanians had to choose, and the history of this country is deeply affected by the choices made during the late 18th and the 19th century.

Russia shared Austria's interest in the principalities because of their unique position next to the Black Sea. During the Russo-Ottoman Wars, Russia won some of the most significant victories in the area, the last one in 1812. Russian influence extended to the principalities, and at one point, it even exercised an unofficial protectorate over them. Empress Catherine the Great (r. 1762–1796) made it her prime objective to create stable communications and a link between the Russian Empire and the Romanian principalities. During her reign, she fought for the expulsion of Turks out of Europe. To achieve this, she planned the restoration of the Byzantine Empire and the union of Wallachia and Moldavia into the "Kingdom of Dacia." Further plans revealed that the Russian empress planned to install a prince of her liking to rule the Kingdom of Dacia, and the territories would serve as a buffer zone between her empire and the Austro-Hungarian and Ottoman Empires.

The Russian authority over the principalities was such that they appointed a consul in Bucharest (the capital of Wallachia) in 1782 and a vice-consul in Iasi (the capital of Moldavia) in 1784. Under the terms of the Treaty of Iasi (Jassy) in 1792, Russia annexed the territories between the Bug and Dniester Rivers, bringing the Russian border to Moldavia. Only two decades later, with the Treaty of Bucharest, Russia reached the Danube and annexed parts of Moldavia between the Dniester and Prut Rivers. This area would later be known as Bessarabia. After the Napoleonic Wars, the prestige of Russia grew significantly in the principalities, and the

Romanians looked toward the East, hoping their liberators would come from there.

Other nations played a significant role in the principalities, but they were not nearly as influential as Russia. Austria planned the expansion of its territories beyond the southern Carpathians so it could take complete control of the Danube and its exit to the Black Sea, but the Habsburgs were more concerned with the affairs of central Europe, and their plans of expansion never came to see the light of day. Even the French displayed an interest in the principalities once Napoleon Bonaparte started conquering Europe. However, Wallachia and Moldavia were only to be used as a bargaining chip with the Russians in Napoleon's plans for Europe. Great Britain saw the principalities as an opportunity to gain more allies, which they could use for their interests in the Middle East. While Russia and Austria saw an economic gain from the principalities and their control over the ports on the Black Sea, France and Great Britain saw them as useful for their political interests, each in its way. Either way, none of them managed to assert their influence as much as Russia did, and in the end, none of them ever took full control over Wallachia or Moldavia as they had hoped.

The Question of a Nation

The educated elite of the principalities started feeling that they belonged to a new, rising community, one that was based not on social status or religion but rather shared history and language. The same idea was born in all three principalities and on both sides of the Carpathian Mountains. However, the forms it took differed, which influenced the historical development of Transylvania, Wallachia, and Moldavia. In Wallachia and Moldavia, the sense of ethnic distinctiveness was based on Byzantine Orthodox cultural and political traditions, as well as their historical origin. However, by the 18th century, the theory of Roman origins was far more attractive, as it implied that Romanians belonged to the rest of Europe. The idea that Romanians were the descendants of the

Roman conquerors of Dacia wasn't only historical and cultural. It was also so popular that politicians started using it in their diplomatic works and as political weapons.

During the Russo-Ottoman Wars, the Romanian boyars continued calling themselves Roman colonists in their communications with the Russians. Calling on their noble ancestry, they tried to get a seat at the peace conferences that would decide the fate of their principalities. In 1807, an anonymous author wrote a memorandum to Napoleon, trying to convince him of the idea of a free Moldavia. In this memorandum, he cited the Roman origins of the people of Moldavia and insisted that Romans remained in the territory even after Emperor Aurelian retreated. Many other authors wrote of the Roman origins of the Romanian people, claiming that they had to be returned to the fold of Europe. It's important to understand that the educated elite of the 18th and 19th centuries didn't invent the idea of Roman origins. There are medieval texts with the same claims, and there are even Byzantine and Roman sources that state the same. Although the continuity of the Roman settlements cannot be proven archaeologically because of the lack of excavation funds, there are many written sources that support this ancestry idea.

Some intellectuals went even beyond the Roman idea of ancestry and allowed Dacians to play a role too. This mixture of Romano-Dacian ancestry represents the modern opinion of Romanian ancestry and ethnicity. The Dacian sentiment was created in the 18th century, and the evidence for it doesn't exist in the historical texts. It is only speculation, as there is no evidence of what happened to the Dacians after the Roman conquest. How well did they adapt to the new culture, were they fully assimilated, or did they simply disappear? Still, no one can dispute the importance of the Dacians in the creation of the Romanian nation, but the majority of 18th-century intellectuals dismissed the idea of Dacian ancestry simply because they regarded these ancient people as uncivilized.

The ethnic consciousness flourished, and at its heart was the recognition that Romanians were European people. Intellectuals accepted the thesis that the principalities of Wallachia and Moldavia stood as the defenders of Europe against the Ottoman Empire. Even the Orthodox Church started writing about Europe as a place of greater civilization and culture. During the 19th century, such a view of Europe was common among the whole population of Moldavia. The idea of getting rid of Ottoman dominion grew stronger, and the politicians and boyars asked themselves how an Eastern ruler could secure the well-being and prosperity of European nations such as theirs.

In Transylvania, a similar sentiment was born among the intellectuals. Almost all of them were members of the clergy who belonged to the newly founded Catholic Greek branch of Christianity and were educated at the Roman Catholic or Greek Catholic schools in Transylvania, Vienna, or Rome. They maintained Eastern Orthodoxy in some forms of their religious expression, but culturally, they were oriented toward Europe. They supported the modern era of the Enlightenment, which was famous for its respect for reason and learning. Under the influence of the Enlightenment of central Europe, they promoted the idea of Roman ancestry to strengthen the link between Transylvania and Europe. They accepted the historical evidence of Romanians being the remnants of Roman conquerors, finding evidence to support this thesis in the Romanian language.

Samuil Micu (1745–1806) was the first to present this idea, doing so in a four-volume series called "The History and the Concerns and the Events of the Romanians." In this work, he described modern Romanians as the descendants of the Roman conquerors of Dacia. He claimed they all came from Italy and that they remained in Dacia once Emperor Aurelian removed the legions from the area. He further claims that these Roman settlers managed to survive the barbarian invasions by retreating to the mountains, where they lived in isolation and avoided mixing with other nations. According to Micu, when the Hungarians entered Transylvania in the 10th century, they encountered already-organized duchies, which had been settled by the surviving Romans. Micu continues his history by lamenting the decline that occurred after the Hungarians took over and created an alliance with the Saxons and Szeklers. Micu was strongly influenced by the Habsburg imperial plans to bring Romanians to an equal social level, so his works are not unbiased. Direct Roman descendancy inspired other nations to feel noble respect toward the Romanians, who were, until now, seen only as peasants.

In 1792, Romanian Transylvanian scholars presented a statement of national identity, called the *Supplex Libellus Valachorum*, to Holy Roman Emperor Leopold II (r. 1790–1792) in Vienna. In it, they gathered all their theories of Roman ancestry and references to the historical evidence they had found. They claimed that this heritage gave them the right to enjoy the privileges their neighbors had. In this document, the Romanian scholars used the term "nation" for the first time to describe the ethnic belonging to a community of Romanians. In their mind, it didn't matter if the person was a peasant or a noble or if he belonged to Orthodoxy or Greek Catholicism. They all shared the same ancestry, which means they all belonged to the same nation. Unfortunately, their efforts were in vain. Neither the court in Vienna nor the Hungarian, Saxon, and Szekler communities accepted Romanians as a privileged nation, so their position in Transylvania continued to be formidable, depending on political currents and needs.

Autonomy

While Austria, Russia, and the Ottoman Empire had their interests in the principalities of Wallachia and Moldavia, they took quite a while to decide the fate of the region. The Romanian boyars saw an opportunity in this indecision of the greater powers to promote the autonomy of the principalities. In the first rows of the autonomy fight were the middle- and high-class boyars, who were occasionally joined by the princes and the ever-growing middle class. These patriotic boyars led the fight to preserve autonomy, and they were the ones who convinced the Austrian, Russian, and Ottoman Empires that Wallachia and Moldavia had never renounced their autonomy and that the peace in the region could only continue if everyone respected it. The boyars never resorted to violence to defend autonomy. Instead, they tried to reason with the greater powers and inform them of the true nature of the principalities. The Russian diplomats were the most sympathetic to the boyars' cause, and because of this, the boyars tried to appeal to Russia first.

The high treasurer of Moldavia, the great boyar Iordache Rosetti-Roznovanu, sent a memorandum to the Russian ambassador in Constantinople in 1818. In it, he urged the ambassador to convince the sultan that Moldavia's many obligations to the Ottomans should be reduced to only an annual "gift." He also demanded that the Ottomans stop interfering in Moldavian internal and external politics. He claimed Moldavia could govern itself as an independent state. However, the Ottoman court remained deaf to these appeals. The economic contribution of the principalities and their strategic importance didn't decline during the 19th century, and despite Russian victories in the region, the Ottomans were reluctant to let go of their grasp. After all, the principalities were the first line of defense against the invading Russians and Austrians, and the sultan could not allow the formation of a free state, which would grant it the freedom to make alliances with foreign powers and create a national army. If the Ottomans lessened their grip on the principalities of Wallachia and Moldavia, they knew it would mean the beginning of the end of their empire in Europe.

However, the patriotic boyars were not afraid to continue with their efforts. When the Phanariot rule ended in 1821, the boyars were deeply committed to the idea of independence. Nevertheless, they realized they would never achieve their goals by working alone. They turned to Russia for help, and the patronage of the

Russian tsars brought the end of the Ottoman Empire in Europe earlier than had been expected. In 1821, the Greek War of Independence broke out and set in motion a series of events that would shake the whole of Europe. Over the next half a century, the status quo of the principalities would change. Moldavia and Wallachia took the opportunity created by the chaos of the Greek War of Independence to move closer to each other and shake off the Ottoman yolk so it was a little looser. The first outlines of modern-day Romania took shape even before the revolutions of 1848.

The first changes were in the administrative institutions of the principalities. The boyars experimented with representative assemblies and started gathering political groups that were different from each other, not only politically but also socially. Society became cosmopolitan and complex, as the number of cities grew. The changing economy and the myriad of cultural patterns brought diversity and mobility to the social classes. Production increased, and both agriculture and industry flourished. However, at their core, they continued to resist innovation. Romanian society turned to the West when it came to ideas and politics, but it remained traditionally Eastern when it concerned technical innovation. In other words, although it was European in mentality, Romania lagged in technology.

In the spring of 1821, in the Wallachian village of Oltenia, a peasant uprising occurred. Soon, it spread across almost the whole principality. The reasons for the movement were many, but the main one was the hard conditions of peasant life, as well as the land and fiscal abuses of the local administrative officials. At the same time, the boyars fought to end Ottoman suzerainty, and the people of the principalities united under the common idea of a nation. The economic and social demands of the peasants and the political aspirations of the boyars found common ground in the movement led by Tudor Vladimirescu, the revolutionary mind of Romania.

Tudor was educated by the boyars, whom he served as a peasant boy. He rose to the position of estate administrator, which would later help him understand the divide between the social classes. He served in the Russian army during the Russo-Ottoman War (1806–1812) and enjoyed the Russian protectorate. Once he came back to his homeland, he was granted the ownership of land and rose to the position of a lesser boyar. But he never forgot that he used to be a peasant. He understood the political needs of the boyars to get rid of the Greek Phanariot rulers, and he sympathized with the peasants and the hard conditions of their existence. The commander of the Wallachian prince's guards, Iordache Olimpiotul (also known as Giorgakis Olympios), included Tudor Vladimirescu in the planning of the uprising against the Phanariots. Constantin Samurcas, the high commissioner of the Wallachian prince in Oltenia, also advocated for Tudor's inclusion. They all met each other during their service in the Russian army, and the two agreed that Tudor's military abilities were needed in the uprising. However, Vladimirescu wouldn't allow others to use him as a tool. He had his own agenda; he thought it possible to free Wallachia from Ottoman rule and to bring about social and economic reforms that would put peasants in a better position.

In 1821, Tudor spent time in his native Oltenia raising his army. To peasants who would join his movement, he promised membership in *Adunarea Norodului*, the Assembly of the People, which he planned to integrate as a part of the Wallachian government. He also promised the end of their abuses and the end of the boyars' tyranny. However, Tudor had no concrete plan for abolishing labor service or granting the peasants the right to own the land they worked. Nevertheless, just the promise of reforms was enough to gather peasants from all over the Oltenia region to his side.

At the time, eastern Europe was, in general, rising against the Ottoman Empire, something that had been initiated and led by the Greek secret organization of *Philike Hetairia* (Friendly Society). Its founders believed they would free Greece of Ottoman rule if they started a Christian uprising in southeastern Europe. One of the founders was Alexandru Ipsilanti (Alexander Ypsilantis), the son of Wallachian Phanariot Prince Constantin Ipsilanti (Constantine Ypsilantis; r. 1802–1807). Using his father's connections, Alexandru thought he could draw upon the boyars of Wallachia. But he greatly misunderstood the boyars' opinions on the Greek princes. Although some boyars and clergy welcomed the Greek insurrection, the principalities were determined to abolish the Phanariot regime. Nevertheless, they hoped they could use the *Philike Hetairia* to overthrow the Ottomans first. In Moldavia, Alexandru Ipsilanti and his army of 2,000 Hetairians entered Iasi on March 6th, 1821. He issued the proclamation of war against Ottoman rule and was welcomed in Moldavia by Prince Mihai Sutu (r. 1819–1821), who believed the Russian army was on its way to help too. However, the tsar condemned the Greek secret order and the actions of Alexandru Ipsilanti. The leader of the Hetairians continued to Bucharest, where he hoped to meet Vladimirescu, but the support crumbled away, as people no longer believed he would be able to protect Moldavia and Wallachia without Russian support.

Tudor Vladimirescu was willing to help Alexandru's army cross the Danube and continue southward, but he made it clear that he wanted the Greek Phanariots out of his principality. While he also relied on Russian help in overthrowing the Ottoman Empire, he also didn't want Wallachia to become a Russian protectorate. He firmly believed in Wallachian independence and its ability to govern itself. By the time Vladimirescu reached Bucharest from Oltenia with his army of 8,000 peasants, all hopes of Russian intervention had disappeared. He had to turn to the boyars to present a united Romanian nation against the Ottomans and the Greeks. Tudor also had a personal motive for turning to the boyars, as he hoped to become the prince of Wallachia after the successful uprising. For that, he needed to be elected by the boyars.

In the end, Vladimirescu failed all of his objectives. On May 25th, the Ottoman forces marched into Wallachia and Moldavia, and Alexandru suspected that Vladimirescu had formed a secret alliance with the Turks. He ordered the arrest and execution of Tudor Vladimirescu on June 8th. The peasant army dispersed after the death of their leader, as the hopes for any reforms died with him. Ipsilanti's army was soon defeated by the Turks, and he escaped to Transylvania, where he was imprisoned. Tudor Vladimirescu failed to bring the changes to Wallachia that had been desired by both the boyars and peasants. However, he remains a symbol of the freedom fight, and the independence movement continued to live. The people needed political and economic reforms, and the death of one man could not stop their determination.

The Ottomans occupied the principalities but only for a short time. Pressured by Britain and France, the boyars and the sultan reached an agreement in 1822 to end the occupation, but the Ottomans preserved their suzerainty of the principalities. The native princes were restored to the thrones, and the rule of the Greek Phanariots officially ended. The new princes, Grigore IV Ghica in Wallachia and Ioan Sandu Sturdza in Moldavia (both ruled from 1822 to 1828), continued expanding their own privileges, and for this, they made the boyars their enemies. The boyars believed they deserved greater involvement in politics, and the conflict between them and the princes extended into the post-Phanariot period.

In 1826, the Russian tsar forced the Ottoman sultan to sign the Akkerman Convention, by which Russia gained "protecting power" over the principalities. This meant that the princes, the sultan, and the boyars had to take into consideration Russian interests in Wallachia and Moldavia and to listen to the observations of the tsar's ambassador and adjust their policies accordingly. However, that wasn't the end of the Russo-Ottoman conflict. They continued to disagree about the principalities, as well as about the status of

Greece and the Caucasus. A new war sparked in 1828, and the Russians occupied the principalities to ensure safe passage for their troops and supplies to the front, which was south of the Danube. A year later, the Russian army was ready to march on Constantinople, and the Ottomans sued for peace. On September 14th, 1829, they signed the Treaty of Adrianople, in which the sultan admitted the autonomy of Wallachia and Moldavia. The principalities were also relieved of their obligations to supply Constantinople and the Turkish army. Economic recovery followed, as both Wallachia and Moldavia gained the right to export their goods wherever they wanted. As a consequence, agriculture bloomed, as the people were no longer pressured to produce a certain amount of food for the Ottomans. The only obligation that remained in place was the annual "gift" to the sultan and the sultan's right to confirm or disapprove of the elected princes.

Russia occupied the principalities while waiting for the Turks to pay the war indemnity. However, they didn't stand idle. They brought modernization to the public life of Wallachia and Moldavia through the Russian official who acted as the prince until 1834. His name was Pavel Kiselyov, and his task was to make sure the governmental and economic growth of the principalities so they could serve Russia's plans in the future. To accomplish this, Kiselyov introduced the Organic Statute, a fundamental law that defined the rights and obligations of each social class. This improved the efficiency of the principality's economy, production, and political life. In turn, the relationship between Russia and the boyars became tighter because the statute ensured that they remain as the leaders of Romanian political life. They were given all the positions of the central administration and were exempted from paying taxes. The new middle class was also included in the statute and gained some political privileges, but peasants were completely ignored.

Another innovation to the governance of the principalities imposed by the Organic Statute was the separation of powers between the executive, legislative, and judicial branches. However, the prince remained the key figure in the political system, as all the executive power was in his hands. The statute also made the government centralized, as it had to appoint officials to supervise village affairs and the administration of the cities. These officials only answered to the central government. The state also gained the power to supervise Orthodox Church affairs, which reduced the role the clergy had in civil and public affairs. Thus, the secularization and modernization of the principalities happened at the same time. The unplanned result of the Organic Statute was the speeding up of the union of Wallachia and Moldavia, as the governmental institutions were the same in both principalities. Later, this would be of great help to the process of unification. However, the greatest result was the introduction of double citizenship. People were granted both Wallachian and Moldavian citizenship, which sparked the idea of common ancestry and a unique nation.

The Generation of 1848 and the Nation

Before the revolutionary year of 1848, the principalities of Wallachia and Moldavia had been culturally and politically influenced by two generations that were driven by similar motives and goals to improve their home country. They were the generation of the Enlightenment movement and the Romantics of the newly risen epoch. The boundaries between the two generations were fluid, as they both worked energetically to raise the Romanian nation into the modern world of western Europe. After the revolution of 1848, these people would remain known as the "forty-eighters," and their movement and revolutionary thoughts would be known as the *pașoptism* (forty-eightism). It was a somewhat liberal movement that sought to unite all social classes into one ethnic community: the Romanians.

The idea easily spread through the principalities because there was an audience. Literacy had increased, and the nation picked up a new habit of reading. At first, they read newspapers, whose authors were careful to take into account their readers' tastes. The new middle class represented the majority of readers, and they were not yet sophisticated enough to read high literature. However, in time, this changed. Literature became available to everyone through the mass publication of books, and both poetry and prose conveyed the message of national unity and independence. The writers sympathized with the lower classes, and to make their works available even to peasants, they turned toward folklore and history. Suddenly, even the boyars understood their ethnic connection with the peasants, and a new type of respect between various social classes was born. To the Romantic idealists, belonging to the nation was based on two main principles: ethnicity and religion, mainly Orthodoxy.

In the spring of 1848, the idea of the nation reached its triumph. In Wallachia, Moldavia, and Transylvania, Romanians sought to unite into a single dutchy and advocate for independence or political autonomy by invoking the right of an ethnic community to self-govern. The people of Moldavia and Wallachia wanted to get rid of the Russian protectorate and deal with the Ottoman Empire on their own. Transylvania was sandwiched between the two regions of Banat and Bukovina, which strove to unite all Romanians into a single political entity. The union of all Romanians, on both sides of the Carpathians, was contemplated because they shared a similar culture, language, and history. However, the political realities of the time made such a union impossible. Transylvania was a part of the Habsburg monarchy, which would never give up its possession without a fight. But the persistence of the Forty-Eighters continued. All around Europe, small nations fought to get rid of the oppressive rule of the bigger powers. Nationalism was on the rise, and the Ottoman Empire slowly retreated from Europe.

The liberal intellectuals of the Romanian principalities were the leaders of the revolution in 1848. They defined its goals, gave it direction, and led it with certainty. This new liberal intellectual elite had been educated in western Europe, primarily France. They brought back liberal ideas, mainly the idea of freedom from foreign powers. But despite their admiration for Western progress, the leaders of the Romanian revolution were aware that their nation's history lay with the East. They understood that bringing Western institutions and values to the people with deep Eastern tradition was almost impossible. Therefore, they were highly selective of the Western ideals they wanted to implement in their home country, and they acted with caution and patience.

Events in western Europe, such as the overthrow of King Louis-Philippe I of France in February 1848 and the spread of revolution to Germany and Austro-Hungary, made the Romanian intellectuals act. Romanian students in Paris rushed home to Iasi and Bucharest to support the domestic revolution and, in some cases, even to lead it. The boyars and the middle class of Moldavia drew up a statement of grievances, in which they demanded the moderate liberal political system and the stimulation of the domestic economy. However, they never wanted to act like revolutionaries, and they didn't seek to overthrow the existing political system. Prince Mihail Sturdza of Moldavia (r. 1834–1849) resisted their demands, and the leaders of the reforms were forced to seek exile. In Wallachia, the reforms took the shape of a revolution. Western-educated boyars assaulted the old regime, and they formed a committee that would organize the armed revolution. On June 21ˢᵗ, 1848, they issued a proclamation stating their revolutionary goals, namely, the liberation of Wallachia from foreign suzerainty and the new social structure of Wallachia, which would be based on the Romanian ethnicity of its people rather than on their previous social ranks. The committee agreed to respect the treaties with the Ottoman Empire, but they viewed Russia with open hostility and demanded the abolishment of the Organic Statute. The Wallachian revolutionaries promised the equality of rights for all citizens; a progressive income tax shared by all social classes; the freedom of the press, speech, and assembly; the abolition of forced labor services of peasants; an expanded school system that would make itself available to all social classes; an end to all noble titles and ranks; and the ability to elect a prince from any social category, one who would only serve for a term of five years.

On June 26th, 1848, the Forty-Eighters replaced Prince George Bibescu with a provisional government that was composed of young liberal revolutionists. They sought to implement these reforms at once by introducing new institutions. The first institution played a role in the government's defense, i.e., the army. However, other promises were never implemented. Some reforms of agriculture started, but the new government was afraid of an economic collapse and was slow to bring changes. They tried to organize an assembly that would draft a new constitution for the principality, but their work was cut short by the interference of foreign powers. The Russians were determined to keep the principalities under their protectorate, and on July 7th, the tsar sent his army over the Prut River to occupy Moldavia. To avoid international scandal, the Russian tsar allied with the Ottoman administration to suppress the revolution in Wallachia. Thus, the Ottomans gained the tsar's approval to occupy Wallachia, and on September 25th, the Turkish army entered Bucharest. There, it met fierce resistance, but the Ottomans were simply more numerous, and they hunted down all the revolutionaries. However, the Russian tsar wasn't satisfied with the Ottoman methods, and he sent his own army to occupy Wallachia on September 27th.

When it came to the Habsburg monarchy, the Romanians didn't resist the revolutionary movement of 1848. They, too, were under the influence of the events happening in western and central Europe. They saw their opportunity to demand civil liberties and national political autonomy, and their demands were more or less successful, depending on the province. In Transylvania, Romanians countered the Hungarian aspiration to unite the region with Hungary. In Banat, it seems that Romanians and Hungarians didn't have much to fight about between themselves, as they both had to resist Serbian domination. In Bukovina, Romanians attempted to unite under the ethnic and historical characteristics of the province, but they met opposition in the Orthodox Church.

In Transylvania, the Romanian leaders found themselves torn between two decisions. On the one hand, they supported the civil rights that Hungarian liberals would bring to the region if Transylvania united with Hungary, but on the other hand, they sought the independence of their nation and its existence. That could not be achieved under foreign rule. Hungarian liberals, in both Transylvania and Hungary, demanded the union of Transylvania. Some Romanian intellectuals were willing to sacrifice their national aspirations to receive the civil rights that would extend to Transylvania. However, they needed the guarantee that the Romanian language and culture would be untouched by the union. Other Romanian intellectuals took a completely different stand and opposed the union with all their hearts. For them, the preservation of Romanian nationality was paramount, and they couldn't see how that would happen under Hungarian rule. Unfortunately, Hungarians wanted Romanians to pay the price of national renunciation to receive full civil and political freedoms. In the eyes of Romanians, Transylvania should have been autonomous, with Romanians as its majority. Only then, in their minds, would the nation be preserved and even allowed to thrive and prosper.

On May 15th, 1848, a national assembly took place in Blaj, where the Romanians presented their program of action. The main item of the program was the declaration of the independence of the Romanian nation and its equality with the other nations of Transylvania. The program also sought to establish a liberal political system that would defend the rights of the Romanians. However, this Romanian opposition to the unification of

Transylvania and Hungary was unsuccessful. On May 30th, 1848, the Diet of Transylvania (the legislative and judicial body of the government) held a vote in the city of Cluj. The majority of the Diet were Hungarians, and they overwhelmingly voted for the unification of the principality with Hungary. Disappointed, Romanian opposition turned to the court of Vienna, which also opposed the Hungarian claims over Transylvania, as it was their principality. Just like everywhere in Europe, the Hungarian liberals sought to bring down the monarchy and gain independence for Hungary. The Habsburg court was against liberal changes, and by siding with it, the Romanian liberal leaders found themselves supporting the conservative side so they could preserve their national identity.

Romanians of other Habsburg principalities (Banat and Bukovina) joined forces with the Romanians of Transylvania to appeal to the court in Vienna. Delegations from all three provinces gathered, and under the leadership of Bishop Andrei Saguna, they presented their national program to Emperor Franz Joseph I. In it, they called for the political union and autonomy of the Romanian nation under the Habsburg monarchy. Unfortunately for them, the court of Vienna rejected the Romanian proposal for autonomy, and it implied that Romanians should stay loyal to the emperor for their well-being.

Nicolae Bălcescu, the leader of the Wallachian revolution of 1848, tried to save the liberal and national rise of the Romanians by bringing about the reconciliation between the Hungarian government, which had just gained independence from the Habsburg monarchy, and the Romanians of Transylvania. He met with Lajos Kossuth, the leader of the newly independent Hungary, and Avram Iancu, a lawyer who led the revolutionary army of Transylvania. While the trio agreed to discuss the problems of a Romanian nation under Hungarian governance, Austria allied with Russia, and their joined forces brought about the end of the organized resistance to the Habsburg monarchy. Hungary lost its independence in August 1849, and the Habsburg order was restored. The failure of Hungary to maintain its independence brought new hope to the Transylvanian Romanians that one day they would get their autonomous duchy. However, the court of Vienna sent Austrian officials to Banat, Bukovina, and Transylvania, whose task was to return the principalities to the status of imperial provinces as soon as possible. These officials expected and demanded that Romanians resume their place as loyal subjects of the emperor.

Chapter 7 – The National State of Romania

King Ferdinand and Queen Maria visiting Transylvania (1921)
(https://en.wikipedia.org/wiki/Union_of_Transylvania_with_Romania#/media/Fil
e:Reyes-ruman%C3%ADa-transilvania--secretsofbalkans00vopiuoli.png)

The Principalities Unite

On May 1ˢᵗ, 1849, the Ottomans and the Russians met at the Convention of Balta Liman, where they agreed on a joint protectorate over the Romanian principalities. New princes were chosen: Barbu Stirbei in Wallachia and Grigore Ghica in Moldavia. But both the Russian tsar and the Ottoman sultan were worried about the return of nationalism and liberalism, so they closely monitored the activities of the new princes. Stirbei was a conservative ruler who aspired to be an autocrat, although an enlightened one. Ghica, on the other hand, was sympathetic to revolutionary ideas, and he allowed some of the Forty-Eighters to return to Moldavia from exile. Some even became members of his government. Although the greater powers intended to make the princes their puppets, both of them proved to be much more than that. They worked on improving the economy and education and refused to be docile instruments of Ottoman and Russian politics.

In 1853, a new international crisis rekindled the war between Russia and the Ottoman Empire, known as the Crimean War (1853-1856). Over the next years, France and Britain joined as Ottoman allies against Russia, and with their involvement, the union of the principalities came closer. Although all of the European powers had their own agenda in the principalities, the Romanians ended up determining their future. At the end of the war, a treaty was signed in Paris on May 30th, 1856. The decisions made in this treaty deeply affected the Romanian principalities. They remained under Ottoman suzerainty, but Britain and France forbade any great power to meddle in the internal affairs of Wallachia and Moldavia. The principalities finally gained worldwide recognition for their administrative independence. They also gained the right to mobilize an army, to legislate, and to engage in commerce with any other country they wished.

But the Treaty of Paris wasn't the end of the freedoms granted to the principalities. A special commission of inquiry was formed by the great powers that gathered information and recommendations on how to base the future governance of the Romanian territories. The commission was based in Bucharest, but they elected a special advisory assembly (*Adunări ad-hoc*), which was to communicate public opinion on various matters to the commission. All the gathered information was to be considered during the future Paris conference, in which the final decision would be made and communicated to the principalities by the sultan. Furthermore, according to the Treaty of Paris, Russia was to cede southern Bessarabia to Moldavia. Local politicians looked forward to the Paris Convention, as they hoped they could push for the union of the principalities through the *Adunări ad-hoc*. The assemblies of both principalities met in October 1857 and immediately passed the resolutions of union and autonomy. Both assemblies took a liberal stand on the matters of civil rights and government reform, but neither of them was ready to suggest the agrarian reforms that would help the position of the peasants. By January 1858, the Wallachian and Moldavian assemblies finished their work and presented it to Paris.

On April 7th, 1858, the commission of inquiry issued its report on the wishes of the Romanian people to the great powers that were to decide its fate. The debate was lengthy, but Britain, France, the Ottoman Empire, and Russia finally reached an agreement in August of the same year. The principalities finally gained a definite political organization approved by all the great European powers. The principalities remained under Ottoman suzerainty, but they were now united under the name "United Principalities of Wallachia and Romania." The administration of the newly united principalities remained in the hands of the Romanians, and the Ottoman Empire was forbidden from interfering. The sultan still had the power to invest in the prince and to gather the annual tribute, but these obligations remained in place as mere formalities. Although the main task of the Congress of Paris was to decide the international status of the Romanian principalities, it did so much more. The people gained fundamental civil rights, and the obligations of the political leaders were now clearly defined. Those who drafted the Paris Convention were liberals who had spent time in Bucharest and saw firsthand what the will of the people was. Each principality was provided with a legislative assembly that had a mandate for seven years, and the Central Commission was also elected. They were to meet periodically in Focsani, a town on the Wallachian-Moldavian border, and decide on the common laws of the principalities. The boyars' ranks and privileges were abolished, as the people were all proclaimed equal in the eyes of the law. Public offices were now open to all citizens who had sufficient education and experience.

The Central Commission also had the task of supervising the election of legislative bodies, which would, in turn, elect new princes. There were many candidates for the princes, but ultimately, the people decided on a Forty-Eighter named Alexandru Cuza, who supported the union. He was elected as the prince of Moldavia on January 17th, 1859. In Wallachia, the assembly couldn't agree on who should be elected as their prince. In the end, they voted for the union too and also elected Alexandru Cuza. On February 5th, he became the prince of united Wallachia and Moldavia, and the Romanians of both principalities welcomed the union.

Prince Alexandru Ioan Cuza (r. 1859-1866)

Alexandru Cuza came from a noble family that held many high-ranking offices in Moldavia ever since the early 17th century. However, his family never held the rank of high boyars. He was born in 1820 and was schooled in a French boarding school in Iasi, from which he was sent to Paris to continue his studies. In 1848, he came back to Moldavia and took part in the reformation movement, for which he was proclaimed a Forty-Eighter and was exiled. Under the rule of Prince Ghica, he was invited back to Moldavia, and he took various administrative posts. At the time of his election as a prince, he was serving as the commanding officer of the Moldavian militia. Cuza was elected a prince because he displayed continuous patriotism, even during his exile. He was also a liberal, but he was not radical, and he believed in the union of the principalities. On September 7th, 1859, the great European powers accepted the double election of Alexandru Cuza.

The final union of the principalities demanded more negotiations with the Ottoman Empire and the European powers of France, Britain, Austria, and Russia, but the Wallachian and Moldavian politicians couldn't wait for them to settle on an arrangement. Instead, they went and merged some of the main institutions, such as the army, currency, telegraph lines, and customs service. The Central Commission at Focsani worked feverishly to unite the laws and administration of the two principalities. Formal recognition of the union occurred at the Constantinople Conference on December 6th, 1861. On December 23rd, Alexandru Cuza proclaimed the union was complete. The Law of February (1862) was the final act by which the union was completed, and it abolished the Central Commission at Focsani. The name Romania was chosen as the official state name because it had been in use since the 1850s, though unofficially.

Cuza's reign was marked by two political sides that often clashed: the liberals and the conservatives. As a Forty-Eighter, the new prince was eager to see the revolutionary ideas take hold in Romania, but the conservatism of the pre-1848 era was still there to appeal to the sense of tradition. The conservatives of Romania wanted to preserve the social structures and privileges that had existed before. They also wanted to reserve the administrative offices for the higher social classes. In opposition, the liberals looked at western Europe as a model for political and economic progress. They insisted that the development of political life in Romania needed to meet the demands of Romanian society. After the union was completed, a divide among the liberals occurred, mainly in Wallachia, although it didn't go unnoticed in Moldavia either. A radical group named the "Reds" broke away from the moderate liberals. They were the most ardent Forty-Eighters who were committed to the union and a liberal political course. They were also very well organized under the leadership of C. A. Rosetti and Ion C. Bratianu. To counter the efforts of the conservatives, the "Reds" gathered masses of supporters in the cities. By controlling the majority of the population, they were able to introduce several political reforms and innovations to politics.

Cuza himself had much in common with the liberals. He wanted to bring fundamental changes to the social, political, and economic organizations of Romania. However, when it came to political reforms, he was on the side of the moderates, and when it came to social reforms, he stood with the radicals. Nevertheless, he chose to work closely with the moderates to try and form the central party, through which he would push his programs through the legislature. Alexandru Cuza wanted to be the leader, and he was repulsed by the intentions of the radicals to democratize the political system, as this would diminish the prince's powers significantly. He also thought the radicals were too revolutionary, especially because they tended to arouse the masses. The last thing the new state of Romania needed was a revolution, as this would prove to the foreign powers that Romanians were not able to govern themselves, making the efforts of the union and the Congress of Paris worthless.

The legislative assembly was made up mainly of conservatives, who stubbornly refused to pass his program of reforms, mainly the agrarian reform. Prince Cuza thought the reforms were necessary to elevate Romania and bring it closer to the progress of other European countries. In the end, Alexandru was so outraged by the assembly's refusals that he decided to dismiss it on May 14th, 1864. To consolidate his power, he came up with the new electoral law and constitution. Even though the prince belonged to the liberals, the law and the constitution, while having some liberal tendencies, were mainly conservative. Cuza increased the number of the voters as the liberals demanded, but the new electoral system seriously diluted the voting strength of the majority, especially the peasants. The new law, although it was infused with the democratic spirit, essentially promoted authoritarianism. The new constitution made the legislative assembly subordinate to the prince, who had far-reaching powers, such as the sole right to initiate legislation and the ability to veto everything and anything the assembly passed.

By bringing about the new law and constitution, Cuza was able to swiftly carry out his economic and social program. The main reform was the so-called Rural Law of 1864, by which the land was redistributed. Peasants now had the full rights to own the land, but the amount of land was very limited. Only two-thirds of the landlord's estate could be owned by the peasants, never the whole estate, and forests didn't even enter these calculations, remaining fully in the hands of the landlords. Compulsory labor service was abolished, as well as the tithe and other obligations the peasants had toward the landowners. The immediate consequence of the Rural Law was the granting of land to the peasant families, roughly four hectares per family. Most of the peasants received enough land to build a house with a small garden that could sustain them. However, the landholdings didn't disappear. After the land grants, more than 70 percent of the land was still in the hands of the landlords. The taxes still weighed the heaviest on the social class that was the least able to pay them. Therefore, the state treasury was poor, and the prince had no funds to develop other branches of the economy. He was forced to borrow money from foreign countries, but his hopes that the same powers that created Romania would be eager to invest in it were soon crushed. Although the Anglo-French consortium opened the first Romanian bank, Banca României, it didn't attract the foreign capital that Cuza hoped it would.

Cuza also gave special attention to the judicial system of Romania, as he wanted to modernize the state with new institutions. In 1864, he brought about the new civil code by which individual and personal freedoms were guaranteed to all citizens of Romania, no matter their social status. All citizens were equal before the law, and their private property was safeguarded by the state. The prince also wanted to create a productive society, and to achieve this, he wanted everyone to have an equal right to education. The same year, he promulgated an education law, which regulated school institutions at all levels, with special attention to primary education. He also established the principle that primary education should be free and compulsory for all citizens of Romania.

Cuza's tendency to create a centralized government that would extend its control over all institutions of the state is best seen in the example of the Orthodox Church. Cuza promoted the secular state, and he was determined to bring the Orthodox Church under the supervision of the government. Alexandru Cuza was largely successful in this plan. He brought about a series of laws that seriously reduced the role of the Church in civil affairs. Besides that, he also put Church administration under the direct surveillance of the state. But his most important church-related law was the secularization of monastery land. This represented around a quarter of the Romanian land, and after the law was presented in 1863, it belonged to the state. The role monasteries had in the economic and agrarian life of Romania since the Middle Ages had finally ended, and the state was able to take an active role in its cultivation and production.

Cuza was very successful in bringing about the desired reforms to the government's bureaucracy, but ultimately, his position was undermined. His political enemies, both left and right, formed an unlikely coalition. In the end, the conservatives condemned him as being too liberal because of his agrarian and electoral reforms, while the liberals thought of him as not liberal enough. In the end, both sides put away their differences because the prince made the legislatures subordinate to his own office. At the time, Cuza was ill, so it was easy to isolate him politically. Due to his illness, he was already contemplating abdication, and he voiced his intention in a letter to the assembly in December 1865. But the plotters didn't only want him removed; they planned on bringing a foreign prince to the throne of Romania. The coup was led by C. A. Rosetti and Ion C. Bratianu, and Cuza's opponents tried to avoid public scandal and foreign intervention by swiftly replacing the prince.

They persuaded the army to arrest Alexandru Cuza, and on February 23rd, 1866, the prince willingly signed the abdication documents. He was forced to leave Romania, and he chose Austria as his place of exile, where he spent the rest of his life, dying there in 1873. Cuza's departure marked the beginning of a new era for Romania, one that would last until the end of the Second World War.

Independence and Political and National Thought

The plotters who overthrew Alexandru Cuza immediately founded the provisional government, which would choose a new prince. The majority favored a foreigner to occupy the throne, as they believed he would diminish internal political rivalries and ensure the stability of Romania. The throne was offered to Prince Karl of Hohenzollern-Sigmaringen (1839-1914). Napoleon III of France suggested him, and since Romania was heavily influenced by the French at the time, the people didn't have much issue with it. Karl accepted the offer of the Romanian throne and traveled to Bucharest on May 7th, 1866, to assume his new position as the prince of Romania. He was the second son of Prince Karl Anton, the prime minister of Prussia. Upon his arrival to Romania, he became known by the name of Carol I of Romania. He was a Catholic, and he didn't know much about Romania when he accepted the rule. Carol had to endure many trials and errors before grasping what it meant to rule a country under Ottoman suzerainty. It must have been difficult to oversee a buffer zone between two powers constantly at war in addition to being a newly founded state that had just organized its national institutions. Nevertheless, Carol was a successful ruler, and he occupied the throne of Romania for a long time. He was aware of his lack of knowledge, and he concentrated his efforts on the familiar aspects of the rule, army, and foreign affairs. In time, his knowledge of internal politics matured, and he became a decisive force behind internal politics too.

The sultan and the rest of the European powers recognized Carol as the legitimate ruler of Romania. His title was recognized as being hereditary, which means his descendants would continue the rule and that there would be no more elections for the prince. On July 11th, 1866, Romania received a new constitution with Carol's approval. The new constitution was the work of the conservatives and liberals who overthrew Cuza, but it was mostly a liberal document. It made sure that the powers of the prince were limited, making him a constitutional monarch. As for civil liberties, nothing really changed. They were still equal before the law, and their freedoms were guaranteed, which included the freedom of the press and public meetings. In order to please the conservatives, the constitution also guaranteed the full rights of possession to property owners, making personal property a sacred and inviolable right. This way, large estate owners were protected from any further agrarian reforms and land confiscations. However, the land that had been given to the peasants in 1864 was protected by Article 20, which guaranteed it must never be confiscated.

The parliamentary system of 1866 enhanced the position of the legislature. The parliament was composed of two houses: the Chamber of Deputies and a Senate. It was almost equal to the office of the prince when it came to making laws. However, parliament also had the right to question ministers about policies and abuses of power. A parliamentary investigation would ensure the proper and orderly work of every minister. The Romanian Constitution was now very similar to those in western Europe, and it ensured that the West remained open to Romania. Authors of the constitution mainly drew their ideas from the Belgian Constitution of 1831, in both form and substance. However, it was by no means a transcription of it because Romania's unique position in the world had to be taken into account. Property, education, and localized government demanded special attention, as Romania lagged behind Europe due to the Ottoman rule.

The parliamentary system came fully into being with the formation of the two political parties almost a decade after the constitution was adopted. The National Liberal Party and the Conservative Party dominated the political life of the pre-World War era. The founders of the parties were the same people who had drafted the constitution in 1866. However, while the world was opening up to the possibility of women's involvement in politics, Romania remained closed to the idea. Women had no mention in the constitution, and they remained in the same status that had been prescribed to them in the 17th century. The wife was legally dependent on her husband in all matters. This also meant that wives could not legally take care of their inheritance or property and wealth earned during the marriage. Women were discriminated against in public employment, and even though they were allowed to attend universities, their degrees were seen as less worthy. Even if they finished university, women were unlikely to find employment, as certain professions remained reserved only for men. Women were deprived of all political rights, and it would take drastic measures and many years to change this opinion. In 1884, some parliamentarians proposed that married women who were rich enough should be allowed to vote for the parliamentary candidates. The response to such a proposal was widespread laughter.

Another class also had to overcome many difficulties to gain their social rights. The Gypsies (also known as the Roma or Romani; not to be confused with the Romanians) arrived in the region of Romania in the 14th century from northern India, and ever since then, they had been regarded as slaves. Usually, they were agricultural laborers who had to pay taxes, but their position in society varied depending on if they were settled or nomadic, as well as if their masters were the boyars, princes, or the clergy. They contributed much to the economic life of Romania through their labor services and craftsmanship, but their lifestyle was very different. Therefore, they were ostracized, perhaps even more than women. They didn't lack support for emancipation, especially from the 19th-century liberals, as many boyars freed their gypsy slaves to support them. But their emancipation and integration in Romanian society came in 1855 in Moldavia and a year later in Wallachia. After the unification, Romania made a part of the land available for the Gypsies to settle, although they weren't prohibited from settling in the cities. However, the majority of Gypsies chose to continue their nomadic way of life, even if that meant remaining marginalized.

When it came to the independence of Romania, both conservatives and liberals were aware they needed foreign friends, but they had different ideas to whom they should approach. The liberals wanted to work with Romania's immediate neighbors of southeastern Europe. They were afraid, and rightfully so, that the greater European powers only cared about their agenda in the region. However, the conservatives thought it would be wiser to gain the trust and partnership of at least one of the big powers. In the end, the uprising of the Bosnians against Ottoman rule in 1875 showed the Romanian politicians the wisdom of the conservatives. Throughout 1876, Romanians demanded the immediate recognition of their independence by the Ottoman government. They even dared to threaten dire consequences. However, those were only empty threats, as Romania had no power to do any damage to the sultan or his empire. They needed the support of the greater powers to do so, and Romania turned toward Austro-Hungary and Russia. In the end, Russia won out, as its relations with the Ottomans had deteriorated quickly. This meant that if the Romanians sided with Russia, they would have their chance to demand independence much sooner. During the negotiations with Russia about the military involvement of Romania, Prince Carol insisted on a general treaty that would guarantee the recognition of Romania's independence. The Russian tsar was only interested in a limited treaty that would allow him to move his forces across the territory of Romania and south of the Danube. In the end, the two countries reached a compromise. Romania would allow Russia's army to cross its territory in exchange for the respect of the country's political rights and territorial integrity. Romania's parliament agreed to these terms and declared war on the Ottoman Empire. The public demanded an immediate declaration of independence, and Mihail Kogălniceanu, Minister of Foreign Affairs, declared that the ratification of the treaty with Russia meant there were no longer any ties left between Romania and the Ottoman Empire. On May 21ˢᵗ, 1877, the parliament declared the absolute independence of Romania.

The relations between Russia and Romania during the war with the Ottomans was very tense. Carol I wanted full involvement in the war, as it would make Romania an equal partner to its ally, Russia. But the tsar wanted no help, as he wanted to be free of any political involvement in Romania's internal problems. When the Ottomans stopped Russian progress at Plevna in August 1877, Russia was forced to ask the Romanians for help. The tsar accepted Carol's terms, which included a separate base and command for the Romanian army. At the siege of Plevna, the Romanian army proved to be the decisive force that brought about the defeat of the Ottomans, and the Romanian soldiers opened the way for the Russians to Constantinople. However, when the Ottomans finally agreed to negotiate peace with the Russians, the Romanians weren't even invited. The Treaty of San Stefano, which was signed on March 3ʳᵈ, 1878, recognized the independence of Romania, but the Russians slipped in their agenda and requested the immediate return of the southern Bessarabia. They offered Dobruja and the Danube Delta as compensation, but Prince Carol I still accused the Russian tsar of breaking his promise to respect the territorial integrity of Romania. He demanded the revision of the treaty, and he wasn't alone. Other European countries demanded it too, and on June 13ᵗʰ, 1878, the Congress of Berlin took place to reduce Russian influence in Europe. However, the points of the treaty that involved Romania was left intact.

The final treaty recognized the independence of Romania, but it came with two demands, or conditions, to its independence. Firstly, Romania had to grant religious freedom to all citizens. The second condition was the acceptance of returning Bessarabia to Russia. Religious freedom was demanded because of the growing number of Jews in Romania, who had settled during the 1830s and 1840s from Austria and Russia. Since the politicians of the time intended to create a national state that focused on Romanians and only those foreigners who were Christian, the Jews were treated as non-citizens. There were some attempts to grant them citizenship during the rule of Alexandru Cuza, but they all failed, as the state had other urgent matters to deal with. Eventually, the Romanian government agreed to accept these conditions. The constitution was modified in 1879, allowing all foreigners, regardless of their religion, to acquire Romanian citizenship. However, the procedure to get citizenship was so complex that by 1919, only a few hundred Jews had received it. Nevertheless, Jews became an integral part of the state's economy, for they were largely producers and crafters.

For Romania, the most important result of the Congress of Berlin was the recognition of its independence from both the Ottoman Empire and the great powers of Europe. After four centuries, the land was finally free of its links with the Ottomans, and national pride started awaking. The independence of Romania allowed its politicians and intellectuals to concentrate on the building of a nation. But this great moment was shadowed by the realization that Romania was just a small country in the sea of big powers that continued to fight for their interests in the region. Even though it was independent, Romania was under the heavy influence of other countries, and to reinforce its position, they proclaimed it a monarchy. Prince Carol I became the first king of Romania on March 26th, 1881.

Romanians in Transylvania, Bukovina, and Bessarabia

Even though Romania became an independent state, some Romanians continued to live outside its borders as a minority. By the end of the 19th century, in Hungary, there were approximately three million Romanians, although the majority of them lived in Transylvania, Banat, and Maramures. Bukovina had at least 230,000 ethnic Romanians, while Bessarabia counted over one million. These Romanians developed under foreign rules and became a part of Hungary, Austria, and Russia. No matter which rule they lived under, they were administered in very similar ways. They had no right to take part in the political life of the country as an ethnic community, and their culture was under constant pressure from unsympathetic governments. Of the three different countries, the Romanians in Transylvania organized the heaviest resistance against the oppression of their national identity. They were very conscious of their historical place in Transylvania and of their long struggle to coexist with those who continuously sought to dominate them. But Transylvanian Romanians had the help and support of two major institutions, the Orthodox Church and the neighboring Kingdom of Romania, which advocated for their rights. In Bessarabia and Bukovina, Romanians had a different destiny. As soon as they were cut off from their motherland of Moldavia in the early 18th and 19th centuries, they were put through rigorous centralization ambitions of the Russian Empire. They had no national institutions, and they lacked a distinct political identity.

In the later decades of the 19th century, the leaders of Romanians in Transylvania were all members of a small but growing middle class. Most of them were lawyers, and they replaced the Orthodox and Greek Catholic clergy as the national leaders of Romanians, for the society as a whole became more secular. They fought for political autonomy and self-determination, and they were also aware of the Romanian role in the economy. They were certain that without modernization, they would remain behind those who ruled them; as a result, they would always be seen as inferior. But they wrongly believed that the economy would only progress if it was based on ethnicity. They fought for the foundation of Romanian agriculture, Romanian banks, and Romanian industries. However, they were not completely wrong. Most Romanians living in Transylvania were peasants, and agriculture was their main source of income. Modernization and urbanization would greatly push the whole community of Romanians forward. The leaders of the Romanians wished to modernize the industries in predominantly Romanian cities and bring Romanization to other larger cities of Transylvania as soon as possible. To achieve this, they organized the Romanian National Party in 1881.

The main goal of this party was the restoration of Transylvania's autonomy, which had dissipated since it became a part of Greater Hungary with the Austro-Hungarian Compromise of 1867, which established the dual monarchy in Austro-Hungary. In 1890, the Romanian hopes of cooperation with Hungarians were destroyed when the government passed a law that made the teaching of the Hungarian language obligatory in Orthodox and Greek Catholic elementary schools. This was only the first of many laws to bring Hungarianization to Romanians and other nationalities in Transylvania. In 1883, a law was passed that required the explicit use of Hungarian in public elementary schools and kindergartens. Many other laws were implemented that solidified the government's control over Romanian teachers, priests, and schools. In 1894, the Hungarian government dissolved the Romanian National Party to undermine the political activities of the Romanians. Because of all these government efforts to subject the Romanians to Hungarian rule, the political activists stopped prioritizing Transylvania's autonomy and instead fought for the preservation of their Romanian national identity. The Romanian National Party continued to gather young activists and promote the idea of a nation and its rightful place within the Austro-Hungarian Empire. At one point, young nationalist Aurel C. Popovici even suggested the federalization of the empire in his book *Die Vereinigten Staaten von Groß-Österreich* (*United States of Great Austria*), which was published in 1906.

Between 1910 and 1914, the Hungarian government negotiated with the Romanian National Party to reach an understanding. On the side of the government was Prime Minister Istvan Tisza, who thought that it was time to answer the "question of the Romanians," but he had no intention of satisfying the minority. His only goal was to strengthen the Hungarian state. He desired a national state of Hungarians and the preservation of Hungarian political supremacy. The Romanians chose Iuliu Maniu as their leader, and he advocated for the urgent federalization of the Austro-Hungarian Empire. However, he considered that the best tactic for fighting for Romanian rights was to start small. First, he demanded the right for all citizens to vote freely, as this would ensure that each ethnic community gained a representative in the government. After they were a part of the government, it would be much easier to continue the fight. In February 1914, the negotiations between Tisza and Maniu reached a dead end, as both parties convinced themselves that the matter was greater than a simple compromise. They firmly believed that the survival of their nations was at stake. Soon, the outbreak of World War I would forever halt the negotiations.

Bukovina had been taken from Moldavia during the 18th century, and it belonged to the Habsburg monarchy since then. By the 19th century, the Romanians were no longer a majority there. The Ruthenians, an Eastern Slavic people, were deliberately resettled to this region from their native Kingdom of Galicia and Lodomeria (an Austrian territory in Poland). As if it wasn't enough that Romanians were being expelled from their own homes, they also couldn't find employment in the civil service, as it favored the Germans and Jews. Nevertheless, once the national awakening started, and the Romanians began to demand more rights in Bukovina, Austria was willing to compromise and accommodate its minorities.

In Bessarabia, things went completely different, as it belonged to Russia. This region was often exchanged between Moldavia and Russia, but the people who inhabited it gradually lost their Romanian character. The population of Bessarabia was very mixed since Russian resettled Jews and Ukrainians there to purposely diminish the significance of Romanian national influence. Even the Romanian Orthodox Church went through rigorous Russification as it fell under the supervision of the Holy Synod of the Russian Orthodox Church. As a part of the empire, the Romanian cultural and political life in Bessarabia was eradicated. Their language was taught in schools as a second language, and all publication of literature in Romanian stopped. However, on the village level, the Romanian language and folklore survived. When the empire was shaken to its foundation during the Russian Revolution of 1905, the Romanians gathered their courage to fight for national recognition. They even went so far as to demand the autonomy of Bessarabia, but they were too weak to make any difference. After 1906, further efforts to recognize the Romanian ethnicity and political activity in the region ceased.

Chapter 8 – Romania and the Great War

Romanian troops in Transylvania during World War I
(https://en.wikipedia.org/wiki/Romania_during_World_War_I#/media/File:Tro
pas-rumanas-c%C3%A1rpatos--rumaniassacrific00neguuofi.png)

Romania's Place in the World

Romania, with its newly gained independence, needed to find its place among the countries of Europe. The king and the Romanian politicians sought the best possible solution to the lack of support of one of the greater European powers. They carefully waged their options and concluded that Russia was out of the question because of its treatment of Romania during the last Russo-Ottoman War and the Treaty of San Stefano. The tsar was seen as an enemy of the state. The king was aware that public opinion favored France as an ally, but he also knew that France had no interest in supporting Romania politically or economically. The most appealing superpower in Europe was Germany. It had a well-developed economy, it was rushing toward complete modernization and industrialization, and it had the biggest and most modern army at the time. Germany was a role model of successful politics, and to bind itself with such a great power, Romania joined the Triple Alliance made between Austro-Hungary, Germany, and Italy in 1883. The terms of the alliance were that if any of these countries were to suffer a Russian attack, the other states would come to its aid. They also promised they would not step into an alliance with other powers who wished to start a conflict against either of them. To keep the public ignorant of such an alliance and to avoid the rage of pro-French politicians, Carol I decided to keep it a secret. Because of this, the parliament never ratified the alliance, meaning the alliance depended solely on the word of the king.

The Triple Alliance was a foundation of Romania's foreign policy for the next three decades. However, when France signed a similar alliance with Russia in 1891, King Carol and the Romanian politicians who were aware of their commitment toward the Triple Alliance watched carefully how the power balance of Europe shifted. In 1904, France signed an alliance with Britain, pulling it into an agreement with Russia too. The stage in Europe was set, and the Romanians realized that things were troubling. With such strong alliances on both sides, Europe was torn apart by the power struggle. The first test of Romania's commitment to the Triple Alliance came with the outbreak of the First Balkan War in 1912. For their own reasons, Germany, Austro-Hungary, and Italy supported the integrity of the Ottoman Empire, while France, Britain, and Russia wanted to see it fall. In the middle were the Balkan nations, who only wanted to get rid of Ottoman suzerainty over Serbia, Bulgaria, and Greece. The victory of the united Balkan nations seriously disturbed the balance of power in Europe. Romania wanted to seize a piece of the land that had belonged to the Ottoman Empire, which the Bulgarians took during the First Balkan War, but Romania lacked the support of Austria. In turn, Austria was trying to win over Bulgaria to join the Triple Alliance and attack Serbia and Greece. The Second Balkan War broke out in 1913, stirred by the Austrian fear of Serbian national awakening after the retreat of the Ottoman Empire from their region. Still wanting the disputed territory in Dobruja, Romania declared war on Bulgaria. This war was very brief, and with the Treaty of Bucharest signed in August 1913, Bulgaria ceded southern Dobruja to Romania. The great powers of Europe now saw Romania as the guarantor of the power balance in the Balkan region.

With its action during the Second Balkan War, Romania alienated itself from the Triple Alliance. However, at the end of 1913, its relations with France warmed, and it started approaching the Triple Entente, the alliance signed between France, Britain, and Russia. Even Russia's foreign minister, Sergei Sazonov, seemed to desire good relations with Romania, and he organized the tsar's visit to the Romanian seacoast city of Constanta in June 1914. The two countries entered a new era of foreign relations, even though Romania never formally joined the Triple Entente. They refused to do so because they had no desire to degrade their already bad relationship with Austro-Hungary.

The Great War

The First World War began when Archduke Franz Ferdinand, the heir to the Austro-Hungarian throne, was assassinated in June 1914. As a response to rising Serbian nationalism and afraid of losing its possessions and subjects in Bosnia, Austria sent a series of impossible demands to Serbia as compensation for the assassination. Knowing Serbia would not be able to fulfill all the demands, the great powers started preparing for the imminent war. King Carol I, together with the representatives of both the liberal and conservative parties, held a Crown Council on August 3rd, deciding that Romania would stay neutral in the upcoming conflict. However, the decision of neutrality wasn't immediate or desired by all. The king wanted to join the war early on as part of the Triple Alliance. He was sure of Germany's military superiority, and he thought Romania would benefit as an ally to the victor. But no one supported the king, and the majority of Romanian politicians were reluctant to support Austro-Hungary, which kept denying civil rights to the Romanians in Transylvania. In the end, the decision was to stay neutral.

King Carol I of Romania died on October 10th, 1914, and Ion Bratianu, Prime Minister of Romania, took full charge of the country's foreign policy. But nothing changed in regards to Romania's stance toward the upcoming war. Bratianu himself sympathized with France and the Triple Entente, but the king's successor, Ferdinand I, ensured him that neutrality was the best choice for the time being. He wanted to wait and see the course of the war and join late once the victor was certain. By doing so, he hoped he could achieve the national goals of Romanians, not only in their country but in the neighboring empires too.

During the Great War, Bratianu negotiated with the Triple Entente, but he avoided joining the war prematurely. During the negotiations in 1915 and 1916, he continued to persuade France, Britain, and Russia to cede Transylvania to Romania after the victory. Only when they agreed to do so did the prime minister agree to stand in the official alliance. In July 1916, the negotiations between Bratianu and the Triple Entente began to take their final form. The Romanians demanded the guarantee of undisturbed trade of armaments because they were aware of their isolation from their Western allies. At first, the allies thought the Romanian demands were excessive, and they were reluctant to agree to the terms set by Bratianu. However, they urgently needed to open yet another front against Germany, and France stepped in to convince Britain and Russia to accept. The secret solution to the "Romanian problem" was to accept all the demands on paper, and if they couldn't meet them after the war ended, they would simply force Romania to accept less.

Romania's alliance between France, Britain, Russia, and Italy was signed in Bucharest on August 17th, 1916, and Romania officially entered the First World War. The Crown Council approved the alliance on August 27th, and the following day, Germany declared war on Romania, with Turkey and Bulgaria following. Romanian military operations started with a swift invasion of Transylvania, but in the south, they had to defend against attacks from German and Bulgarian forces. Because they were forced to fight on two fronts, the Romanians could not hold their success in the north for very long. In November and December of 1916, significant strategic locations of western Wallachia were lost, and the German and Austrian forces penetrated deep into Romanian territory. On December 6th, German troops entered Bucharest, but in Moldavia, along the Danube and Siret Rivers, the Romanians managed to stabilize their positions. After only four months since entering the war, the Romanian losses were significant. Around 250,000 soldiers were killed, territory had been lost, and equipment destroyed. More than half of the Romanian territory was under occupation, and most of it was the agrarian region, the breadbasket of the country.

After evacuating the king and his family from Bucharest to Iasi, Bratianu formed a government of national unity on Christmas Eve of 1916. Some of the conservatives formed political alliances with the liberals, and together, they brought forth immediate agrarian and electoral reforms to avoid social unrest caused by possible famine. When Russia burst into its revolution in 1917, the government of national unity feared it would spread to Moldavia and the rest of the country. To elevate political pressure, King Ferdinand spoke to Romanian troops in April 1917, promising they would receive land and voting rights as soon as the war was over. Seeing that the king's gesture had the support of both conservatives and liberals, army morale was lifted.

Once the war resumed in July 1917, the Romanian troops, under the command of General Alexandru Averescu, began an offensive on the Moldavian front. They performed brilliantly, and the army pushed forward, but their Russian allies and its garrison in Moldavia lost its morale, forcing the general to halt the advance. The German commander took the opportunity of the situation and ordered an offensive of his own. He hoped he could defeat the allied Russian and Romanian forces and knock Romania out of the war. However, he didn't count on the Romanians' ability to defend themselves. On August 19th, at Marasesti, the German offensive was stopped by a Romanian strategic victory.

In Russia, the revolution continued, bringing new worries to Romania. Russian soldiers gave up on fighting because they were persuaded to join the Bolshevik Revolution. They were promised peace and land if they helped bring the tsar down. In November 1917, the fall of the Russian Empire was imminent, and the Moldavians of Bessarabia took the opportunity to gain independence. They appealed to Romania for help, and Iasi responded by sending troops to free the Moldavian capital of Chisinau from the Bolsheviks' grasp. On March 27th, 1918, the Moldavians of Bessarabia voted to unite with Romania. However, this union was of no comfort to Romania. The Russians signed a peace with the Central Powers (Austro-Hungary, Germany, the Ottoman Empire, and Bulgaria) and left the war. As a result, Romania suddenly lost the military support of its neighbor, and its supply lines with the West were cut off. Two months later, the pro-German conservative Alexandru Marghiloman was elected as the prime minister, and he signed the Treaty of Bucharest with the Central Powers, allowing the country to be economically and politically dependent on them.

But the events on the far-off Western front changed Romania's fortunes. The Allies managed to defend themselves against the German's final offensive attempt and started advancing toward Germany. In Italy, they defeated the Austro-Hungarian armies, which held the north, and on November 3rd, Austria agreed to a ceasefire, followed by Germany on November 11th. Back in Romania, the Marghiloman government fell, and Bratianu returned to the office of prime minister. With the war at its end, he was determined to pursue the unification of the Romanian national state with Transylvania, as well as to finish his agrarian and electoral reforms. King Ferdinand ordered the army to rejoin the war on November 10th, and by December, it returned to Bucharest in triumph.

After the war, the territories of Austro-Hungary dissolved, and the Romanians in Transylvania, Bukovina, and Bessarabia declared their wish to join Romania. However, at the peace conference in Paris, on January 18th, 1919, the great powers refused to treat Romania as an equal partner of the alliance. Great Britain, France, the United States, and Japan constituted the Supreme War Council, and even though Bratianu pressed for Romania vigorously, he was unable to make them understand the importance of national unity for the Romanians. In defiance of the decisions of the Supreme Council, he sent Romanian troops to invade Hungary all the way to Budapest. It was this offensive that led to the fall of the Hungarian Soviet Republic on August 1st, 1919. Three days later, Romanians occupied Budapest and attempted to install a government in Hungary that would cede Transylvania. But Bratianu's aggressive stance only managed to turn the Western allies against Romania.

The pressure on Bratianu to accept the peace terms imposed by the Allies who wouldn't treat Romania as equal partners led to his resignation on September 10th, 1919. But despite these setbacks, Romanian territorial questions were settled when the new Romanian government agreed to sign the treaty with Austria that concerned national minorities. According to the treaty, Romania was obliged to treat all of its citizens equally, regardless of their nationality. On November 27th, 1919, in a separate treaty with Bulgaria, Romania confirmed its border in Dobruja, which had been drawn at the end of the Balkan Wars in 1913. Soon, the Supreme Council divided Banat between Yugoslavia and Romania, giving two-thirds of the region to Romania. They also recognized the acquisition of Bessarabia in June 1920, and with the Treaty of Trianon, Romania was awarded Transylvania and part of eastern Hungary. The new provinces added to Romanian production, and the economy flourished. However, with the acquisition of the new territories, Romania gained many new minorities. Roughly 30 percent of the total population of the country were non-Romanians. Before the war, that number was only 8 percent. All these new citizens had to be integrated into already existing social structures and institutions.

The Interwar Period

In the two decades between the two world wars, Romania managed to build an internationally recognized state, which hurled itself forward into modernization. For the Romanian people, this was an era of enormous vitality and creativity. The leading classes experimented with new political trends, as well as with philosophy, poetry, business, and economics. But at the same time, Romanians experienced division and internal conflict, as they had to reorganize all of their institutions, administration, and cultural and religious traditions. They also faced the problems that follow fast urbanization, which included the rise of the middle class. Agriculture remained the main source of funds for the Romanian economy. It supplied its people with food, but since production was very high, most of it was exported to other countries, guaranteeing the financial health of the country. The industry was making extraordinary progress and started bringing in national income too. Due to the rising industrial sector, the urban working class started developing, but the peasants still remained the most numerous class. Nevertheless, it was the middle class that left the deepest impression on life during the interwar period.

The center of politics during the interwar period was the debate about national identity and development, in Romanian history known as the Great Debate. The main point of the conflict between politicians was the issue of Romania's place in the Western world. The question was asked if the nation should follow the Western model and become a modern and industrialized state, or whether it should cleave to the peasants, agrarians, and Orthodox traditions. Many thought that only the latter option would make Romania stay true to its primordial national values and traditions. However, some politicians saw the possibility of taking a third path, which would ensure that Romania preserved all the best aspects of its traditional way of life but also made strives to join the economic progress of the rest of Europe. Thus, the intellectual social class was divided into two main groups: the Europeanists and the traditionalists.

The Europeanists regarded Romania as part of the greater European political and economic scene, and they thought their country had no other path of development but the one that would follow the latest standards set by Europe. Two figures among the Europeanists stand out: Eugen Lovinescu, a literary critic, and Stefan Zeletin, an economist and sociologist. Together, they undertook a serious investigation of Romania's economy to decide its future. They wanted to modernize the country further, and the result of their investigation showed that Western-style capitalism was the only possible solution. Lovinescu believed the ideas of capitalism would force the change in Romania, while Zeletin thought the economic and social aspects of capitalism would propel the country into the new era. However, they both agreed that the "Westernization" of Romania was necessary if they wanted their country to emerge as a modern nation within the greater context of Europe.

The traditionalists, on the other hand, wanted Romania to remain an agrarian country, as that had been the main aspect of its economy for so long. It worked well enough, and they saw no reason to risk experimenting with new economic models. They thought that if they kept to the traditional ways, Romania would find its rightful place in the world. However, even though they agreed that the country's future should be based on the political and economic models that had worked in the past, they could not agree on what constituted the tradition of Romania. They believed in the rural character of their country and that it should continue developing as a primarily agrarian nation. They resented all Western cultural and institutional influences, but they still recognized the need for modernization. For some of them, that modernization would come through ideas and religious experience. To them, Westernization would degrade Romanian morals and values, which had led to social decay since the 19th century. They sought to reverse the trends and bring back what they regarded as true Romanian ideology, based on Eastern ideas and Orthodox values. Traditionalism was very popular among poets and artists. Lucian Blaga was the embodiment of a true traditionalist, perhaps because he looked even beyond the Orthodox traditions. He believed folklore and mythology would lead to national prosperity, but he never denied the importance of Eastern Orthodoxy in developing the national and cultural image of Romania. Blaga also experimented with the ideas of Oriental religions, as well as with the philosophy of western Europe.

Oddly enough, the advocates of the third path, the one that wished to reconcile Romania's agrarian past and the European future, were part of the National Peasants' Party (*Partidul National-Țărănist,* or shortened *Țărăniști*). They wanted Romanian society to remain agrarian, which would be supported by native institutions, but also sought a modernized system of production, which would follow European trends. They saw the future of Romania as a third-world country, standing between the capitalist West and the socialist East. The leading figure of the *Țărăniști* was Virgil Madgearu, an economist who was guided by his theory that Romania's social and economic progress needed to remain separate from both Western and Eastern models. He believed that peasants, who represented the most numerous social class of Romania at the time, differed both economically and psychologically from the upper classes. Because of their vast numbers, Madgearu thought the peasants should lead the country. He named this new political and social entity the peasant state. His favorite political government was a parliamentary democracy, as he believed it perfectly reflected his idea of the peasant state.

The participants of the Great Debate had different stances on Romania's future, yet they all agreed on one point: their country had gone through a significant change during the past century. They recognized that Romania was nearer to Europe and that it couldn't avoid Western influence. However, they were not all certain if this influence was good or bad, or if the country should continue on the same path or return to the more traditional one. The political changes that swept the world during the 1930s would open up various possibilities for Romania's politicians, who tested their visions of Romania's future. One of the most important aspects of politics was international relations, and with the approach of the new war, Romania would find it impossible to stay neutral, as it could not remain uninfluenced by the currents of world politics.

The political life in Romania between the world wars was quite vibrant, as more social classes gained the right to indulge in it. Various political parties were formed, and since all the males of Romania had gained the right to vote, it seemed as if the oligarchy would be easily brought down. Both peasants and Europeanists were advocates of the parliamentary government, and they enjoyed the support of the general population. In the elections held in 1928, the parties that represented democracy won overwhelmingly. But there were various obstacles to be passed. Peasantry lacked political experience, and because of this, they refused to take part in the political life of the country. This diminished the voting body greatly, as peasants were still the most numerous social class of Romania. The National Liberal Party came out as the strongest during the 1920s, but the Liberals were pulled down by their apathy. In theory, they wanted a parliamentary system, but in practice, they preferred the industrial oligarchy, which enabled them to gather financial wealth, although they never became incredibly wealthy. Because of this, various groups who were against industrialization, Westernization, and the democratic political systems rose up. They were from the traditionalist parties, and they created a mood in Romania that favored extreme nationalism and authoritarian governmental systems.

The increase of nationalism, together with the world economic crisis of the 1930s, brought about anti-Semitism. This gave strength to the new extreme nationalistic movements, which made anti-Semitism ideological the core of their vision of the future nation. One such organization was named the Iron Guard, and it reached the peak of its popularity in the mid-1930s. But it wasn't only totalitarianism organizations that brought Romania's democracy into a crisis. King Carol II ascended the throne in 1930, and he made it immediately clear that he had no intentions of sharing his power. He loathed the parliamentary institutions and made no effort to hide his intentions of becoming an oligarch. The rise of fascism in Italy and of Nazism in Germany only encouraged the opponents of Romanian democracy. The advocates of democracy were unable to survive the pressure that was placed on them by their opponents from both inside and outside of Romania. The result was the establishment of a dictatorship in 1938, with King Carol II as the sole ruler of the country. Democracy would not return to Romania for half a century.

The Rise of Nationalism

Anti-Semitism in Romania was no post-World War I phenomenon. It can be traced back to the early years of the 19th century when Jewish immigration to the principalities started rising. But during the interwar period, Alexandru C. Cuza, a professor of political economy, advocated the expulsion of the Jews from all areas of economic and political life. In 1923, he founded the National-Christian Defense League, which, among the rest, demanded an end of Jewish cultural life and their forceful Christianization. One of the members of Alexandru's League was Corneliu Zelea Codreanu. He was an extreme nationalist who thought the League's principles weren't strong enough. In 1927, he decided to start his organization named the Legion of the Archangel Michael. The Legion gained a military wing three years later named the Iron Guard. Soon, the whole organization would be called by this name.

The Iron Guard members resembled those of the Italian and German armies, with dark-colored uniforms and the glorification of their leader, to whom they would salute. The essence of Romanian fascism was anti-Semitism, Orthodox Christianity, and the cult of an unspoiled man, which they saw only in the Romanian peasants. These were all unique aspects of Romanian fascism, and they originated from the native sentiments of the principalities before unification. However, the organization lacked a cohesive ideology. During the early 1930s, the Iron Guard became a violent organization that used force to intimidate and bully its opponents. In 1933, Prime Minister Ion G. Duca outlawed the Iron Guard to establish peace within the country. They responded by assassinating him. His successor, Gheorghe Tatarescu, proved to be more tolerant of the extremist organizations, even though he came from a political party named the Young Liberals.

The Iron Guard continued its activities, and by 1937, they had become a massive movement. During the elections of that same year, they won 15.58 percent of the popular vote. They owed their success to their tireless work in appealing to all levels of society, including peasants and rural clergy, the working and middle class of the cities, and those on the margins of society. The most numerous members of the Iron Guard were young intellectuals who regarded the organization as the youthful vitality Romania needed to return to its true values. The elections brought sixty-six parliament seats to the Garda de Fier (the Iron Guard). This made it the third-largest party in the government. However, King Carol chose Octavian Goga as his new prime minister, who belonged to the very small National Christian Party. The king hoped that by bringing the party, which had won less than 10 percent of the votes, to the forefront, he would be able to manipulate them and fulfill his ambitions. He also demonstrated to the public that their votes didn't matter and that it was his will that would set the future course for Romania. In the next year, he replaced Goga's government with an "advisory government," which was headed by the patriarch of the Romanian Orthodox Church, Miron Cristea, who was nothing more than the king's puppet. In February, the new government abolished the constitution of 1921 and formed a new one that put all the power in the hands of the king.

To consolidate his power, King Carol II issued a decree in which he abolished all political parties, although he promised their return as soon as Romania adapted to the new political scene of Europe. However, the National Peasants' Party and the National Liberal Party informed the king they would continue their work, openly opposing him. The king had no time to deal with the two parties, as he was more concerned about the growing influence of the Iron Guard. He needed to deal with their violence and bad influence on the public, and he instructed the minister of internal affairs to immediately deal with this organization and use any means necessary to get rid of them. Many of the Iron Guard were rounded up and imprisoned in concentration camps. The government was brutal in dealing with the organization because they considered it an enemy of the state and a German agent. But when King Carol visited Germany in November of 1938, Adolf Hitler urged him to free the imprisoned Iron Guard members and to form Codreanu's vision of the government. However, Codreanu, the leader of the Iron Guard, was soon shot dead while trying to escape one of the concentration camps.

Chapter 9 – Romania during the Second World War

Ion Antonescu and Adolf Hitler in Munich (1941)
*(https://en.wikipedia.org/wiki/Romania_in_ World_ War_ II#/media/File:Bundes
archiv_Bild_183-B03212,_M%C3%BCnchen,
_Staatsbesuch_Jon_Antonescu_bei_Hitler.jpg)*

The political situation in Europe changed drastically with the outbreak of World War II. Hitler became one of the most powerful figures, and he put the smaller and newer European countries in danger. The lack of action from the greater powers allowed Nazi Germany to play the bully in Europe. Even when Hitler dismembered Czechoslovakia, France and Britain were silent. In the Munich agreement, which took place on September 29th, 1939, they even formally accepted the new division of Czechoslovakia, signaling Germany's political dominion in Europe. Those who had no power to oppose Hitler were forced to adhere to German political influence.

Germany had shown interest in Romania earlier because of its oil fields in Ploiesti. Germany needed this oil to fuel its war machine, and in 1939, they made a deal with Romania, promising to develop its mineral mining system in exchange for oil. Aside from oil, Germany relied on Romania to supply its army with food, and in turn, they brought modern military equipment. Germany also bought Romania's grain supplies, providing them the best prices in Europe and thus greatly contributing to its economic rise. Nevertheless, Romania tried to be neutral during the ensuing conflict. It still had an obligation to help the allies of the Triple Entente, but since Britain and France were silent about Germany's threat in Europe, and since Germany invested so much in Romania, King Carol had no other choice but to remain neutral. However, things changed when France was occupied in the spring of 1940, as Germany came out as the probable victor of the conflict. To survive, Romania had to rely on Germany's support. The Soviet Union demanded Bessarabia and part of Bukovina, and Carol hoped Hitler would offer to protect the country's territorial integrity. But what he didn't know was that Hitler had already signed a non-aggression pact with the Soviet Union and expressed his disinterest in what would happen to the Romanian territories other than Ploiesti.

Romania lost Bessarabia and part of Bukovina to Russia, but Carol made it his prime task not to yield to the territorial demands of Hungary and Bulgaria. On July 4th, he installed a new government, one that was pro-German. Carol hoped good relations with Hitler would secure his country, even though Germany failed to do so against Russia. Romania officially withdrew from the League of Nations and joined the Axis Powers, but Hitler again showed to be of no help to Romania. He demanded that Romania reach an agreement with Hungary and Bulgaria immediately and that the territory in Dobruja, which had been gained in 1913, had to be returned to Bulgaria. Transylvania proved to be a bigger problem, as the Romanians did not want to give it up, so no deal between Hungary and Romania was reached. Hitler was forced to take the initiative and settle the matter, as he needed both of these countries within his fold so he could use them during the war. Hitler himself drew the new border, which split Transylvania between the two countries. Romania was given an ultimatum; either it would accept Hitler's solution, or it would suffer the consequences of war with Hungary, which was supported by the Axis. Romania had no other choice but to accept. Hungary was awarded a large part of Transylvania, together with the city of Oradea and Maramures County. To the south, it encompassed the city of Cluj and the Szekler districts along the western slopes of the Carpathians, reaching Brasov. This loss of territory for Romania is known as the Vienna Diktat, and it brought about the loss of independence in foreign relations. The whole Romanian economy became subject to Germany's war aspirations.

By losing more than a third of Romania's territory to Hungary, Bulgaria, and Russia before the war even officially started, King Carol faced a national catastrophe. To save himself, Carol needed to quickly reconcile his relationship with the Iron Guard, which would offer some protection to his rule. Since its leader, Codreanu, had been shot dead, Carol invited General Ion Antonescu to form a new government. Antonescu had ties with the Iron Guard, as he, too, was a nationalist. But Carol miscalculated the intentions of his new prime minister. He believed Antonescu was pro-German, but he only accepted German influence because he saw no other choice once France fell. Ion Antonescu was a pro-Westerner and, above all, pro-France. He wanted to create a strong national state of Romania but only as a part of Europe. His prime intention was to overthrow the king and take control of the whole country, turning it into one that wasn't subordinate to Germany. However, for the time being, the international situation in Europe favored Romania's alliance with Germany, and Antonescu was aware he had to wait for the right moment to start enacting his plans.

In the summer of 1940, Antonescu came to an agreement with Germany, guaranteeing Romania's compliance with the war efforts. But once Antonescu tried to negotiate with the domestic political leaders about internal state matters, it became evident that nobody was willing to work with the government of King Carol because he had caused this national catastrophe. Antonescu seized the chance to fulfill the first part of his plans, and on September 5th, 1940, he asked the king to abdicate. When Carol hesitated, Antonescu pushed the matter of abdication, convincing the king his life and the lives of his family were in danger. The next day, King Carol II renounced the throne of Romania, leaving it to his nineteen-year-old son Mihai I (Michael I), and left the country. Mihai gave all the powers of the state to Antonescu, which allowed him to form a coalition government with the Iron Guard. With its rise to power, the Iron Guard gained control over some of the key positions in the state. They held the ministries of interior and foreign affairs, education, and cults. The Iron Guard also controlled the media and propaganda services, and soon, Romania was proclaimed a "National Legionary State," with the Iron Guard as the only political party allowed to function.

With Germany's growing influence over Europe, Antonescu had no other choice but to pursue better relations with the Nazis. He carried out the territorial swap that had been ordered by the

Vienna Diktat and ensured that the military strength of the country and its economy remained tied to Germany. Romania was an extremely important ally for the German plans in southeastern Europe, not only because of its oil supplies but because it was also crucial to the army's movement to Greece after the Italians failed to occupy it. As the relations with the Soviet Union deteriorated, Germany saw Romania as a perfect place for a military base on the Eastern Front. The first German troops arrived in Romania on October 10th, 1940.

On November 23rd, Antonescu arrived in Berlin to officially sign the alliance with the Axis Powers, which consisted of Germany, Italy, and Japan. Hitler's meeting with Antonescu left a deep impression on the Nazi leader. Hitler saw a person he could trust, and Antonescu remained in Hitler's favor until his downfall in 1944. The Romanian prime minister insisted that Hitler revise the Vienna Diktat, but the German dictator could make no immediate promises. He only stated that the situation after the war would be different. This brought hope to Antonescu, who now saw Germany as the only way to regain Transylvania. Although he was pro-France, Antonescu committed to working with Germany for the good of his own country. Once the prime minister clashed with the Iron Guard in the power struggle, Hitler showed him his full support, naming him the only person capable of leading Romania to a better future. Encouraged, Antonescu returned to Romania, determined to deal with the Iron Guard and arrest all of its leaders. However, the Iron Guard leaders appealed to the chief of the German secret police, who secured them safe passage to Germany.

The War

Antonescu was now the sole ruler of Romania in all but name. He implemented a military dictatorship regime, but unlike Hitler's Nazism and Mussolini's fascism, it had no coherent ideology and no massive support from the political parties. Antonescu told the people they needed such a regime for security and order. He refused to rely on politics and the support of the people. Instead, he only relied on the army, which was his tool to bring order and suppress any disdain coming from the masses. But Hitler himself had his doubts about the Romanian army, and he limited its role in the upcoming occupation of the Soviet Union. Once Germany made its plans to attack Russia known, Antonescu promised Romania's full military and economic support. The German invasion of the Soviet Union began on June 22nd, 1941. On the same day, King Mihai and Prime Minister Antonescu declared a "holy war" for the freedom of Bessarabia and northern Bukovina. This was a cause the Romanian people supported because they needed to remove Russian influence from their territories. Because of the active propaganda, the people believed in the superiority of the German army, and they trusted the victory would be fast and complete. The offensive on the Romanian front started on July 2nd, and within a month, Bessarabia and Bukovina were again part of Romania.

Antonescu was determined to send his army further to the east to support the German invasion of the Soviet Union. He was sure a victory would arrive very shortly, and he wrote to Hitler of his intentions to fight alongside his allies until the Soviet Union fell. Another meeting between the two leaders occurred on August 6th, 1941, and Hitler agreed Romania should occupy the territory between the Dniester and Dnieper Rivers. From there, they should continue east and take the territory that would be known as Transnistria, placing it under the Romanian administration. Antonescu also wanted the Romanian army to take Odessa, and even though they tried, they proved unable to occupy it without German help. The siege of Odessa lasted from August 18th until October 16th, during which the Romanian army suffered enormous casualties. More than 18,000 soldiers were killed, 63,000 were injured, and 11,000 went missing. As retaliation for the casualties, the Romanian army destroyed the remnants of the city's Jewish community.

The end of 1941 saw Romania entering into conflict with the Western Allies. On December 7th, pressured by Russia, Great Britain declared war on Romania, and in turn, Romania declared war on Britain's ally, the United States, which had just entered the war. It soon became evident that Romania's leaders and people were reluctant to step into open conflict with the Western powers. Their allegiance to Germany lay solely in its ability to crush Russian influence in their country. On the Eastern Front, Romanian troops engaged in a massive German offensive of southern Russia during the summer of 1942. However, the main part of the army fought at the Volga River, where the decisive battle of the winter offensive took place on November 19th. By December, the siege of Stalingrad had begun, but the Romanian army was ill-equipped for further conflict. The Third and Fourth Armies sustained the heaviest damage, as they were reduced from 228,000 soldiers in November to 73,000 in January 1943.

In domestic affairs, the main problem during World War II was the "Jewish question." The problem of the increasing number of Jews had preoccupied Romanians since the early 19th century, but with the rise of Nazism and Romania's allegiance to Germany, it became a burning question that had to be solved immediately. Nazi sentiment allowed the Iron Guard to conduct their anti-Semitic ideology after the establishment of the National Legionary State. But with them gone, Antonescu was left alone to deal with the Jews how he saw fit. His primary goal was to remove not only the Jews but all foreigners from the Romanian economy. He issued a series of decrees that expropriated Jewish property, from rural and urban homes and land to forests and businesses. In another decree, he demanded all industries to fire their Jewish employees and replace them with Romanians. However, those Jews who proved to be indispensable were allowed to stay in their positions. After Romania took back Bessarabia, the measures against the Jewish community took a more ominous form. Large numbers of them had already fled the provinces, but those who remained started being deported to Wallachia. In Iasi, 4,000 Jews were killed by German and Romanian troops, and 110,000 were deported to Transnistria. However, the conditions in which the people were transported were so horrible that more than half of them died.

But it wasn't Antonescu and his government who organized or participated in the transportation of the Jews. The whole project was part of Hitler's final solution to the "Jewish question," and it was the German officials in Romania who planned it all. Antonescu became aware of the uncertainty of the German victory in the war, and he did not want to be associated with the extermination of the Jews, for he knew that after the war, he could end up answering for these war crimes. Instead, he opted for traditional anti-Semitism, which meant ostracizing the Jewish community.

The crucial turning point of the war for Romania was the defeat at Stalingrad. For the first time, Antonescu saw the weakness of the Nazi regime and their inability to protect Romania from the Soviet Union. He realized the Nazis wouldn't win the war, so he put all of his efforts into protecting his country from the great danger that Russia represented. After all, this was his prime motive for joining the Axis Powers in the first place. But he couldn't suddenly break off the alliance. He continued supplying the Nazis with men and with provisions for the war, but at the same time, he started diplomatic relations with the Allies, trying to convince them that Romania had no other choice due to its difficult position between Russia and Germany. Of the two evils, Antonescu believed he chose the lesser one and concentrated on persuading the European powers that the Soviet Union was dangerous to them all. By the spring of 1944, all other political parties, which, until then, didn't even formally exist, started joining in the efforts to pull Romania out of the war.

The leader of the democratic opposition to Antonescu's government, Iuliu Maniu, played a key role. During 1942 and 1943, he communicated with Great Britain through his secret channels, which often proved to be Swiss and Turkish diplomats.

He explained Romania's position in the war and its aspirations and motives for joining the Axis Powers, and he convinced the British government that the Romanian people strongly opposed continuing the war with the Soviet Union beyond the Dniester River, as their only motive was the return of Bessarabia and northern Bukovina. He also voiced his worries that the Soviet Union would occupy Romania at the first chance they had, and he sought protection from the Western powers. The first response from the British government was very disheartening. They simply said that the borders of Romania would be drafted after the war to adhere to the Allies' best interests and the security of the Soviet Union. To Maniu, it was clear that Britain implied Romania would simply have to reach a deal with Russia before the end of the war.

Antonescu continued working with Germany even though he was aware of the disaster it would bring Romania. He couldn't see any alternative, though, as Hitler announced he planned to occupy Romania to avoid an anti-German coup. At a meeting on February 28th, 1944, Antonescu reassured Hitler of Romania's loyalty, and the two leaders reached a new economic deal that guaranteed supplies for the German army. However, the opposition continued to work on withdrawing Romania from the war, and Maniu intensified his communications with the Allies. In early 1944, in Cairo, Barbu Stirbey, the descendant of Wallachia's most powerful boyar family and the representative of Iuliu Maniu, negotiated with the Allies. He met with a Soviet representative, who promised that Russia would not strive to acquire any Romanian territory and would not influence its social order. The British and American governments helped Russia draft the minimal requirements for an armistice with Romania, and in it, they demanded a complete break from Germany and assistance in their struggle against the Nazis. They also asked for the reestablishment of the border between Russia and Romania as it had been on June 22nd, 1941, as well as reparations to the Soviet Union, the liberation of war prisoners, permission for the Soviet army to move across

Romanian territory unhindered, and the nullification of the Vienna Diktat, which would guarantee Transylvania's return to Romania.

Maniu accepted all of these terms but wanted no foreign army to enter Romanian territory unless invited to do so. He had no faith in the Soviet Union's promises to respect Romania's territorial integrity and sovereignty, as he still believed Russia would launch an occupation at the first chance. But the Allies refused his counter-proposal and demanded he accept all the terms of the armistice. Reluctantly, Maniu accepted, but he still refused to work directly with the Russians. Instead, he communicated all diplomatic efforts through the Ally base in Cairo so that he was certain Britain and the United States remained full partners in the agreement and checked on Russian intentions.

In early June of 1944, the political parties that opposed Antonescu's regime and the war organized a coalition. The National Liberal, the Social Democratic, the National Peasants', and the Romanian Communist Parties formed the National Democratic Bloc (*Blocul Național Democrat*, or BND for short). Their goal was an immediate armistice with the Allies and the withdrawal from the Axis Powers. They also worked on overthrowing Antonescu's dictatorship. But what the Romanian politicians didn't know was that in May, Great Britain and Russia had agreed to divide southeastern Europe into military zones. In this deal, Greece would belong to Britain and Romania to the Soviet Union. In June, Winston Churchill, the British prime minister, proposed that Bulgaria should belong to Russia and Yugoslavia to Britain. US President Franklin Delano Roosevelt accepted this agreement on June 12th, but none of the parties involved planned for this division to be final even after the war. Nevertheless, the course of events locked Romania under the Soviet sphere of influence for a long time after the war.

On August 20th, the Russian Red Army started its massive offensive on the Romanian front. They broke through the German defenses quickly, pushing the front line farther south toward the

Focsani-Galați defense line. Antonescu was sure that if this defense fell, Romania's fate would be sealed, and the country would fall under Soviet influence. In the meantime, the opposition was planning Antonescu's overthrow. The Russian offensive only made them eager to hasten the pace of events. Maniu and King Mihai organized the coup and put their plans in the works on August 23rd. Antonescu was invited to the royal palace by the king, where he was presented with the terms of the armistice. But when he refused to acknowledge it, the king had him arrested and put General Constantin Sanatescu in his place as the prime minister. Sanatescu immediately organized a new government of the National Democratic Bloc, and the same evening, the king broadcasted the proclamation, in which Romania officially broke off its ties to the Axis Powers and entered an armistice with the Allies. He also declared that Romania joined the Allies against Germany and would start mobilizing the army to liberate Transylvania. German officials in Romania didn't expect this course of events and were surprised. They organized an elaborate retreat from Romania by August 31st. On that same day, the Russian Red Army entered Bucharest.

The Seizure of Power

The Red Army poured into the country, and the Sanatescu government had no other choice but to accept the terms of armistice drawn up by the Soviet Union. On August 31st, Great Britain and the United States received the news and had a clear insight into the Soviets' terms for an armistice. It became clear to them that Russia regarded Romania as an occupied country, not as an ally. One of the main terms of the agreement was the provision of the Russian High Command in Romania. The Allies pressured Russia to modify this term and approve the creation of the Allied Control Commission. The British and American representatives would be included, but the Soviet High Command would be able to make all the important decisions. The Romanian delegation traveled to Moscow to sign the armistice deal on September 13th.

Romania was to provide at least twelve infantry divisions, equipment, money, and supplies for the Allied military operations in Hungary. It also had to pay 300 million dollars in reparations to the Soviet Union for the loss of Bessarabia and northern Bukovina, and it also had to return these territories to the Russians. The only positive term for Romania was the abolishment of the Vienna Diktat, but the fate of Transylvania was to be determined after the war was over.

The Romanian politicians had no choice but to sign the armistice, and they left Moscow deeply worried about how the Soviet officials in Romania would interpret it. They feared for the safety of their people, as the newly signed deal treated Romania as an occupied country. Even the American ambassador in Moscow, who took part in the negotiations, admitted that with this armistice, Romania handed political and economic control to Russia, at least until the end of the war. The Sanatescu government cooperated with the Russian High Command on the battlefield, but it often clashed with the Soviet occupation force and their officials in Bucharest. The Soviets didn't only bring their massive army to Romanian territory; they also brought many civil service personnel that would decide the political path Romania took. The Allied Control Commission proved to be impotent, which only proved the Soviet's predominance in southeastern Europe.

In domestic politics, 1944 was the year of the awakening of the political parties, which had been deemed illegal under the dictatorships of Carol and Antonescu. They started mobilizing people into their ranks, and soon, the rivalry between the political parties brought about the end of the National Democratic Bloc. Of the four parties that were part of the Bloc, the Communist Party was the weakest. They were completely outlawed, and by the time of the coup that August, they numbered around 1,000, members with most of its leaders in jail. With the arrival of the Red Army, the Communists who escaped to Russia during the Antonescu dictatorship came back. The leaders were also released from prison after the coup and soon joined forces with the Muscovites, the returning communists from Russia, to revive the party. They benefited from the Soviet presence in Romania, and only a week after the coup, they announced they wished to transform the Bloc into a massive organization. They called on workers to organize their political parties and join the Bloc.

The National Peasants' and National Liberal Parties also worked on their revival, but they failed to present a plan of action and soon went through internal division. By October 12th, the determined Communists succeeded in transforming the Bloc into the National Democratic Front, gathering worker parties around them as allies. They abandoned the Sanatescu government and advocated the formation of a new government under the leadership of Petru Groza. He was the leader of the peasant party that had allied itself with the Communists, known as the Ploughmen's Front. The Soviet Union supported the National Democratic Front and approved of its aggressive methods of leading. Under such pressure, the Sanatescu government resigned on December 6th, 1944, but the new government wasn't formed by Groza; instead, General Nicolae Radescu took power. His effectiveness was greatly diminished by the Communists, who took the initiative over the political life of Romania. In January of 1945, Communist leaders Gheorghe Gheorghiu-Dej and Ana Pauker went to Moscow, where they were assured of Soviet support to seize power. Upon their return home, the power struggle over the political leadership of Romania began.

The Soviet Union did more than just quietly support the Communists. They took the matter into their own hands. In February, they sent their official, Foreign Minister Andrey Vyshinsky, to coordinate the Communists' seizure of power. He spoke directly to King Mihai, asking him to dismantle Radescu's government and install Petru Groza as prime minister. The king declined, saying he needed to consult the leaders of the other political parties. Vyshinsky gave him only two hours to do so, threatening the termination of Romania's independence. King Mihai lacked the support of the Western Allies, so he was forced to accept the Soviet demands, and on March 6th, he announced the formation of the new government under the leadership of Groza.

Earlier in 1945, the Allies signed the Declaration of Liberated Europe at the Yalta Conference, in which they discussed the future of Europe after the end of the war. Great Britain, America, and Russia reached an agreement that they would help all the countries liberated from the Nazi regime in establishing a democratic political system. But the Soviets' treatment of Romania proved that the declaration did not dictate their policy toward Romania. The declaration's intention to establish democracy through elections and the free will of the people was contrary to Soviet political principles. The Soviets needed a friendly and docile government in Bucharest, and if they allowed free elections, the outcome would certainly be different. The Romanian people felt resentment toward Russia, so the chances that they would elect a pro-Russian government was very slim. But for Russia, Romania was a place of enormous strategic importance, as it opened the way to the whole Balkan region and, with it, central Europe. The Allies didn't bother to protest the Russian treatment of Romania, as they considered the war to be a more important matter. It was nearing its end, and Britain and the United States were fully concentrated on its outcome. They only voiced a very restrained criticism of the Soviets' behavior.

The new communist government headed by Petru Groza by no means represented the will of the Romanian people. The Soviets secured all the key governmental positions for the members of the Communist Party, while the National Peasants' and the National Liberal Parties had no seats. Because the Communists were hated, they had to make sure their position was secure, and so they made sure to install prefects who were members of the Communist Party. In every country, a Communist-dominated council was installed, and they played the role of executors of the central government's decisions. They had extensive authority to conduct economic and administrative reforms of the counties and to secure people's support for the communist cause. Similar bodies were installed in villages and the cities to work on an even more localized scale. The peasants were encouraged to form committees that would seize land from the landowners and redistribute it. In cities, worker committees were organized with the task of taking control of the factories and businesses from their owners. The ultimate objective of the Communist Party was to undermine the existing economic and political system of the country and pave the way for the new communist order.

Iuliu Maniu established himself as the leader of the opposition to communism. He gathered all those who wished to form a parliamentary democracy based on the Western model. Maniu strived to protect Romania from Soviet influence and domination, but he had no greater hopes for the future. By June 1945, he had come to the conclusion that Romania was no longer a free, sovereign country. Everyone in the government was willing to do whatever the Soviet Union ordered, and slowly but certainly, they were "communizing" the country's economic and political structures. Maniu urged the king to immediately dismiss the Groza government on the grounds of its violation of the armistice with the Allies. But to do that, the king needed the support of Britain and the United States, which he didn't have. The Allies didn't want to put the outcome of the war in danger by alienating the Soviet Union, and they had no intention of helping Romania. Romania had been an active part of World War II for the last four years, and in May 1945, the war ended with German capitulation. The Romanian army took part in some of the last major offensives of the war, one of which was the Budapest Offensive in Hungary, which lasted from October 1944 until February 1945. During this operation, 11,000 Romanian soldiers were killed and wounded. In another operation, which lasted from December 1944 until May of 1945, 250,000 Romanian troops joined the drive through Slovakia and Moravia into Bohemia to liberate Prague. Even though they were ordered to halt their progress toward the city when they were just within 80 kilometers (about fifty miles) since Germany had capitulated, they had already lost nearly 70,000 soldiers.

The Communists continued to grow stronger during the summer of 1945. On October 16th, they held their first national conference where the delegates elected the Central Committee. In it, three prominent figures took the leading roles. Gheorghe Gheorghiu-Dej was elected as the minister of public works, and both Ana Pauker and Teohari Georgescu became secretaries. These three remained the most powerful people in Romania until 1952. To recognize this new Romanian government, the British and American representatives at the Moscow Conference, which began on December 16th, 1945, asked for the inclusion of at least one member of the National Peasants' and National Liberal Parties. A month later, the two members of these parties were included in the Romanian government as ministers without portfolio. The Groza government was officially recognized on February 4th, 1946, before the elections Petru Groza had promised would be held.

The Groza government finally decided to hold the elections on November 19th, 1946, to satisfy the American mission in Bucharest, which pressured the Communists to fulfill their promise. The Communist Party used all the power of the government to hold a campaign that promoted them as the only choice in the upcoming elections. The National Peasants' Party was their main opposition, but the Communists did everything they could to prevent it from holding a successful campaign. Gheorghiu-Dej even admitted all of this to the American mission, stating that the upcoming elections were the historical battle in which the destiny of Romania would be decided. And it certainly was, although it was not without controversy. The government had to promise they would announce the election results the next day, on November 20th. However, because of an unexplained delay, the results came on November

22nd. The Communist Party won the majority of the votes and gained 349 seats in the new parliament. The National Peasants' Party won 32, and various other smaller parties together won 33 seats. However, an investigation conducted in 1989 showed that the actual results of the elections of 1946 were completely different. The National Peasants' Party was supposed to win, but the Communists, seeing their failure, sent an order to the county prefects to "revise" the numbers. Ana Pauker consulted Moscow as soon as it was evident that the elections were lost, and she received clear instructions on how to manipulate the votes and proclaim a Communist victory. The US and Britain accused Groza of manipulating the election, and they declared that the Communist Party did not represent the will of the people. However, they were not ready to pursue the question further, as they didn't want to antagonize the Soviet Union.

The Paris Peace Treaty, which began to be formulated during the Paris Peace Conference in 1946, was signed in February of the next year. For Romania, the biggest gain was the confirmation of Transylvania as an integral part of the Romanian state, as well as the obligation put on the Russian army to leave Romania within three months. Even though the Russians did retreat part of its army, a large number of soldiers and equipment remained until 1958, under the excuse they needed a connection with occupied Austria through Romania. Article 3 of the Paris Peace Treaty obliged Romania to secure civil rights for all of its citizens, no matter their class, ethnicity, or religion. They also had to allow the complete freedom of the press, associations, and assembly. However, under communist rule, Romania had no intention of fulfilling those terms.

With the end of the war and the new government, under the leadership of Communist Groza, in place, Romania had to face the difficult task of recovering from the war. The economy was shattered into pieces, as the war indemnity to Russia had to be paid in money, raw resources, food supplies, and with what was left of

Romanian industrial equipment. The economic treaty Russia imposed on Romania in 1945 obliged the country to form Soviet-Romanian companies, which only helped put the Romanian industry under Russian monopoly. Although this economic treaty was supposed to make both parties equal, in reality, it served the purpose of helping the Soviet Union exploit Romania even more.

During 1947, the new Romanian government did everything it could to make the economy comply with the Soviet model. They prepared the grounds to nationalize the whole industry and to put the control of agriculture under the collective. In April, the new Ministry of Industry and Commerce started collecting and allocating agricultural and industrial goods. They confiscated all raw materials to distribute how they saw fit and had direct control of the national credit. Everything the new ministry did was to prepare the Romanian economy to become a part of the Soviet Bloc. The consequence of Soviet control over the Romanian economy was the end of all ties the country had with the West. This separation from the West grew to influence all aspects of Romanian life, including politics, culture, and religious and civil freedoms. Suddenly, the country felt more isolated than it did during the 17th and 18th centuries while it was under Ottoman suzerainty.

On Romania's political scene, the Communists sought to get rid of the remnants of the opposition. To deal with the opposing political parties, such as the National Peasants' Party and the National Liberal Party, they arrested their leaders under accusations of treason. They claimed they had conspired with the American and British representatives in Bucharest to bring down Groza's government. Iuliu Maniu and other opposition leaders were brought to court on October 29th, 1947, and were charged with treason. They were sentenced to anywhere between five years to a lifetime in prison. The real reason behind their arrests and sentencing was the Soviets' endeavor to cut off all the ties Romania once had with the West. The public sympathized with Maniu, who showed nothing but honor and bravado during his defense, but the outcome of the trial was obvious. The Communists needed to consolidate their power, and the opposition had to disappear. Maniu was sentenced to a lifetime in prison, where he died in 1953. Although opposition activists remained, they were systematically shut down and imprisoned, often even without a trial.

However, the Communists still needed to keep the appearance of a diverse government, so they kept Gheorghe Tatarescu, a member of the National Liberal Party, in the position of foreign minister. He dealt with the Western powers in a manner that suited the Communists, but eventually, the differences between them were too great to be ignored. By the end of 1947, he was forced to resign, and his successor was Ana Pauker, who became the world's first female foreign minister. Tatarescu was arrested in 1950, together with his three brothers and other members of his family.

The final step of the Communist efforts to install a new political order in Romania was to deal with the monarchy. They feared the king would be a symbol around which the opposition could gather, and the monarchy was also not compatible with the Soviet model of politics they wished to follow. On December 30th, 1947, they forced King Mihai of Romania to abdicate and proclaimed a new state, the Romanian People's Republic.

Chapter 10 – Communism Rising

Gheorghe Gheorghiu-Dej giving a speech in 1946
(https://en.wikipedia.org/wiki/Socialist_Republic_of_Romania#/media/
File:IICCR_FA186_Dej_post_1946_elections_meeting.jpg)

The Communist Party stayed in power for the next four decades, from the end of World War II until 1989. Under their regime, Romania became isolated, not only from the Western world but also from the Romania of the past, which had strived to connect with the modern thought of the West, and from the Romania that was yet to be, a modern civilization rushing to meet the standards of its fellow members of the European Union. The Communists tried to modernize the country, but the methods they used were based on the Soviet model. The leaders of the Romanian Communist Party were unwilling to make any concessions with the people, and they disbanded any consultation with civilians. They believed their authority was ultimate, and they forbade all means of opposition. In the end, their inflexibility and complete ignorance of the population and their demands led to the fall of the communist regime in Romania.

The Rise of the Communist Elite and Their Regime

The Communists' efforts to grab power in the period between 1944 and 1947 brought about the rise of a new elite society. The communist elite was a diverse group, mainly made up of individuals who belonged to the working class. They were of modest, if any, education and were mainly ethnic Romanians. But the Communist Party didn't restrict itself on ethnicity; anyone was allowed to join. Therefore, among its members were also Jews and Hungarians, intellectuals and peasants, and people of all ages. However, the communist regime mostly appealed to young people, who felt the need to belong to a certain group and who wanted to feel active in the political life of their home country. Some of them spent considerable time in Moscow, where they learned the true Stalinist model of communism, and they were considered a valuable addition to the domestic party. The communism of Joseph Stalin's Soviet Union was the ultimate goal for these Romanian activists, and it was the one ambition this diverse group shared.

Gheorghe Gheorghiu-Dej remained the leader for the next ten years. He was a perfect image of what a communist elite should be. He came from a poor family and had a very limited education. In adulthood, he worked on railroad construction in Bucharest and joined the Communist Party as a young activist. Soon, he became the organizer of workers' strikes and was often arrested. In 1933, Gheorghiu-Dej spent time in prison for organizing a railroad workers' strike. While in prison, he established various contacts among a diverse set of individuals. He also started learning about human nature and expanded his limited knowledge. Gheorghiu-Dej had a natural intellect that allowed him to move up the ranks of the Communist Party and become one of its elite members and a leader.

The main rival for the communist leadership to Gheorghiu-Dej was a Jewish woman named Ana Pauker. As a young girl, she was sent to Switzerland to study to become a nurse. While there, she became involved with socialist politics, and once she came back to Romania, she joined the Romanian Workers' Social Democratic Party. As she was an ardent activist, she was arrested several times. After serving time in 1940, she was transferred to Moscow under the prisoner exchange program. There, she not only accepted communism, but she also became one of Stalin's personal favorites. Everyone expected her to become the leader of the Romanian Communist Party upon her return to the country, but she had two major setbacks that pulled her down: she was a woman, and she was a Jew. The Romanian population was not yet ready to accept such changes that came so naturally in the Western world.

Another prominent communist individual was Lucretiu Patrascanu, who was also seen as an outsider. Although he was communist, he was an intellectual with a law degree from the University of Leipzig. However, his estrangement from the core of the Communist Party wasn't due to his education. He preferred to think for himself and refused to be a Soviet puppet. He strongly believed that Romanian communism shouldn't look up to the Russian model and that it should be built by Romanians for Romanians. Patrascanu was against foreign influence in the post-war development of Romania, but he still served as the minister of justice under the Groza government. Patrascanu was fully committed to communist ideals, and he didn't mind the perversion of the justice system, as it would better serve communist ambitions. Patrascanu's education became the divisive point that stood between his progress and the Communist Party. Even though he defended many Communist leaders during the 1930s, he ended up in prison himself, as he was not trusted enough to be promoted to higher leadership.

Two of Gheorghiu-Dej's closest friends stood out from the usual Communist social circle, as they were not common workers of modest education. They were Emil Bodnaras, an army officer who spent World War II in the Soviet Union, and Ion Gheorghe Maurer, a lawyer, who had defended the leaders of the Communist Party since 1935. He served as the president of the Council of Ministers from 1961 to 1974. These two individuals acted as personal advisors to Gheorghiu-Dej, and they worked on broadening Gheorghiu-Dej's knowledge about the outside world.

Many other elite members of the Communist Party were known as Gheorghiu-Dej's "workforce," and their main goal was the modernization of Romania. But instead of continuing Romania's path to become one of the European states modeled on Western values, they worked hard to commit Romania to the Eastern Bloc. To the Communists, the modernization of the country meant a radical transformation to set Romania free from previous Western influence. To achieve this, they had to create new institutions, a new elite, and a new universal social class. It also had to destroy the old system of values and social structures. To the Communists, modernization meant industrialization, but only if it was done through the massive nationalization of the means of production. Resources were confiscated and redistributed to the branches of industry that the central government thought was most needed. People were also mobilized, as they were the real workforce, the labor strength that would bring about the new order of society.

The dark side of the Communists' modernization of Romania lay in the brutality and destruction it wrought to reach its goals. The Communists believed that the full modernization of the country could only be achieved through total control. The individual didn't matter anymore. Everything had to be subordinate to the collective. To begin, the Communists installed a monopoly over the political power of the country by brutally eliminating any possible opposition. Once the monopoly was established, they started training their cadres by indoctrinating them with communist ideology. Once an individual showed a certain level of enthusiasm in communist activity, they would be chosen to become the managers of the local branches of the party or state businesses. To be enlisted, one had to have a proper social and political background.

In 1948, the Communist elite thought the time was ripe to install a new security system that would serve the party's goals. Once again, the leaders looked at the Soviet model and established the General Directorate for the Security of the People. At first, they relied on the old system and the Russian occupation force to maintain the security of state institutions. But to effectively defend the regime from both foreign and internal enemies, they needed a stronger force. The new organization became known as simply "Securitate" (the "Security"), and its main task was to protect the communist regime in all spheres of Romanian life. The next year, the regular police force was replaced by the Militia, whose prime task was to secure and maintain public order. In reality, the Militia was an extension of the Securitate, as the two organizations worked together to put the people under constant surveillance. Aside from maintaining order, the Militia also had the right to issue residency permits for the cities, as not everyone was eligible to become a resident. A new organization, named the Security Troops Command, was brought to light in 1951. This was a special unit of the Securitate, and it was equipped with armored vehicles, planes, and artillery. Their primary task was the suppression of the opposition to the regime.

These three security forces acted without restraint to defend the regime against the individuals and groups who were accused of conspiring against the social order or undermining the national economy. Tens of thousands of villagers were removed from their land by these forces when the Communist Party ordered the acquisition of all agricultural land. Tens of thousands of individuals were accused of opposing the communist regime and were arrested. Those who were unfortunate to be accused of working against the state never saw a trial; instead, they were put directly into prisons. These same security forces were in charge of a vast prison network. Under their direct control were hundreds of detention centers that resembled the Soviet Gulag. Some of the prisons had extremely bad reputations. For example, in Pitesti, the prisoners were forced to torture each other. In other institutions, prisoners suffered forced labor and often died from hunger and exhaustion.

During the first decade after the war, the Romanian Communist Party was under close surveillance by the Soviet Union. Because Romanian communists had no support from the people, they needed an external partner and leader who could lift them to power. Since they found such a partner in Russia, the new elite felt obliged to respond to their every request. But in reality, the relationship between Romania and Russia was never one of equal partnership. Russia acted as if it had sovereignty over Romania, and the Soviets even installed their agents into various Romanian institutions. They were called Soviet advisors, and their prime task was to teach the Romanian communist leaders. But they also acted as agents, sending reports directly to Moscow. Gheorghiu-Dej, Pauker, and the others were well aware that the Soviets closely monitored their work, and they knew they would easily be replaced if they made a mistake. The Soviet advisors wouldn't leave Romania until 1964.

The Communist Party, as well as all the branches of the Romanian government, were modeled on the Soviet Union. Even the Securitate was a copy of the Soviet security system. The Romanian Ministry of Foreign Affairs had the largest number of Soviet agents because Stalin needed to control Romania's relations with other countries, especially those of western Europe. He was building the Eastern Bloc, and he couldn't allow the influx of foreign influence to his proxy states. Although the military also had a large number of Soviet agents who trained and organized the Romanian army, Stalin never saw fit to unify the army of the Eastern Bloc. That came later, after his death, as a response to the creation of NATO (the North Atlantic Treaty Organization). When West Germany joined NATO, the new Russian prime minister, Nikita Khrushchev, responded with the creation of the Warsaw Treaty Organization, also known as the Warsaw Pact. This treaty put Romania's army directly into the hands of the Soviets.

The first crisis the Romanian Communist Party experienced was after Stalin's death when Khrushchev accused his predecessor of various crimes against humanity and ordered the de-Stalinization of the whole Eastern Bloc. Up until then, the cult of personality was very important for the regime, but suddenly, Moscow demanded it to be brought down and replaced by a collective leadership. Gheorghiu-Dej was an avid supporter of Stalin's regime, but he quickly realized that to survive the regime change in Russia, he needed to adapt. In 1954, he resigned as the leader of the party and installed Gheorghe Apostol in his place, but everyone was aware he continued ruling the party from the shadows. The crisis continued in 1955 and 1956, as Khrushchev strived to implement his reform into the countries of the Eastern Bloc. In Poland, he removed the communist leaders of the government who remained loyal to the old communist model of Stalin, and in Hungary, he dealt with an uprising that threatened to end the communist regime. This uprising spread to the university centers of Romania in Timisoara, Cluj, and Bucharest, where students gathered to support the people of Budapest, but they didn't have the support of the workers and peasants and remained too small in numbers to make any significant change.

An important segment of Romanian history has always been the Orthodox Church. Its sheer existence was what preserved the tradition and memory of Romania's place in the Christian world through the period of Ottoman rule. The Communists couldn't ignore the importance of religion in the everyday lives of the people, as well as in the building of a new nation. Therefore, they couldn't simply ban religion, even though atheism is one of the main points of communism. The Orthodox Church numbered the highest percentage of followers, 72.6 percent, followed by the Greek Catholic Church with 7.9 percent. For the time being, the Communist Party chose to let the churches function but placed them under the strict control of the regime. The survival of the Church is largely thanks to its patriarch, Justinian Marina (1901–1977), who continuously worked on bringing peace between religion and communism. He and his followers believed that if they abided by the legal framework set by the Communist Party, the Church would thrive. Justinian even wrote numerous volumes of *Apostolat social*, the *Social Mission*, a publication in which he described how necessary it was for the Church and its followers to adapt to the political circumstances of the country and to do whatever was in their power to build a new society.

But when Justinian started reorganizing the monastic lives, the Communists began to be alarmed. The patriarch's reforms of monastic life elevated monasteries as new centers of faith and intellectual thought. The Communist Party saw a threat in such centers, as they could be the perfect hiding spots for the opposition and also produce opposing ideas. In 1958, the party started a campaign against the monasteries, which resulted in the closing of monastic schools and the reduction of the clergy, monks, and nuns. The following year, the government forced the Holy Synod to accept a new monastic reformation, one that worked perfectly in synchronization with the objectives of the Communist Party. The monasteries resisted at first and proved their resilience when threatened with the powerful governmental machinery, and by 1961, the Communist Party and the Church had improved their relations once more. But the destiny of the Greek Catholic Church was completely different. The party was determined to abolish it because of its ties with the Vatican and the West. The Catholic clergy was forced to either convert to Orthodoxy or give up their positions. All the property owned by the Greek Catholic Church was confiscated and given to the Orthodox Church. The Greek Catholic Church was officially abolished in 1948, but many of its followers and priests continued to practice their rites in subtle ways as outlaws. Those who were discovered were immediately arrested and imprisoned, sometimes even killed.

When talking about Romanian communism, it is unavoidable to mention the treatment of ethnic minorities. Although in all aspects, the Communist Party tried to model itself on the Soviet example, they failed to or refused to do so when it came to minorities. The Hungarians and Szeklers were the largest ethnic minority group in Romania, with most of them living in Transylvania (approximately 1.5 million). They were historically bound to the land, and they considered it their home. But communist ideology could never allow them to have their own cultural or economic autonomy. The Communist Party wanted to keep all the power in its own hands. Thus, the Hungarians were allowed to have their representatives in the institutions but only as members of organizations approved by the party. For an organization to gain approval, it had to abide by communist rules and ideals. In 1952, the Soviets pushed for the organization of the Hungarian Autonomous Region, which would allow the Romanians to deal with this minority the Stalinist way. To do so, Romania had to change its constitution, which would then allow the existence of an autonomous region. Nevertheless, the region still had to be approved by the Romanian legislative body, the National Assembly, which decided never to act on the question of the Hungarians. Although the region was formed, it never gained autonomy and continued to be governed from Bucharest. It was dissolved in 1968.

Under the Gheorghiu-Dej and Ceausescu regimes, there was no place for Hungarian business, bank, or culture. Thus, there was no economic model that would finance strictly Hungarian institutions. Both communist leaders undertook strict programs that would end Hungarian businesses, churches, schools, and cultural activities. The schools were the first to be nationalized; in 1948, the Hungarian language was forbidden in schools, and all classes had to be taught in Romanian. During the 1950s, Romania started a program that forced Hungarian students into learning in only Romanian schools. The responsibility for this partially lay in the uprising that occurred in Budapest in 1956. Afraid that the Hungarians of Transylvania would be inspired by their revolutionist cousins from Hungary, the Communist Party decided to diminish, as much as possible, their national sense. In 1959, in Cluj, the Hungarian Bolyai University merged with the Romanian Babes University. It not only demonstrated the Communists' power over the minorities, but it also announced the awakening of a new socialist regime, which would come to life during the 1960s. It was clear that the party's vision of national socialism meant there was only room for one ethnicity, that being Romanian.

The position of the Saxons was significantly different after the war. Because they had joined the German army against the Russians on the Eastern Front, the Soviets couldn't allow their existence. The Romanian Communist Party, pressured by the Soviets, even considered exiling them from the country. But the party settled for proclaiming them a cohabiting nationality, the same status that other minorities had. Thus, the Saxons were allowed to retain their Romanian citizenship and to take part in the socialist transformation of the country. But their fate was very similar to the Hungarians during the Gheorghiu-Dej regime. Between 1948 and 1952, the Saxons went through a strict nationalization of their economy and culture. The Saxon middle class had no means of survival, and their leadership was doomed to failure. Communism destroyed the Saxon village life with the collectivization of agriculture, and many Saxons were forced to leave their homes and search for livelihood in the cities. Because of the lack of funds, Saxon culture couldn't thrive. Saxon schools were abolished as early as 1948, and the use of the German language in national schools was very limited. The Communist Party did allow various Saxon organizations, but they only served to mobilize the citizens to serve communist ideology. They certainly did not represent Saxon interests and were incapable of providing this ethnic minority with proper leadership.

The Saxons, as an ethnic community, had no hope of survival in communist Romania. Because of it, they emigrated to Germany in masses, especially after 1967, when the two countries established diplomatic relations. West Germany signed a secret agreement with Romania, paying anywhere between 4,000 and 10,000 Deutschmarks for every Saxon who was allowed to emigrate. In addition, the credit of another 700 million Deutschmarks was approved to Romania. But the massive emigration of the Saxons only occurred after the fall of the communist regime, and their numbers were reduced to barely 120,000 by 1993. The Saxon community never peaked again, and they stopped being a significant social and cultural force in Transylvania.

After World War II, the Jewish community of Romania started experiencing a revival. Their numbers were cut almost in half due to the horrors of the war, but in the years that followed, they worked vigorously in rebuilding Jewish businesses and the cultural and political life. However, the Communist Party, although it allowed the existence of various Jewish organizations, demanded their subordination. But unlike the Hungarians and the Saxons, Jews got the opportunity of having true representation in the government. They organized the Jewish Democratic Committee as early as 1948, and it represented the interests of the Jews within the parliament. However, this organization was communist by nature and thus followed the general ideology of the ruling party. The Jewish knew they had to bring their community in order, so all the prominent figures who refused to lend their name to communist propaganda were removed from their positions and replaced with more compatible individuals. Rabbis were not spared either, as synagogues were forced to serve the communist ideology. The only Jewish organization that was allowed to exist outside of the communist context was the Zionist Organization of Romania. But in 1949, even the Zionists were accused of opposing the idea of nationalization and were shut down. The Jews responded with massive emigration. With the foundation of Israel in 1948, they had a home country to which they could go, but the communist regime wouldn't allow just anyone to leave. They had to go under rigorous checkups by the Securitate to prove they were not acting as spies for the foreign powers. Nevertheless, the immigration, although slow, was fairly steady, and by 1993, there were only 9,000 Jews left in Romania.

Gypsies were largely ignored in the early days of the communist regime. There were some initiatives to integrate them into Romanian society and make them a part of the national economic program, but they were not a priority. Their nomadic way of life was prohibited, and they started settling in the cities and villages. The state promised them a school and jobs and completely ignored their wishes to be a part of the change of their society. The question of the Gypsies was essentially frozen for the time being, and it only resurfaced during the 1970s. The communist regime of later years tried to integrate the Gypsy minority into society but without much success. They were obliged to send their children to school and to work, but many resisted giving up their nomadic way of life. Due to the act of 1966, which abolished abortions in Romania, the population of the Gypsies rose significantly, and by 1977, their numbers doubled. Today, they are the largest minority in Romania, surpassing even the Hungarians.

Change of Policy

The 1960s were a turning point for the Communist Party, which changed their ideology from simply imitating the Soviet model to building their own communist model unique to Romania and the times. To develop this national communism, the party leaders had to work extensively on getting rid of Soviet control over Romanian politics and the economy. Suddenly, the Communist Party changed its policy against Russia and strived to expel the Soviets from all the state institutions. Romanian people always had an anti-Russian stance, and the fact that the ruling Communist Party shared it only brought popularity to national communism. But the Communist Party did much more than simply renounce its ties with Russia. It started building up a relationship with western Europe and the United States. The people felt as if Romania was returning to Europe, to its rightful place. But the Communists had no such sentiments; they were driven only by the practicality and the greater good for the party. The sense of belonging to the European world would disappear again at the beginning of the next decade with Ceausescu's return.

By the 1960s, the Communist Party had no opposition left. The social elite and the leaders were very diverse, as the party gathered individuals from all social and economic levels. But despite this diversity, they managed to maintain a certain level of cohesion because they were all driven by the same ideology and the same aspiration to bring complete autonomy to Romania. Impressed by the support they got for turning state policy against the Soviets, the Communist Party decided to relax the relations it had with the people, a practice known in politics as the détente. There was no longer a need to put constraints on social activities, such as religion or cultural expressions. Gheorghiu-Dej came to realize that these measures were counterproductive and that the party could gain much more if it enjoyed the support of the people wholeheartedly. Therefore, he concentrated on emphasizing the bond between society and the Communist Party. The party was reconfigured in such a way so that it represented national interests first and communist interests second. The Communist Party became the most ardent defender of progressive change in the country, eliminating the class struggle just so it could build an ethnic nation. But the most significant change in the relations between the ruling elite and the people of Romania was that instead of using commands, the party started opening up a dialogue. The people's needs were listened to, and although the political leaders didn't actively seek to conform to all of them, they started giving instructions for change rather than commands.

Because of the newly established communication with the people, the Communist Party made sure that new apartment buildings were built and that there were enough stocked goods for the consumers. They also made healthcare and education available to everyone, as well as employment and pension plans. The reach of the Securitate was limited, which resulted in a reduction of arrests and imprisonments. By 1964, the Communist Party even started symbolically releasing their political enemies. After all, the support of the people was enough to keep them in power, and there was no need to be afraid of the opposition. Nevertheless, the Communists released only those prisoners who were not a serious threat to their power or ideology. They were well aware that there was a chance a well-organized opposition could form.

But besides these obvious signs of the Communist Party wishing to have a dialogue with the citizens and caring for their well-being, the Communists still couldn't shake off their old habit of asserting their control and manipulating public opinion. This is probably most evident in the cultural and educational spheres of literature and history. Both of these professions were seen as a means of reaching the population. For the Communists, they were the perfect propaganda tools. Soon, the Communist Party came up with a set of rules for writers, ordering them how to modify their style to reach wider masses. They also dictated the themes and mood of the poems, novels, and history works to make sure a writer was conveying the message in the "good spirit of the Party." If an individual refused to abide by the rules and stood up to defend artistic freedom, the Communist Party didn't react. It was the same in all other spheres of life. But even though the Communists opened up a dialogue, they never really stopped trying to control people's professional and personal lives. There could be no cultural organization without the involvement of the Communist Party, and the liberalization of the political system never came, as the party was never really challenged to loosen its grasp. The détente wasn't the result of pressure from the people or foreign powers. It was completely the will of the Communist elite, who saw only good things for the party if they relaxed relations.

National communism wouldn't have occurred in Romania if the stage hadn't already been set for it. After the death of Stalin, his successor, Nikita Khrushchev, accused him of abusing his power, and he set in motion many changes in the Eastern Bloc. The Romanian Communists were ready to prove their loyalty to the Soviet Union if it was asked of them, but it wasn't. In 1958, Khrushchev withdrew the Red Army from Romania and changed Moscow's stance on the relation between the two countries. Russian advisors started leaving Romanian institutions, loosening the Soviet grasp over the country. In the end, it was the Soviet leader who inspired the idea of Romanian autonomy and the building of national communism. But that doesn't mean Khrushchev offered no resistance to Romanian efforts to challenge the policies of the Eastern Bloc, especially when it came to the economy. Russia still wanted to pick up the fruit of the labor of their allies, and Khrushchev hoped to reinvigorate the Council of Mutual Economic Assistance, which had been founded in 1949 by Stalin himself. The whole Eastern Bloc was affected by the series of reforms Khrushchev brought forth, and the result was the affirmation of Soviet control over the economies of the states. Khrushchev's reforms dictated that some countries had to focus on industrial modernization while others should concentrate only on agricultural production. Romania was to be among the latter. Gheorghiu-Dej was aware that the Soviets planned to make the countries of the Eastern Bloc dependent on each other, crushing all possibilities for autonomy and complete independence. He firmly rejected Khrushchev's plan and continued to concentrate on developing Romania's heavy industry.

To speed up the de-Sovietization of Romania, the Communists started renaming the city streets, which had carried the names of prominent Russian figures for the last decade. For example, the city of Brasov, which had been renamed Orasul Stalin (Stalin City) in 1950, changed its name back in 1960. The second step of removing the connections with Soviet Russia was reconditioning Romano-Soviet institutions, such as the Maxim Gorky Institute of Russian Language and Literature, which was simply turned into a department of Slavic studies within the Institute for the Languages. Others were simply shut down. Up until the 1960s, learning the Russian language in schools was obligatory, but now, it was only studied as a second language, and it had to compete with German, French, and English. In the media, there was no more enthusiasm for Russian news and publications, as the Communist Party and the people turned to information coming from the West. This was the result of the improved diplomatic relations Romania had been working on since the death of Stalin in 1953. However, despite their renewed approach, the Communist Party continued to pursue its interests. Gheorghiu-Dej simply wanted strong relations with France and England so he could continue the de-Sovietization of Romania. The Communists never really aspired to accept Western values or to leave the Eastern Bloc. They simply needed the West as a new marketplace to which they could sell goods, ensuring the communist modernization of the country.

The culmination of Romania's efforts to break ties with Soviet Russia came on April 27th, 1964, with the establishment of the Romanian Workers' Party on Issues of the International Communist and Working-Class Movements. No longer was the

Romanian Communist Party obliged to answer to the Soviet Union for its deeds; instead, it simply proclaimed independence. The freedom they gained with the party's independence inspired them to pursue autonomy more vigorously. They started demanding other communist states to obey the principles of non-interference in internal matters. With this demand, they sent a clear message to Moscow: each country was to decide how it would achieve communism without having to report to the Soviets.

The strength of the Communists was probably best displayed in the smooth transition of power when Gheorghiu-Dej died in 1965. He designated Nicolae Ceausescu (1918–1989) as his successor, and no one challenged that decision. Ceausescu had been born in a village to a peasant family. This fact inspired a saying that a peasant replaced a worker. However, this wasn't completely true. Ceausescu left his village after finishing only four grades of elementary school so he could find an apprenticeship as a shoemaker in Bucharest. He started his communist career in 1933 when he joined the Union of Communist Youth. Two years later, he was a member of the Communist Party and started organizing various party activities. Because of that, he was often arrested, and in prison, he met Gheorghiu-Dej. During the 1950s, Ceausescu continued to climb the ladder of the political hierarchy, and by 1960, he was powerful enough to install his own men in key positions within the party. When he came to power in 1965, he continued the party's policy of collective leadership. However, Ceausescu was very ambitious and desired all the power to be in his own hands. In 1969, he started creating a cult of personality, and at the same time, he started removing the old Communists, the followers of Gheorghiu-Dej's ideology, from the party.

Chapter 11 – The Ceausescu Regime

The revolutionaries of 1989 after the Securitate
opened fire on them
(https://en.wikipedia.org/wiki/Romanian_Revolution#/media/
File:PozeRevolutia1989clujByRazvanRotta13.jpg)

At first, Ceausescu continued Gheorghiu-Dej's policy of collective leadership and building national communism. He continued to modernize Romania through industrial development and continued the policy of détente. Ceausescu severely limited the extent to which the Securitate could work, and he significantly increased the quantity and the quality of available goods for consumers. He promised he would lift the limitations on artistic freedom, but he also encouraged them to reevaluate Romanian national history and place value on communist history. Thus, he and his party gained legitimacy. However, Ceausescu's real intentions could easily be seen in his attempts to limit personal freedoms and bind the individual to the Communist Party. No person could pursue their own interests, as everything had to be subordinate to the building of socialism in accordance with communist ideals. Ceausescu needed more workers, but the population increased too slowly to fulfill his plans. In October of 1966, he decided to ban abortion and contraception as a long-term plan of increasing Romania's workforce.

The consequences of the abortion ban were severe. In an ideal socialist state, the government would take care of the unwanted children, and Ceausescu promised just that. But Romania lacked funds for extensive childcare programs, and the result was numerous orphanages across the country filled with unwanted and starving children. The conditions in these institutions were so horrid that many children died of neglect and disease. The children who grew up in orphanages were indeed abandoned, not only by their parents but also by the state. The lack of food, education, and constant confinement in the institutions had a severe impact on child development. Recent studies reveal that those who grew up in Romanian communist orphanages were more likely to suffer mental disabilities due to brain underdevelopment. And women didn't fare any better. Out of necessity, they would turn to the black market to get illegal, back-alley abortions. Since they were performed in an unsterile environment with makeshift tools, many women died. Modern scholars estimate that around 10,000 women died between 1966 and 1989 due to the consequences of these abortions. If they were caught, women and those who performed abortions on them faced imprisonment. Many young women were not even able to confide in their husbands or friends out of fear they would be reported to authorities.

To inspire people to have children, Ceausescu introduced a special tax on childless people in 1977. The number of children who grew up in communist orphanages is unknown because the state never bothered to keep proper records. However, the contemporary belief is that around 500,000 children grew up in orphanages.

The same year Ceausescu assumed power, he changed the name of the state to the Socialist Republic of Romania, and he and his colleagues issued a new constitution. They also changed the name of the party from the Romanian Workers' Party back to the Romanian Communist Party. In foreign policy, Ceausescu followed the example of his predecessor and continued to build good relations with the West. In 1967, he established diplomatic relations with West Germany, an act that disturbed the Soviets, as they had East Germany under their control. Angered, the Soviets started accusing Romania of being out of step with the rest of the Eastern Bloc and for failing to coordinate its economy with other communist countries. But Ceausescu didn't care; he planned to continue the de-Sovietization of Romania, and he needed Western allies to do it effectively. Ceausescu had no intentions of giving up on building communism, and the establishment of diplomacy with West Germany was only the first step to opening a new market for Romanian goods, as well as for acquiring modern Western technology.

To confirm his intention to fully break the bonds with the Soviet Union, in 1968, he condemned the actions of Russia, which had sent the army of the Warsaw Pact to occupy Czechoslovakia. Ceausescu feared the same fate for Romania; therefore, he announced his plans to build a patriotic army that would defend the country from foreign invaders. This act brought him fame among the Russia-hating population, and even the Western powers started recognizing his defiance against the Soviets as a trait of a good leader. Unfortunately, Ceausescu would prove to be far from a good leader. Nevertheless, the summer of 1969 saw an official visit from US President Richard Nixon, and the next year, Ceausescu and his wife visited Washington, DC, where many new economic deals were signed. In 1971, Romania became part of two international economic institutions: the General Agreement on Tariffs and Trade (GATT) and the International Monetary Fund (IMF).

The Dictator

Nicolae Ceausescu started showing his true face in 1971 when he issued a speech known as the July Theses. They were formulated in the true spirit of communism and represented a turning point in the project to modernize Romania. The July Theses announced the return of old communist values, the end of cultural autonomy, and the end of the détente. The Communist Party was returning to its old ways of creating a new order through indoctrination. Ceausescu thought the relaxation of relations between the state and society led to the rise of liberal ideas, which led the country off its path to achieving communism. He believed that because of this renewed liberal spirit among the people, the old bourgeois spirit had returned, which advocated diversity in ideology. For Ceausescu, these were thoughts that would halt communism.

The reason for Ceausescu's turn in policy can be found in his visit to China and North Korea in June of 1971. There, he was greeted with massive displays of communist strength and power through public demonstrations. He saw firsthand how a well-organized party could build a nation ready to commit, sacrifice, and work on changing the country. He was impressed by what the Asians had achieved in regards to communist ideology, and he was prepared to try these firm methods in his own country. In his view, Marxist-Leninist ideology was a perfect guide for society and the party, whether it pertained to education, the media, literature, history, or various activist organizations. Ceausescu called for the party to tighten its grasp on all segments of society. By this point, Ceausescu had no opposition within the party or outside of it. His proposals were accepted by everyone in the state council, and Romania started hurling down the path of a dictatorship regime.

Ceausescu didn't only set Marxist-Leninist ideology as the right path for the country; he also established neo-Stalinism, with a cult of personality growing strong. Even though the regime of Gheorghiu-Dej was just like that at one point, the previous leader had adhered to communal rulership. Ceausescu, on the other hand, turned to complete dictatorship. During his regime, from 1971 until his fall in 1989, nepotism and corruption flourished, becoming a part of everyday life for the citizens of Romania. But the cult of personality was the defining point of Ceausescu's dictatorship. It grew every day, and it knew no limits. A day wouldn't pass without him showing up in the press, on the television, or on the radio. He was ever-present in the people's lives, and the only person who got as much attention as he did was his wife, Elena. By 1974, Nicolae Ceausescu held the three most important offices in the country: the commander of the army, the general secretary of the Communist Party, and the first president of the Socialist Republic of Romania. Other important state offices were filled with members of his own family, and he elevated Elena as the second most powerful person in Romania. Ceausescu relied on her opinion, and it seems he followed her instructions. They even started preparing their son for the succession, which led the Western media to refer to Romania as the "socialism of one family."

During Ceausescu's rule, the Communist Party fell into second place as his cult of personality grew. The Communist Party was no longer seen as the driving machine that pushed Romania into modernization; this was the accomplishment of only one man. Still, the number of the party's members continued to grow, as it was the only way of getting some social benefits, such as education, employment, or even material goods. But the Communist Party was completely subdued to the will of one person, and even though it continued its activities to build up communism, they served only to promote Ceausescu. All the accomplishments of the party were promoted as accomplishments of their great leader. The strong cult of personality that Ceausescu built ensured that there was no room for the formation of opposition within the Communist Party or outside of it.

Romania's economy continued to grow during the first decade of Ceausescu's dictatorship, but during the early 1980s, it completely broke down. The development of the heavy industry was pushed to the extreme, for in Ceausescu's vision, it was the key to progress. It was the economic drive that would secure Romania's autonomy and provide the country with the strength to remain outside of the Soviet sphere of influence. Whenever allocations were made, the industry came first, followed by its auxiliary enterprises. Other segments of Romania's economy fell behind because they were regarded as less important. To invest in the development of heavy industry, Ceausescu borrowed money from foreign financial institutions, such as the IMF. He planned to pay back the loan once the industry was more firmly established, as its products would be sold in the West. But the poor management at the local levels, as it was filled with corruption, took Romania in another direction. During the late 1970s, both the industry and agriculture suffered because of shortages of energy and raw materials. Nevertheless, Ceausescu didn't want to give up on his plan. In his stubbornness, he clung to the vision of the future for Romania he had had since the July Theses, and he did nothing to prevent the upcoming disaster.

When the economic crisis hit Romania in the 1980s, Ceausescu refused to make market concessions or to sell goods quickly and cheaply to save the people. Instead, he opted for saving industry at the expense of the people. He demanded increased production, but he offered no compensation to the workers. In fact, he placed more burden on them, as he found new ways to implement higher taxes on the people and started reducing the availability of food and other resources. In 1982, Ceausescu decided to pay off the country's debt as soon as possible to avoid foreign financial institutions meddling in Romania's economy. As a result, the quality of life drastically fell, not only for the workers but for the Communist elite too. In a way, the lower standard of living tested the loyalty of various state officials.

During the economic crisis of the 1980s, Ceausescu started some of his most demanding projects. He didn't spare the labor force or money to achieve his grandiose plans. The construction of the Danube-Black Sea Canal, which had been abandoned in the 1950s for being too expensive, was continued and even completed in 1986. Although the canal cut short the distance ships needed to travel to reach the Black Sea, the building of the canal proved unnecessary at the time because the crisis resulted in reduced traffic. Bucharest, as the capital of Romania, suffered the most, as the dictator planned to make it into a truly modern European city. Ceausescu had grandiose plans of constructing massive buildings that would display Romania's power, and one of these, the Palace of the Parliament, stands even today. It is the largest parliamentary building in Europe, and in the world, it is second only to the Pentagon in Washington, DC. But to complete his megalomaniac building projects, he destroyed much of the city. The old 19th-century buildings, which gave Bucharest a special charm, were razed to the ground, and in their place, communist blocs were erected.

However, there were benefits for the people who lived under the Ceausescu regime, even though the government sought to dissolve all social structures and pry into the private lives of its citizens. Education was made available to everyone, and with it, literacy grew. The Communist Party needed its citizens to be able to read and understand communist propaganda, and while Gheorghiu-Dej made elementary schools obligatory, Ceausescu made it possible for all social classes to attend secondary schools and universities. The number of students increased during the 1980s, and everyone was guaranteed a job, even though it might not have been what they wished to do. Despite these improvements, Ceausescu was determined to end the détente with the people and tighten his grasp on their lives. The overall mood of Romanian communism was disdain for individuality in all spheres of life.

The Ceausescu regime also prioritized the emancipation of women, and the Communist Party claimed they had equal rights as men. Women joined the party in droves, which provided them with free healthcare and work. But, as with other marginalized groups, the regime's true intention wasn't the liberation of women but rather access to a new labor force. Just like the ethnic minorities, the Church, and other undesired layers of society, the Communist Party had a solution for women too. Another bonus effect of this emancipation was the destruction of traditional family values, which brought the need for individuals to turn to the collective. Ceausescu's wife, Elena, served as the perfect image of the communist woman. She shared political power with her husband, and during the 1980s, the party tried to present her as an equal to Ceausescu himself. But her life hardly reflected the real conditions of women's lives under communism. A common woman had to be a worker, a mother of future generations of workers, and someone who had to navigate everyday tasks, which, during communism, meant the lack of food, resources, power, modern healthcare, and even access to basic human needs.

In foreign relations, Ceausescu remained true to his initial plans to build relations with the West. However, he realized he had to normalize the relationship between Romania and the Soviet Union because he needed the resources provided by the Eastern Bloc for his development of the country's industry. He improved Romania's attitude toward Russia, but he remained defensive about the country's autonomy. Never again would Romania allow Russia such direct and invasive interference in its internal affairs. The Western powers saw Ceausescu for what he was, especially during the country's crisis in the 1980s. They were aware of his failures to repay the national debt, establish basic human rights for his citizens, and provide the country with enough resources for all. Nevertheless, they continued to support him because the Ceausescu regime was the soft spot of the Eastern Bloc, and it acted as a separation line between the West and the Soviet Union.

The Revolution

The Ceausescu regime proved to be very brittle, as its dictator showed no signs of flexibility or realism. When the revolution occurred in the second half of December 1989, Nicolae Ceausescu was brought down in only ten days. The Romanian economy collapsed because the country's leader had stubbornly held to his initial plans and refused to make any concessions with the market or his people. He continued to use his cult of personality, empty promises, and old communist slogans to hold his regime together. He was afraid of innovations coming into the existing order because he saw it as a threat to his authority. Even though the discontent among the population grew steadily, no one foresaw Ceausescu's sudden fall from power.

The Communists in Romania made sure there was no organized opposition to their rule, but the signs of disdain started showing back in 1977 with the first workers' strikes. In the Jiu Valley, thousands of coal miners protested, demanding better working conditions, but the Communist Party quickly dealt with them by using the oppressive force of the Securitate. The miners were intimidated, abused, and arrested repeatedly until they finally gave up. Although unsuccessful, this strike had been the largest opposition to the communist regime since its foundation. Ceausescu continued to abuse the labor force by lowering wages, providing no food for families, and doing nothing to improve working conditions. The result was a street demonstration in Brasov in 1987, where factory workers rebelled. They openly attacked the Communist Party's headquarters and other buildings. To alleviate the situation, Ceausescu's government once again used the Securitate, which arrested the demonstration leaders. The situation was then smoothed over with empty promises of better conditions for the workers in the future, but, of course, that future never came. No one dared to criticize Ceausescu or his regime except for a few intellectuals. However, they created the false image of the existence of a state enemy, which only served to prove how great a leader he was. Ceausescu was presented as the ultimate decision-maker as well as problem-solver, as only he alone could deal with these intellectual dissidents.

In 1987, Mikhail Gorbachev, the last leader of the Soviet Union, visited Bucharest with the sole purpose of persuading Ceausescu to restructure his regime. The Russian politician started reforms throughout the Eastern Bloc because he realized that the growing power of the Western world was making the survival of communism impossible. But Nicolae Ceausescu would not falter. He strove to persuade Gorbachev that everything was going according to plan. He organized it so the Russian statesman only met with individuals who would confirm that Romanian communism was alive and thriving. After Gorbachev visited Bucharest, the relations between the two countries grew cold, which only helped push Romania into complete isolation from the rest of the world.

The first sign of internal troubles came on March 10th, 1989, when some of the former Communist Party officials drew up the so-called "Letter of the Six." It was an attempt of direct communication with Ceausescu, and in the letter, they urged him to raise the standard of living for the Romanian people and to return some of their civil liberties. They also asked for him to return the governing power to the Communist Party and to adjust his modernization policies to follow contemporary trends. Among those who signed the letter were Gheorghe Apostol, the man who succeeded Gheorghiu-Dej for a short time, and Corneliu Manescu, the former foreign minister. Ceausescu never bothered to reply to the letter; he simply had all six of the signatories put under house arrest.

There were many causes of Ceausescu's downfall, among them being the living conditions of the common people. During the 1980s, when Romania stepped into an economic crisis, Ceausescu did nothing to improve the lives of his people. He was so eager to pay off his foreign debt and to continue with the same policy of industrialization that the people suffered the most. It wasn't only food the people lacked; they also had no access to warm water, heating, or even electricity. Everyone was working and received payment for it, so the people had money, but there was nothing to buy with it. The stores were empty, and individuals often had to turn to the black market to buy simple things like milk, meat, fruit, razors, or jeans. Cars were a luxury and rarely seen on the roads because one needed state permission to buy a car. But even if a common worker had a car, there was no way for him to get gas. Nepotism and corruption entered all spheres of life, and even though healthcare was free, one had to bribe doctors to even bother to perform surgery or use anesthetic during simpler but painful procedures.

But even though the people were dissatisfied and eventually raised a revolution, one could argue that Ceausescu himself was the main reason for his fall. His inability to see the reality around him and his stubbornness to continue down the same economic path brought the anger of the people upon him. He even allowed the alienation between himself and the party to occur and, even worse, between himself and the army. Because of that, when the revolution began, he had no other support but that of his closest advisors. The members of the Communist Party, which no longer blindly followed Ceausescu, realized the need for a change within Romania's economy, politics, and society. However, they were afraid to act on their own, so they waited for the first opportunity to mount their frontal assault on the government.

This opportunity presented itself in Timisoara when a local Hungarian Protestant pastor named Laszlo Tokes refused to be transferred to a remote rural parish. The police were sent to arrest him for his defiance on December 15th, 1989, but in front of the pastor's house, a crowd of his parishioners gathered to defend him. They blocked the officers' path to Laszlo's home, and when word of their actions spread through the city, they were joined by a mass of people. Soon, the defense of one house transformed into street unrests. And from there, it turned into an anti-Ceausescu movement, which easily spread from one neighborhood to another. The whole city was out in the streets, demanding the dictator to step down. In response, the government sent in the Securitate and regular police to control the protests, but they were powerless. Even the killings of several protestors didn't slow down the accumulated anger of the people.

Ceausescu didn't understand how serious the situation was. He even left the country to pay an official visit to Iran on December 18th, but he was forced to return only two days later once the local protest of Timisoara started spreading through the country. Upon his arrival back to Romania, he ordered the military to suppress the revolt in Timisoara by any means necessary. Luckily, the army was unwilling to open fire on their own people. In Bucharest, Ceausescu's supporters organized a gathering in front of the Communist Party's headquarters on December 21st, bringing people from all over the city. They hoped that if the leader addressed the people directly, his personality would remind them of the love and devotion they had once held for him. But Ceausescu started his speech by calling the revolutionary instigators "hooligans" and claiming they were aided by "foreign agents" who only wished to destabilize Romania. His speech was cut short, as the gathered mass started booing him and chanting "Timisoara" in support of the revolt. Violence broke out, and the Securitate and army were used to suppress the uprising in Bucharest. Many protesters died that day.

By December 22nd, the army had decided to no longer obey Ceausescu and abandoned him. Still, the Romanian dictator was too stubborn to realize his reign was near its end. Instead, he believed one more speech would convince the protesters that better times were coming. He organized another rally in front of the Communist Party's headquarters, but even before he could start his speech, the gathered people started yelling insults and attacking his supporters. Ceausescu and his wife were forced to flee to the rooftop of the building, where they had a helicopter waiting. The end came quickly, for the helicopter brought them just north of Bucharest, where the army arrested Nicolae and Elena Ceausescu.

A group of Communists led by Ion Iliescu was determined to take power after the downfall of the dictator, so they needed to create the image of supporting the revolution. They ordered an immediate trial for Ceausescu on charges of genocide. On December 25th, a quick trial was organized, and Ceausescu was proclaimed guilty. He and his wife were executed immediately. The haste of the trial and execution is evidence that Iliescu was afraid a real trial would reveal how deep the Communist Party's involvement in Ceausescu's regime had been. Iliescu knew he would lose the party's momentum, the power he had just gained, and probably his own life too. The revolution, Iliescu's involvement, and Ceausescu's so-called trial are still under legal investigation to this day.

Conclusion

Romania's ties to Europe, which had been building for more than two centuries, were severely cut during the communist period. Luckily, time heals all wounds, and for the next twenty years after the revolution, Romania worked tirelessly on mending this break. Since Romania is located right in the center between Eastern and Western cultural influences, the nation had a difficult time choosing which side to join. While its religion and traditional ties were Eastern, Romania always leaned toward the West when it came to culture and ideology. Even though it had been a part of the Eastern Bloc since the end of World War II, it was never the will of the nation. After the end of communism, Romanians were sure where their future lay, and it was not in the East.

Immediately after the revolution in 1989, it was not clear which political direction Romania would take. The 1990s were a period of transition, of getting used to how things worked in the world. The country was isolated, locked away from the influences of its neighbors, as Ceausescu had made it impossible for his people to enjoy everyday items available in the West. Many people tried pineapple or wore jeans for the first time in the 1990s. Suddenly, music, film, and literature from around the world became available; during communism, the only cultural programs available were two hours of propaganda television programs per day and Communist

Party-approved movies and cartoons during the weekend. Even if there was enough electricity to turn on the TV, there were few broadcasting stations to transmit anything. Romania had been locked out completely. With the downfall of the Ceausescu regime, the people were flooded by cultural influences from around the world. This created confusion among native artists. While they were finally free to express themselves however they wanted, these new genres and influences brought new competition to the market. There was so much to learn, so much to experience.

The Orthodox Church remained the only institution resisting the temptation to rush into the Western fold. The Church survived communism because its leaders had been willing to collaborate with the regime. However, this collaboration didn't prove to bring any protection or benefits to the institution. Because of this, the Church was targeted by the public for its failure to protect its clergy and its followers. But as time passed, the people came to understand how little the Church could do, and they saw survival as a good enough excuse for collaborating with the Communists. They made peace with the Church and its leaders, who continued to occupy high positions within the institution. During the confusion of the post-communist years, the Orthodox Church tried to impose itself as the main religious institution of the state. It also refused to acknowledge the European trend of the secular state, claiming that it was the tradition of Romania to keep the link between the state and the Church unbroken. However, none of the ruling political parties was willing to go against the will of the people. To this day, Romania remains a secular state, but the influence of the Orthodox Church remains very high. This has helped the Church retain the properties of other religious groups it had confiscated during the communist regime.

On the political scene, the 1990s were very confusing because there were no active political parties other than the Communist Party. But the party couldn't allow itself to be associated with the Ceausescu regime, so it abandoned the name. The Communists instead organized themselves into the National Salvation Front (FSN), an institution that was supposed to supervise the return of the multi-party system in Romania. On February 6th, 1990, the ex-Communists registered it as a political party, which gave them the unique opportunity to remain in power under a new name. But with this new name came the new goals. No longer did these politicians strive to build a nation under communism. They instead wanted to establish a European-style parliamentary democracy and join European economic and security institutions. The first post-communist election was won by the FSN, and its leader, Ion Iliescu, an ex-Communist, became the president, earning 85 percent of the vote.

When the ex-Communists proclaimed victory in the election, the Western world was unsure of Romania's intention to reform and abandon its Eastern values. However, the FSN proved to be capable of persuading the foreign powers of its intention to fully commit to its new goals. Nevertheless, the economic crisis within the country persisted, and Romania had to make some big steps to be able to reach its full potential. Even today, Romania lags behind the rest of Europe, but it has made significant progress. In the meantime, other political parties started forming and stepping onto the political scene. Iliescu's government officially applied for membership in the European Union in 1995, but Romania still had much to do to adjust its political, economic, and ideological doctrines to be more like other countries of Europe. Since then, Romania has continuously worked on many issues that were practically nonexistent during the communist days, such as the freedom of religion, civil rights, and the rights of minorities.

However, old habits die slowly, and the members of the FSN continued practicing nepotism and corruption to gain personal wealth. Because of this, since the mid-1990s, they started losing popularity, while the Romanian Democratic Convention (CDR), a coalition of smaller liberal parties, has gained in strength. During the election of 1996, Emil Constantinescu, the CDR candidate, overthrew Iliescu from the presidential office. While his government was capable of easing the economic crisis of Romania, corruption continued to flourish.

Although Constantinescu's government gave support to the NATO alliance in the Kosovo War, he became very unpopular among the population who supported Serbia in the war. In the 2000 election, Iliescu won again and reversed the policy toward Serbia. The Western powers were afraid that with the renewed power of Iliescu and his new party, the Social Democratic Party (PDSR), Romania would go on a path of neo-communism. However, the election of Adrian Nastase as the prime minister of the new government ensured that the intentions of the PDSR were completely different. Nastase was an ardent defender of everything European, and he led the country into smooth negotiations for European Union membership. Due to his work to reconcile Romania and Europe, and due to the constitutional changes, Romania joined NATO on March 29th, 2004, and the European Union only three years later in 2007.

But the membership in the EU did not guarantee that Romania would get rid of all of the internal problems caused by communism. To this day, the country struggles with corruption, which often results in an inability to modernize the state. Although Romania has taken enormous steps to improve the conditions of minorities, especially the Hungarians and Gypsies, it lacks investment in other social aspects. The country's healthcare is still considered to be one of the most underdeveloped in Europe, and the economy still lags behind the West. However, with each passing year, Romania is stepping forward. The hardworking people are attracting foreign investments, and the new generations, those born in the 1990s and 2000s, are free from the communist mindset. They are the future that will bring stability and steady progress to a country forever trapped between two worlds, the traditional East and the progressive West.

Part 2: Vlad the Impaler

A Captivating Guide to How Vlad III Dracula Became One of the Most Crucial Rulers of Wallachia and His Impact on the History of Romania

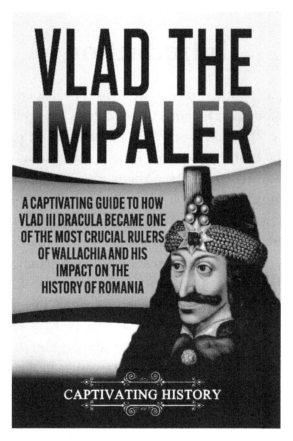

Introduction

The medieval Balkans almost seem like uncharted territory to Western historians. Modern events such as the collapse of the Eastern Bloc, the Yugoslav Wars, the tension with the migrant crisis, and the hostilities between nations overshadow the fact that this area, which connects Asia Minor to Central Europe, is rich with a turbulent, bloody, and fascinating history. Some of the biggest and most important battles were fought in the medieval Balkans, resulting in a series of notable demographic and political changes that resonated throughout the rest of the continent.

But the Balkans aren't mysterious simply due to its history. Another phenomenon seemed to have taken Europe by storm that originated from this area, that of vampirism. Ever since the first official cases of vampiric activity among the Serbian populace were written about by Austro-Hungarian newspapers in the 18th century, Europe could not get enough of the blood-sucking fiends. Other stories resurfaced, but the vampire hysteria reached its peak with the publishing of one novel in 1897, a novel that spoke of supernatural beings in Victorian England but whose main antagonist bore the name, or rather the nickname, of a historical figure who had, at that point, been dead for over 400 years.

The Balkans were the home of both the vampiric stories and the aforementioned monarch, whose name became synonymous with drinking blood and avoiding sunlight. That monarch was Vlad, the third ruler of Wallachia to hold that name, the second ruler to be associated with the Order of the Dragon (and to incorporate that into his name), and the first ruler to be associated with a gruesome act, that of impalement. Vlad III, *Vlad Țepeș* in Romanian, also known as Vlad the Impaler or Vlad Dracula, was (and still is) a never-ending conversational piece among Romanian historians, medievalists, political analysts, literary critics, and even the common folk. This voivode ("prince" or "duke") from a small Balkan land would not only become a terrifying figure that some of even the most powerful monarchs at the time would fear but would also become a fascinating individual worthy of entire poems, legends, and art pieces being devoted to him. And despite ruling very briefly compared to other monarchs at the time, he still left a very notable imprint on the political and social life of his native medieval Wallachia, as well as the countries surrounding it. He would become a man to take the throne no less than three times, get captured and held as a prisoner for decades no less than twice during his life, a father to children whose descendants would rule Wallachia well over 200 years after his death, and a man whose heroic and patriotic acts were overshadowed by literally hundreds of thousands of corpses.

In this book, we will focus on the turbulent and fascinating life of Vlad the Impaler. Before we delve into it, however, a fair warning to the fans of Bram Stoker's novel should be issued. Though he wasn't a vampire himself, Vlad III did lead a life that would rival some of the best fictional characters out there. By reading onward, you might leave with the impression that Dracula, the figure who seduced young British women and bore himself as an aristocrat of elegance with a penchant to drink blood, pales in comparison to the historical figure he is merely based off of. That's right; this book will illustrate that Vlad the Impaler, a seemingly insignificant lord of a small nation who barely had a few years to his reign, has more appeal than a fictional monster with otherworldly powers.

Naturally, there are many details about Vlad's life that we simply do not know. Contemporary documents definitely exist, even some written by the man himself, but in terms of the necessary documentation to complete the picture, they are few and far between. In addition, there are decades of his life where almost nothing was written about him, making it even more difficult to maintain a single, unified image of Vlad. Fortunately, the interest for the voivode has not waned in the 21st century, as the scientific community keeps discovering new details about his life and adding to the significant wealth of information we already have.

The bulk of the book will deal with what Vlad's political career looked like, what wars he waged, and how his life eventually ended. But we'll go one step beyond and cover some areas that historians don't typically focus on. In addition to raw facts, we'll also focus on what Vlad III's character was, what drove him forward, and what his chief traits might have been. In addition, we will give a much-needed focus on his successors and what life was like in Wallachia after his passing. Furthermore, you'll also get a glimpse into some of the most popular myths and legends about Vlad III, some of which were written and passed on by both his supporters and his bitter enemies. All of these are needed to get as complete an image of Vlad as possible, which will help us understand what kind of man he was and what kind of impact his life had on those around him, as well as those who came after him.

Portrait of Vlad the Impaler at Ambras Castle, Innsbruck, Austria, circa 1560.

Chapter 1 – Early Years: Birth, Captivity, First Reign, and Exile; Wallachia and the Balkans in the Early 15th Century

Birth of Vlad III

The exact year of Vlad's birth is still debated among historians. In fact, most of the facts regarding the Impaler's life have to be pieced together from fragments of available information, considering that most of the official records kept in the Balkan countries from that time period have disappeared after the Ottoman invasions. At best, we can ascertain that he was born anywhere between 1429/1430 and 1436.

Interestingly enough, though we might not know the exact date of Vlad's birth, we have a reasonable idea of where he might have been born. Modern-day Sighişoara in Romania's province of Transylvania still contains a house that Vlad II Dracul, i.e., the father of Vlad the Impaler, supposedly lived in with his first-born son, Mircea.

The house and the town itself aren't arbitrarily chosen as the birthplace of Vlad the Impaler, of course. Sighișoara, then known as both Schaäsburg (in German) and Segesvár (in Hungarian), was an important trading and crafting hub of Transylvania. Over fifteen guilds and twenty handicraft branches found their home in the city, and Vlad Dracul himself minted coins there. The town was populated by both Wallachians and Hungarians, but a growing population of German artisans, originally from the Holy Roman Empire, made their home here as well. In fact, a significant part of Vlad's early childhood was spent in Transylvania among the local Saxon communities.

While most people today associate the Impaler with Transylvania, the truth is that Vlad was a Wallachian voivode, and most of his time spent in Transylvania did not see him rule over that land. During the early 15th century, Dracula and his family were predominantly Wallachian voivodes, but they did get involved in the state affairs of both Transylvania and neighboring Moldavia.

In order to understand the whole situation, we need to examine how the ancestors of modern Romanians and Moldovans went about their days during the Late Middle Ages. Both Wallachia and Moldavia were semi-independent lands that were predominantly inhabited by Romanian-speaking people who practiced Eastern Orthodox Christianity and were under the direct cultural influence of the Greeks (the Eastern Roman Empire, i.e., the Byzantines) and various Slavic groups (predominantly Bulgarians and Serbs). For example, most of their religious customs came from the Byzantines, but their court titles and architectural layouts of castles were mostly Slavic-like. In addition, Old Church Slavonic was the "diplomatic" language of the elites, and most rulers in this era wrote and spoke it (similar to semi-independent Albanian territories during the same timespan). However, the territory known as "the land beyond the forest" (*ultra sylvam*) isn't that easy to pinpoint in terms of populace. While it was definitely home to a large Wallachian population, from the early 11th century up until the modern day, the Wallachians were never a majority there. In fact, based on all the archeological evidence and contemporary written sources, we can safely say that the majority of Transylvanians were not Wallachian, didn't speak or write predominantly in Slavic, and were the polar opposites of Eastern Orthodox Christians. Transylvania was officially a Hungarian vassal territory subjected to the Hungarian king, who had the power to instate his own voivodes as protectors of the land. However, the territory boasted a large number of German Saxon inhabitants who began to show up en masse during the beginning of the new millennium (Saxons also inhabited neighboring Serbia and Bulgaria, working largely as miners and smiths). Finally, there were the Székelys (referred to as Szeklers in further text), a sub-group of Hungarians whose origins are still somewhat debated but who served as frontier guards for the Kingdom of Hungary during the Early Middle Ages. All three groups were primarily Catholic and swore loyalty to the Hungarian Crown, often acting in direct opposition to any Wallachian voivode who would come to power.

The reason the composition of the populace of Transylvania is important for the history of Vlad the Impaler is due to the fact that it shaped most of his later worldviews. We'll delve more into this in later chapters, but to sum it up, Vlad was someone who grew up in a multiethnic environment with diametrically opposing religious and cultural beliefs, and while he did work hard on ensuring the stability and well-being of his own multiethnic state, he was still as xenophobic and mistrusting as a medieval prince would be. And he's by no means alone in this: most medieval rulers throughout the world, on all permanently inhabited continents, were outright antagonistic toward neighboring tribes and would frequently exert efforts into assimilating or annihilating them.

Dracula's house in Sighişoara"

Balkans in the Late 15th Century

As stated earlier, Vlad was most likely born between 1429 and 1436. It was a time of great turmoil within the Balkan Peninsula. The emerging Ottoman Empire kept growing in size and strength, and the effects of this growth were felt across the independent lands whose own influence was waning. The once-powerful Eastern Roman Empire had, by the 1450s, been reduced to a few territories in modern-day Greece and the territory of Constantinople, which had, by that point, become a shadow of its former self. The majority of its inhabitants were long gone, and from a perspective of a local citizen, it looked not unlike a ghost town. The incumbent emperors at the time, the Palaiologoi dynasty (sing. *Palaiologos*, meaning "old word"), were effectively vassals to the Turks. Not only would they have to pay a monetary tribute to the sultan, but they would also be subjugated to the system known as Devshirme, i.e., paying tribute "in blood." The system was simple enough: Ottoman troops would take a group of boys and young men between the ages of eight and twenty, transport them to a major Ottoman center, and forcefully convert them to Islam. Once they were Islamized, the boys would either become soldiers (as a part of the elite troops called the Janissaries) or would enter the civil service as diplomats and viziers. Hundreds of thousands of Christian boys were converted through this system until it was abolished in the early 18th century, with the vast majority of them being of Greek origin.

However, the Turks had other nations to deal with during the early years of Vlad's life. Right around the time of the collapse of the Eastern Roman Empire, Serbia had risen to prominence, having been elevated to the status of empire in 1346. After the fall of the empire several decades later and the famous Battle of Kosovo in 1389, Serbia became a vassal state of the Ottomans, with its territory greatly reduced and ruled by a despot (a royal title one rank below that of an emperor). Between 1427 and 1456, the despot would be Đurađ Branković, the first ruler of the Branković family to sit on the throne and the last effective ruler of the Serbian lands. At the age of fifty, he had the experience and the prowess of a decent ruler, as well as an incredible amount of wealth. However, his territory was independent in name only; just like the Palaiologoi, the Branković dynasty also had to pay tribute to the Ottomans. Still, he wasn't necessarily a loyal vassal of the empire, nor was he really loyal to their enemies. Though he maintained good relations with Sultan Murad II, largely because his daughter, Mara Branković, was married to the sultan in 1434, he was also a close ally to the Hungarian Crown, as well as the Republic of Venice and some parts of medieval Zeta. Of course, Đurađ Branković's rivalry with the Hungarian general and Christian hero John Hunyadi would result in him constantly either refusing to help the Christian cause against the Ottomans or even helping the Ottomans (such as when he captured Hunyadi after the lesser-known Second Battle of Kosovo in 1448 and kept his older son as a hostage for a ransom), which was, in and of itself, bizarre considering the exchange of estates between Hunyadi and Branković not too long ago. Both men would die in 1456, several months apart from one another. The death of Đurađ Branković was possibly the biggest blow to late medieval Serbia since a succession crisis ensued, with his remaining family members feuding over the inheritance. A mere three years later, the Serbian Despotate would finally succumb to the Turks, and the country would not regain its independence until the late 19th century.

Bosnia was in a similar situation to Serbia, with its reigning Kotromanić dynasty being weakened by regional rulers who tore the country apart. Its last ruler was Stephen II Tomašević, who was, interestingly enough, the last official despot of an independent Serbia before surrendering it to the Ottomans in 1459 and returning to his native Bosnia, where he was crowned as king soon after in 1461. His own death in 1463 at the hands of Sultan Mehmed II himself (or one of his close military officials), as well as the deaths of his closest living male family members, marked the end of Bosnia and the subsequent Ottoman rule that would last until the territories were annexed by Austria-Hungary in the late 19th and early 20th centuries.

Of all the Balkan-based lands, Hungary was probably the biggest rival of the Turks during Vlad's time. It was the Hungarian king, Sigismund of Luxembourg, who decided to act against the Ottomans by forming the so-called Order of the Dragon. This Order contained prominent members of European nobility, including Đurađ Branković's predecessor, Despot Stefan Lazarević (the son of Lazar Hrebeljanović, the Serbian prince who led the Serbian army against the Ottomans during the Battle of Kosovo in 1389); Hermann II, Count of Celje and the father-in-law of King Sigismund; Pippo Spano, an Italian general and magnate who was Sigismund's personal friend and a talented statesman; Karlo Kurjaković, a Croatian nobleman and one of the Order's founders; Fruzhin, a Bulgarian noble who was descended from the last Bulgarian emperors and who was a staunch fighter against the Turks; King Alfonso V of Aragon, an exceptionally important figure during the early Renaissance; Gjergj Kastrioti Skanderbeg, an

Albanian noble who became renowned all over Europe for his fierce battles against the Ottoman troops; and Vlad II Dracul, Vlad the Impaler's father. In fact, Vlad's sobriquet "Dracul" actually derives from his position as a member of the Order, as it means "dragon." Subsequently, Vlad III's own sobriquet can be read as "little dragon" or "the son of the dragon."

Hungary's importance during the early years of Dracula's life cannot be overstated. Sigismund's general John Hunyadi, for example, had been so influential in the region that he was able to instate his own voivode in Transylvania, and after dethroning Vlad Dracul in 1447, he even referred to the contemporary Wallachian capital of Târgoviște as his city. Hunyadi's influence had been strong even within Hungary itself. As a regent of young Ladislaus V the Posthumous, the underage son of the late Albert II of Germany, who had been the legitimate heir of the late Sigismund of Luxembourg, Hunyadi had enjoyed a life of absolute privilege and was one of the richest men in the region at the time, wealthier than even some contemporary rulers. The people had admired Hunyadi so much that, not long after his death, his son Matthias Corvinus was declared king, following a bloody rebellion that caused the young king Ladislaus to flee Hungary, unexpectedly dying soon after. Corvinus himself would be instrumental in Vlad the Impaler's adult life, both as an enemy and as an ally.

Naturally, this is but a brief overview of some of the major players among the Balkan states in the Late Middle Ages, and it merely scratches the surface of the political picture at the time. Other countries, such as Bulgaria, Albania, Zeta, the Republic of Ragusa (today's city of Dubrovnik in Croatia), the Republic of Venice, and the semi-independent Croatian and Slovenian territories also played a vital role throughout the century, but covering everything would require a whole other book to be written. But based on these simplified examples above, we can clearly see just how convoluted the Balkan political scene was during these turbulent times. If we were to include the religious relations between the countries, their economic statuses, their day-to-day lives, major battles, forming of alliances and their break-ups, and so on, there would be no end to this book. And we should also take into account that most of the contemporary sources we have are often incomplete, contradictory, or outright fabricated. Naturally, Wallachia itself was just as complicated, which made Vlad's ascension(s) to the throne quite exciting but equally convoluted and dangerous.

Vlad's Childhood and Captivity under the Ottomans

As a child, Vlad was most likely taught the same things that his brothers Mircea and Radu were. At an early age, he had to be a skilled horse rider, sword fighter, and marksman; the knowledge of several languages was a must, especially in a region as diverse as the Balkan Peninsula, as well as the knowledge of several different scripts like Latin and Cyrillic. Moreover, there was the question of faith. With the Muslim Ottomans slowly encroaching on the Balkan states, it was of vital importance that Christianity prevailed. However, Wallachia was an Orthodox country, while Hungary, which was the overlord of Wallachia, was Catholic. Vlad's older brother Mircea was more than likely baptized in a Catholic church, but history isn't entirely sure about Vlad and Radu. Most likely, they were baptized secretly in an Orthodox church in Wallachia, but Vlad himself would convert to Catholicism some years before his death, which he did in order to prove his loyalty to the Hungarian Crown and to regain (and retain) his title of the Wallachian voivodeship.

By the age of eleven, young Vlad would have been taught several skills, including jousting, fencing, swimming, court etiquette, archery, and horse riding. By all accounts, he was a gifted and quick learner, acquiring all the necessary skills that a Balkan monarch needed at an early age. However, Vlad's early adolescence would prove to be a difficult one, mainly due to the dealings of his father.

During the reign of Sigismund, Vlad II had been an ally of the Hungarians, becoming acquainted with some of the most prominent figures in Hungarian nobility, including John Hunyadi in his early years. Even in those days, Hunyadi was a cunning strategist and a favorite among the Christian communities despite being a man born in low nobility and hailing from Wallachia (though there are conflicting sources over his origins, most scholars consider the Hunyadi family as ethnically Wallachian/Romanian). By the time Vlad II had ascended the throne, Hunyadi had already been in the service of the late Serbian despot Stefan Lazarević and had since been serving as one of Sigismund's most efficient military leaders. One of the many reasons why Hunyadi was so effective was his undying loyalty to the Christian faith and his desire to defend Christianity at all costs, a trait that would eventually put him at odds with Vlad II and start a chain of events that would affect young Vlad III.

As a ruler, Vlad II had been an enemy of the Ottomans during Sigismund's reign, but after the Hungarian king's death in 1437, he signed an alliance with the Turkish sultan Murad II, agreeing to pay him a yearly tribute of 10,000 ducats and provide military aid. This act on Vlad II's behalf was in direct contradiction with his obligations to the Order of the Dragon, whose name he still used. At the time, the united Christian effort wanted to engage in another crusade against the Ottomans, but Sigismund's death had led to a succession crisis. Several rulers were claimants and held the throne for a short time, including Albert II of Germany, who ruled roughly two years before dying of dysentery while preparing for a crusade; the infant Ladislaus the Posthumous, with his mother Elisabeth of Luxembourg (the only surviving child of King Sigismund) serving as a regent; and the Polish king Władysław III, a member of the Jagiellonian dynasty. Władysław was crowned in 1440 and was backed by Hunyadi, but Ladislaus was named as his successor should he die without issue. A year later, having somewhat secured the Hungarian throne and calmed the succession crisis a bit,

Hunyadi visited Vlad II in Târgoviște in 1441. And even though he was sternly reminded that his loyalties should lie with the Order of the Dragon and the Christian cause, Vlad II still refused to end his relations with the Turks. However, oddly enough, he had only been a half-hearted ally of the sultan to begin with. When the Turks marched into Wallachia on their way to invade Transylvania, Vlad II remained neutral, simply allowing them to pass. This action resulted in a humiliating defeat of the Turks and put further doubt into Murad II's mind when it came to the Wallachian voivode's loyalty. It didn't help matters that other local princes wrote to the sultan warning him not to trust Vlad, among other rulers.

Sometime between 1442 and 1443, Murad II decided to act on his suspicions and invited both Vlad II and Đurađ Branković to his court. The Serbian despot shrewdly avoided going, but the Wallachian voivode set out to see the sultan in the city of Gallipoli, taking his two youngest sons with him and leaving his oldest heir, Mircea, to rule during his absence. To young Vlad and the even younger Radu, this trip would prove to be one of the most traumatic events of their lives. Upon their arrival in Gallipoli, the voivode and his sons were put in chains. Vlad II himself was kept in the city dungeon, but his sons were sent to Eğrigöz (modern-day Doğrugöz in Turkey), a grim mountain fortress. All three would eventually end up in Adrianople, the Ottoman capital (modern-day Edirne), at the court of the sultan. Less than a year after his capture, Vlad II was made to swear an oath of loyalty to the Turkish court all over again, on both the Bible and the Quran, but this time, the tribute was more than a "mere" 10,000 ducats. In addition to the money, Vlad II had to send at least 500 young men under the Devshirme system, and more importantly, both young Vlad and Radu were to be kept as hostages at the sultan's court. That way, the Ottoman ruler had the means of directly punishing Vlad II should he not honor his tribute.

Of course, the deal that Murad II forced onto Vlad II offered some obligations on the sultan's part as well. As long as the

Wallachian voivode did what he was told, no harm was to come to the boys. In addition, they were to receive the best education and the best treatment, just like any other child of an obedient nobleman. The young Dracul boys were taught everything from theoretical mathematics to basic precepts of the Quran and Aristotelian logic, as well as some of the fine Eastern Roman traditions that the Turks themselves inherited. Young Vlad's knowledge of the Turkish language also improved, which would prove invaluable in his future exploits. However, the two boys took to their captivity very differently. Even at this early age, Vlad was showing signs of disobedience to his Turkish overlords, often lashing out against his teachers and receiving severe punishments for it. Radu, however, became somewhat of a court favorite. Because of his outstanding good looks, he was to gain his own sobriquet of *Radu cel Frumos*, "Radu the Handsome," and would become a source of infatuation for both the women and men at the sultan's court. Some contemporary sources even mention that Murad's son, Mehmed II, treated Radu as his lover. Whatever the case might be, Radu proved to be more loyal to the Turks than either his father or his brothers, which would again prove to be instrumental in later years when Vlad III ascended to (and descended from) the throne multiple times.

During the captivity of the three Draculs, typical medieval Balkan politics once again shook the throne of Wallachia. The country itself was, at one point, ruled by the unified House of Basarab, named after the first independent ruler of Wallachia, Voivode Basarab I. However, after the death of Dan I, the step-uncle of Vlad II Dracul, the throne was succeeded by his step-brother Mircea, known in Wallachian history as Mircea the Old due to his long reign and the respect he commanded. Both Dan's and Mircea's descendants would constantly try to usurp the throne from one another, forming two main branches of the House of Basarab, called the House of Dănești and the House of Drăculești. And much like Vlad the Impaler himself, several rulers from both noble houses would come to ascend and descend the throne several times during their lives.

Of course, a rival royal house was not the only issue that the Draculs had to deal with in their lifetime. It's of vital importance to know that ascending the throne at Târgoviște was somewhat different than, for example, ascending it in Buda at the Hungarian court, or at Constantinople, or anywhere else in the Balkans. Namely, the notion of bastardy didn't really affect who would sit on the throne next. Many of the Wallachian rulers had been born out of wedlock, oftentimes to low-born women. In practice, this meant that literally anyone could ascend to the throne, a practice that had far more setbacks than benefits. For instance, Vlad II himself was an illegitimate child of Mircea, yet he still managed to rule over the country for several years. In addition, he had other children besides his three legitimate sons and one daughter, Alexandra. There was a bastard son named Mircea, on whom we barely have any historical data, and another Vlad who would rule Wallachia on several occasions as Vlad IV Călugărul, or "Vlad the Monk."

Before Vlad II returned to his country, the throne had been seized by a Dănești noble, Basarab II, the grandson of Dan I. Basarab had actually enjoyed secret support from John Hunyadi years before Vlad II went to visit the sultan and got captured. After deposing Vlad's oldest son Mircea in 1442, Hunyadi placed Basarab on the throne, but the voivode would only rule for a little over a year. Upon Vlad II's return to Wallachia from the Ottomans, he would swiftly depose the new voivode, although we don't have any reliable data letting us know how he did it. Considering his new treaty with the Ottomans and an already strained relationship with Hungary, we can speculate that the sultan might have helped him in this endeavor. We also know that Basarab II, though deposed, wasn't killed or otherwise harmed by Vlad II, though he would not rise to prominence until his death during the reign of Vlad the Impaler himself.

By the end of 1443, Hunyadi and Władysław III were undertaking their so-called "Long Campaign" against the Ottomans, a crusade that would have devastating results for the Christian forces. In its early stages, the campaign had been successful; the crusaders actually managed to liberate vast areas of Serbian and Bulgarian lands, so much so that even some of their defeats (such as the one at the Battle of Zlatitsa Pass on December 12th, 1443, and the subsequent retreat to Buda) were treated as victories and used as pro-Christian propaganda at the time. Because of these circumstances, Hunyadi and Władysław openly rejected a treaty with the sultan, despite him vehemently pursuing peace talks. Vlad II decided against helping the crusade openly, as did Despot Branković (his daughter Mara, Murad's wife at the time, was actually instrumental in convincing the sultan to sue for peace). Both rulers had heavy ties with the Ottomans, but Vlad II's situation was slightly worse off because of his obligations to the Order of the Dragon, on the one hand, and his young sons being the sultan's prisoners, on the other. Despite trying and failing to convince the crusaders against waging war, he sent a battalion of 4,000 horsemen led by his son, the deposed voivode Mircea II, in 1444. The Polish king Władysław died during the battle, with the Ottomans beheading him and impaling his head on a pike as a display of victory. Hunyadi himself retreated but was subsequently captured by Vlad II and held prisoner for a brief period of time. The reasons behind Vlad's capture of John Hunyadi aren't entirely clear to historians, but he did release him soon after, allowing him to return to Hungary but demanding a large ransom in return.

Vlad II would remain in power until 1447. Several important events took place that further complicated his relations with both the Ottomans and the Hungarians, all of them involving a military campaign between 1445 and late 1446. Assisted by both Hunyadi's forces and a band of crusaders from the Duchy of Burgundy, Dracula's father waged a few successful battles against the Turks, retaking some important forts (such as the one in Giurgiu) and even taking in 11,000 Bulgarian refugees who rebelled against Sultan Murad II. In his final years, Vlad II would return the refugees to the Ottomans and refuse to participate in any other Christian efforts against the overwhelming Muslim force. In late July 1447, Hunyadi openly supported a different pretender to the Wallachian throne, Vladislav II of the Dănești line. The people of Brașov, a city important to both the Transylvanians and the Wallachians, were ordered by Hunyadi to extend their support to the new ruler, and the antagonism for Vlad II grew. Not long after, Hunyadi invaded Târgoviște, the capital of Wallachia. Vlad II managed to flee, but he was captured and killed, more than likely by Vladislav II himself. Vlad's eldest son Mircea was also killed around the same time. In terms of regular rules of primogeniture, Vlad III was, by all rights, the successor to the throne since Mircea had no issue. However, with Wallachia having its own laws regarding the succession, and with the Hungarian general intrusively involved as he was, the throne was anything but secure, no matter who occupied it.

Murad II, painted circa 1800[ii]

Vlad's First Reign (October–November 1448)

Vladislav was the puppet ruler in charge of Wallachia, though, in reality, he had to answer to John Hunyadi. Hunyadi himself might have held direct power over the country for a short while, possibly appointing Vladislav in December as a "legal" successor to the late Vlad II. Strategically speaking, this would have been a savvy move on the Hungarian noble's part; not only would Hunyadi have the loyalty of a ruler whom he had supported for months and reap the material benefits from such an arrangement (in the form of taxes, lands, and privileges), but he would also avoid all the hassle that would come from dealing with the common folk of Wallachia and the members of the nobility, the so-called boyars. It's fascinating to know that the commoners and the members of the nobility, both minor and major, had more of an influence on the current ruling state of affairs than modern history tends to give them credit for. If provoked or unsatisfied, they would rebel, regardless if said rebellions would be fruitful or not. Transylvania and Wallachia, in particular, were notorious for how often the boyars and the commoners of major forts and cities (Târgoviște, Giurgiu, Chilia, Brașov, etc.) would successfully overthrow the ruler they deemed unworthy. It didn't help that various pretenders (legitimate or otherwise, Wallachian/Transylvanian or outsiders) all had different ways of influencing the boyars' opinions directly. Before Vlad III took the throne, the boyars' sense of entitlement and the rebellious attitude of the common folk was such a major issue that even someone as powerful as Hunyadi would end up dead if a few dozen commoners got offended one afternoon. Therefore, appointing a puppet voivode was a way for Hunyadi to avoid all of that hassle and maintain a living head on his shoulders. But there was one more benefit to the general's supposed shifting of the Wallachian throne to Vladislav instead of maintaining it himself. Namely, as a Hungarian noble who had Wallachia's loyalty in the bag, Hunyadi would enjoy major privileges at the court of Buda. By 1446, he had already been appointed regent to the young king Ladislaus V and had been one of the richest barons in Europe, but that didn't stop him from trying to extend his influence further, as he launched several military campaigns in a row, starting with an unsuccessful spat against Ulrich II, Count of Celje. By August 1448, Hunyadi was in a full-on war against the Ottomans, and he wanted to unite his forces with Skanderbeg, the contemporary lord of the Albanian lands and one of the fiercest enemies of the Turks. For the purposes of this unification, Hunyadi took a force of over 16,000 men through Serbia, whose despot remained neutral but was considered a Turkish ally. Vladislav II also contributed to this military effort with 8,000 troops, but more importantly, he himself joined the crusade, leaving the court at Târgoviște wide open.

Eventually, Hunyadi would face the Ottomans during the Second Battle of Kosovo in September 1448, which resulted in a catastrophic and humiliating defeat for him. His subsequent capture by the Serbian despot during his retreat from the battle was just another nail in the coffin of this humiliation, though, interestingly enough, even this sequence of events didn't tarnish his reputation significantly with the Christian nations of the Balkans. Even among his contemporaries, the Hungarian baron enjoyed a great deal of respect amongst the Wallachians, the Transylvanians, the Bulgarians, the Serbs, and the people of the Crown he served.

Naturally, all of these events were perfect for Vlad III to step onto the Balkan political scene in 1448. In October, while Hunyadi and Vladislav II were on their way to battle the Ottomans, the young Wallachian voivode in exile returned to his country and, via a bloody coup and with the assistance of the Ottoman forces, took the throne at Târgoviște. By this time, Vlad had proven himself a capable military commander and a leader at heart. As early as his initial stay at Edirne, the young prince was given the rank of an officer within the Turkish army. Sultan Murad II had clearly considered Vlad his preferred choice to take the throne of Wallachia. This was, in large part, due to Vlad's many years of Ottoman "brainwashing"; after all, he had been kept as a prisoner at the royal court and was a valuable hostage, along with his younger brother, to be used as a bargaining chip against Vlad II. But those weren't the only reasons why Murad II (and even Mehmed II during his early reign) favored Vlad. Despite his rebellious behavior against his captors, the youth had proven himself to be cunning and ruthless, just the kind of man to head an army and sit on the throne in the name of the sultan.

It's impossible to know what Vlad had been thinking during this time. Based on his later actions, we can safely say that he had no love for the Turks and that his upbringing at both Eğrigöz and Edirne had been viewed by him as a strategic means to an end—he would learn everything he needed to know about Ottoman battle tactics, and when the time was favorable, and he occupied the throne in Târgoviște, he would use the Turks' own methods of warfare against them. However, as he was alone at the Ottoman court with few real allies, the prince still had to recognize their sovereignty, at least for the time being. During his reclaiming of the throne, Vlad was witness to the Turkish claiming of the fortress of Giurgiu, which would remain under their domain even after his first deposition.

As is more or less expected of medieval Wallachia, Vlad III's first rule barely lasted a month. Though the defeat of the crusaders at Kosovo had been monumental, Vladislav II had managed to survive, as did an unknown but probably significant portion of his army. We can't really estimate the number of the Wallachian survivors, but they must have been sizable since the Dănești voivode managed to reclaim his throne when he returned to Wallachia in November. With his army, Vladislav defeated Dracula's forces, and the new voivode had to flee south of the Danube River. By December 7th, the news of Dracula's deposition had even reached Constantinople; some of the news was clearly false, such as Dracula's death by decapitation or the fact that he had been defeated by Hunyadi rather than Vladislav.

And speaking of both Hunyadi and Vladislav, the end of 1448 saw them both suffer the consequences of their recent actions. Hunyadi's capture by Despot Stefan Lazarević had been a humiliating experience, and it didn't help matters that Vladislav had decided against helping Hunyadi during their retreat from Kosovo (after all, Vladislav had still been in the Serbian lands in October and could have reached the despot in a matter of days). Vladislav's decision to reclaim Wallachia was important politically, but his failure to support Hunyadi had cost him dearly. When Hunyadi was eventually released from the despot's dungeon and returned to Wallachia, he took away two important territories from Vladislav, namely Amlaș and Făgăraș. These settlements had been predominantly Saxon in terms of demographics, but as fiefdoms, they had been the "ancestral home" of the Basarab dynasty, and they were equally important to both branches vying for the Wallachian throne in the late 15th century. By taking them away from Vladislav but still keeping him in power, Hunyadi humiliated the voivode and, at the same time, proved just how much influence he could still exercise even after a major defeat.

Vlad's Exile

Vlad had originally fled to the Ottoman court at Edirne. History doesn't know a whole lot about this brief period, but soon enough, the deposed Wallachian voivode would move again, this time as a guest at the court of Bogdan II of Moldavia. As mentioned earlier, the two lands had always had a form of kinship: both spoke the same language, were largely homogenous in terms of religion, had their royal families intermarry several times, and had provided support for one another during crucial events such as wars, dethronings, and rethronings. And while they didn't always see eye to eye (which we will cover in later chapters), their relations had remained largely stable, even decades after Vlad the Impaler's death.

The deposed voivode had extremely sound personal reasons to find refuge at the Moldavian court. For instance, Bogdan II's sister was his second wife. Bogdan's own wife, Princess Oltea, was of Wallachian origin and probably a member of the Basarab dynasty. She was also the mother of Stephen the Great, who was at Bogdan's court and who would develop a close friendship with Vlad the Impaler. Finally, Bogdan himself had a valid reason to receive Vlad at his court, in what would become the current city of Suceava. During Vlad II's reign, Bogdan had to seek refuge at the court of Târgoviște. The reason behind this event is unknown, but it was more than likely a struggle for the Moldavian throne. Bogdan himself would be assassinated by Petru Aron, the bastard son of Bogdan's father Alexander the Good, in 1451. With a new, hostile ruler on the Moldavian throne, Vlad had to flee again, finding refuge with his father's old enemy, John Hunyadi himself. His plan was for Hunyadi to help him reclaim the throne, which the Hungarian noble would initially refuse to do. However, though his early reign had ended in a series of setbacks, this was merely the beginning for Vlad III. Soon enough, all of Europe would come to know his name.

Chapter 2 – Second Reign: Vlad as a Ruler, Domestic Affairs, Foreign Relations, Wars, Dethroning, and Capture

Most casual history buffs have an idea that some of the best-known monarchs had long reigns that lasted for decades. And while there were people throughout human history that ruled for exceptionally long periods of time, most of them had only a few years of ruling to their name. In fact, some would barely last over a month. Let's be a bit more concrete with this and use the medieval rulers we've mentioned thus far to illustrate the point. Bogdan II of Moldavia, the ally of the Draculs, ruled for a little over two years. Ladislaus V the Posthumous, although he is officially recognized as a ruler from his birth in 1440, didn't actually independently take the throne until 1452, which means he ruled for around five years. And though Vladislav II technically ruled for nine years in total, his first reign (before Dracula seized the throne) was barely a year long. Vlad's own father, Vlad II Dracul, had been a ruler of Wallachia for a grand total of ten years, which was split between two reigns. His predecessor, Alexander I Aldea, had only been a voivode for five years. The son of Despot Đurađ Branković, Lazar, ruled the despotate after his father for roughly two years and was followed by his cousin Stefan, who only ruled for fourteen months.

With so many examples of brief reigns, which seemed to be as frequent as local wars and uprisings, it's no wonder that Vlad III's longest and most notable period in power lasted a little over six years. When compared to some of the highest-regarded rulers of both Wallachia and Moldavia, such as Mircea I the Elder (ruled for a total of 29 years) and Stephen III of Moldavia, also known as Stephen the Great (ruled for an astounding 47 years), this particular rule of Vlad III seems almost insignificant in comparison. However, it was during these years that Vlad would establish himself as a powerful political player who wasn't afraid of using any means necessary to achieve his goals and bring some stability to his land.

Stephen the Great of Moldavia, Gospel miniature, from the Humor Monastery, 1473

Events that Led to the Second Reign

We don't know the exact course of events that placed Vlad the Impaler back on the throne of Wallachia. However, we can piece together what happened in the few years before he did so. During his exile in Moldavia, Vlad began to repair his relations with the Hungarian Crown; more precisely, he was trying hard to get in the good graces of John Hunyadi.

This wasn't an easy task at the time. The Hungarian kingdom was, effectively, just as hungry for Wallachian territory and influence as the Ottoman Empire. What made them almost a bigger threat than the Turks was their proximity; Wallachia and Hungary were literally neighboring states, while the whole of Bulgaria, Serbia, and what was left of the Eastern Roman Empire stood between Vlad's land and the Ottomans. Moreover, thanks to the efforts of both the current political establishment at Buda as well as the rulers active during Vlad II's time, the Hungarian nobles could lay legitimate claims over large swathes of territory in Wallachia. In addition, they would intermarry and produce offspring that would have hereditary rights over any of the lands. Hungary was effectively in the same position that the Habsburg Monarchy, i.e., the Austrians, would enjoy only a few centuries later.

In one sense, Vlad III was a bit cornered due to this situation with Hungary; outright refusing them would not be an option, as Hunyadi would not only refuse to offer help in case the Ottomans wanted to invade the voivode, but they could also very well attack Wallachia itself. However, Vlad's decision to ally himself with the Hungarian kingdom more closely was actually a prudent political move. Most of his father's Dănești-born rivals and claimants to the throne had outside help, and 90 percent of the time, it was the Hungarian king who provided it. Therefore, Vlad would simply use his enemies' tactics against them, and he would do so preemptively.

Despite Vlad's showing of goodwill toward Hunyadi, the Hungarian baron did not immediately (and openly) declare his support right away. After all, Vlad's father was still fresh in the baron's memory, and supporting his hot-blooded, shrewd son might have ended up backfiring on Hungary. There was a general aura of distrust, which was not unwarranted on Hunyadi's part; immediately after taking the throne, Vlad would undertake actions that would do damage to the Hungarian economy and strain their relations even further.

However, Hunyadi himself also proceeded with some steps that would ensure Vlad's mistrust in him. On February 6th, 1452, the baron had instructed the people of Braşov not to shelter Dracula. However, soon after, the Wallachian voivode would return to this city with a task to defend it, a task proclaimed by none other than Hunyadi himself. While we know little of these events, we can safely say, judging by their proximity and outcomes, that the voivode and the baron made peace with one another between 1452 and early 1456.

Wallachia upon Vlad III's Return; Demographic Makeup, Domestic Affairs, Early Issues

The year was 1456, and depending on the source, it was either early spring or mid- to late summer when Vlad III Dracula invaded his homeland of Wallachia and reclaimed the throne from Vladislav II. Some sources even claim that the voivode killed the acting prince himself before declaring his sovereignty. Vlad achieved this victory in no small part thanks to the Hungarian forces sent by Hunyadi. And as a son of a former ruler, he had as much legitimate claim to the throne as the pretenders, some of whom were born bastards and all of whom tried to dethrone the voivode at one point or another. One of these pretenders was Dan

III, while another was an unnamed priest mistakenly referred to as Vlad's namesake brother, later known as Vlad the Monk.

Vlad's coronation was not recorded, but based on how some of the later rulers of Wallachia were crowned, we can assume that most of the customs from the past coronations were used in these later ones, albeit with some changes. A typical coronation would involve the presence of all the court dignitaries, members of the clergy, local boyars, and regular folk. The church service itself was held in Church Slavonic, though most of the particularities of the coronation itself were derived from East Roman customs, as was the case with every Orthodox Balkan nation at the time. Typically, a ruler would receive a scepter, a sword, a gold crown with precious gems, the country's standard, its coat of arms, a saber, and a lance. However, judging by the clothes that Vlad wore in the many contemporary descriptions of the voivode, some Ottoman customs must have crept their way into the event. After all, the Impaler's regal clothing had some interesting Ottoman elements to it, including a caftan (a type of robe) made of velvet and silk that the sultans would wear, which was embroidered with gold filaments, buttons made out of precious stones, and fine sable lining.

Naturally, Vlad's coronation and early rule were not without its problems. Just like any ruler at the time, Vlad III needed to have a council. Usually, around twelve people would serve as council members, tending to different duties regarding the court and the state. However, this number is not set in stone, and with scant data on Vlad's reign, we can't know for sure how many members his council(s) ultimately had, nor who they were. Based on what we do know, however, Vlad had the habit of disposing of any council member he deemed unworthy, often in brutal ways.

From 1456 to 1462, we have records of several key people during Vlad's reign. One individual who, at first, hadn't held any real office position during most of Vlad's early childhood and adolescence was an elderly court scholar named Manea Udrişte. He held the title of vornic, which would be the equivalent of a supreme judge. This was the same position he held during the reigns of several rulers, but in 1453, his own son Dragomir would succeed him, serving as a vornic to Vladislav II. Because of this circumstance, Vlad III saw Dragomir as a staunch adversary, so vornics disappeared from the political scene altogether during the Impaler's second reign, coming back well after Vlad had been deposed and held captive by the Hungarians.

Of course, Manea was merely the first council member attested by historical documents to have served under the Impaler. Some of the other notable members include:

- Codrea, a vornic in 1457, stationed in Braşov
- Dragomir, son of Ţacal, a high-ranking boyar and possible vornic between 1457 and 1459
- Voico, son of Dobriţa, first counselor between 1457 and 1461
- Stan, son of Negrea, a high-ranking boyar who also served under Vladislav II; his service ended probably around 1459
- Duca (also Doukas), a Greek jupan (or *župan*, a Slavic title with the rough meaning of "grand prince") who also served during Vladislav II's and Radu the Beautiful's reigns, attested only in 1457
- Cazan, son of Sahac, a council member of the Wallachian court since the 1430s, attested as a chancellor in 1457
- Calcea, attested in 1457 as Vlad's secretary, later promoted to chancellor
- Linart (also Leonard or Leonhard), a Transylvanian Saxon from Braşov, attested as Vlad's Latin secretary and promoted to chancellor in 1461
- Iova, attested as a constable in 1457 and a treasurer in 1458

Vlad's reign was infamous for the way he dealt with insubordinate or inefficient council members. Quite a few of the ones listed here disappeared from court documents altogether after less than a year since they were appointed (or at least attested to be in power). That's because Vlad had the habit of executing any high-ranking boyar who didn't perform his duties as prescribed. There were a few exceptions, however. The most notable was Cazan, a man who had been in the court's service since the reign of Alexander Aldea in 1431. More impressive is the fact that he remained a court official until 1478, having been everything from a boyar to a chancellor and even a jupan.

One other key aspect of Vlad's "revolving" council is the fact that some of its members had openly served his enemies, mainly the pretenders from the Dănești line. It would seem that Vlad was wise to execute them since those who were banished or managed to escape later came back to serve Vlad's opponents. Duca is the best example of this phenomenon. Initially being Vladislav II's councilor all the way back in 1451, he didn't resurface until 1457, the first and only year he would serve under Vlad III. Historians speculate whether he was in league with the Saxons of Transylvania and the Hungarians, which would undoubtedly lead Vlad to believe that Duca was working toward deposing him in favor of a more docile pretender-ruler. Considering that Duca had served Vlad's younger brother Radu for almost six years after Vlad's own deposition, the voivode had been right to get rid of him as early as he did.

Somewhat paradoxically, even though Vlad had obvious xenophobic tendencies, which were almost always justified in some way and, lest we forget, not uncommon for contemporary monarchs, his court of "revolving" council members didn't merely consist of Wallachians. We already saw from the official documents that both Greeks and even Saxons could end up in high positions at Dracula's court. Laonikos Chalkokondyles, an Eastern Roman historian, wrote at length about the Balkans in his famed work *The Histories*, written in ten tomes. Regarding Dracula, Chalkokondyles mentions that the voivode had a court where no council member could trust each other due to how devious they all were. In the historian's own words, Vlad would employ Hungarians, Serbs, Turks, and Tartars if they would serve his purposes. It's also highly likely that a few Moldavians held some important positions, considering Vlad's amicable relations with the rulers of this Romanian-speaking realm. It's fascinating to learn that one of history's most arguably chauvinistic rulers had such a diverse court, with their only common trait being how corrupt they were, a trait that ultimately besets any government body, even today.

As stated earlier, one of the major problems that the Wallachian court had to deal with was the shifty nature of the boyars and the rowdiness of the commoners. Vlad's desire to have full control over who got to sit on his council, as well as his swiftness in removing those that would undermine him, resulted in a country that was a bit more uniform than before. Granted, he wouldn't always reward loyalty on the part of his advisors. Codrea, for example, was staunchly loyal to Vlad III, but that didn't stop the voivode from executing him in 1459.

Vlad's Wallachia was a small, largely rural country. Based on certain estimates and educated guesses, it must have had, at most, 400,000 inhabitants. Of those, more than 90 percent lived in villages. There were only seventeen major market cities, of which three would serve as court capitals. The first was Câmpulung, and it would remain a capital from at least 1300 to 1330, which was when it was replaced by Curtea de Argeş. Târgovişte, Vlad III's capital, would rise to prominence in 1408.

Some of the other major cities in Wallachia included:
- Chilia (or Kilia, modern Kiliya in Ukraine)
- Brăila
- Târgul de Floci
- Giurgiu
- Turnu

- Turnu Severin

Interestingly, no city in Wallachia had strongholds like other cities in the medieval Balkans. The few that did would usually be held by the Hungarians or the Turks. Instead, the local populace would choose to hide in forests or monasteries if there was a major war or a disaster. The cities themselves were poorly fortified, with either flimsy brick or wood enclosures around them. To the native Wallachians, that lack of fortification was a blessing in disguise since most fortified cities were constantly fought over by different regional powers; thus, living inside such a city would see a lot more deaths and hold a lot more danger.

Coming back to the population of Wallachia in the Middle Ages, the estimated figures show just how brutal and efficient Dracula's regime had been. When the 1470s came, the same area that was ruled by the Impaler had, at the very least, 60,000 people less than during his time. Of course, wars and uprisings account for some of those losses, but even if we take that into account, the number of people who died during Dracula's reign is staggering.

Within that population, Vlad III actually did have people who were willing to lay down their lives for him, and the majority of them constituted his army. The voivode's troops consisted of two major regiments. The first was the so-called "small army," made up of sons from lesser nobles, certain boyars, and the landowning free folk known as *curteni* (the term being a plural form of *curtean*). There were no more than 10,000 people that made up the small army, which made it merely a third of the larger "great army." This massive regiment consisted mostly of commoners who were old enough to bear arms, and the absolute majority were men.

Vlad III and Foreign Affairs

Vlad and the Hungarians

The Impaler's rise to power bore new challenges and issues. As a voivode, he had to establish or reestablish foreign relations with the surrounding monarchies, including heavyweights such as Hungary and the Ottoman Empire. In terms of the former, Vlad was, at the moment, somewhat safe. John Hunyadi had finally provided open support to him, though it wouldn't last for long, as Hunyadi would soon die in August 1456. However, Hunyadi's word was an important political advantage to Vlad, considering how much influence the baron had had at the court in Buda. With his early death, however, nearly all of the state affairs of Hungary were squarely in the hands of the king, the young Ladislaus V the Posthumous. Vlad immediately set about to swear loyalty to the king, which can be attested from several treaty documents that the voivode signed with the Saxons of both Brașov and Sibiu. These treaties obliged Vlad to defend the Transylvanian Saxons from Turkish invasions and allow the Saxon merchants to move freely without having to pay taxes (though this last privilege was not afforded to the people at Sibiu); in return, the Transylvanians and Hungarians had to provide shelter to the voivode should he be attacked by either an external force or an internal traitor (and with the pretenders to the Wallachian throne emerging on an almost yearly basis, this wasn't an unreasonable request on Vlad's part). Naturally, the Impaler did not uphold his end of the agreement, considering that the Turks were already raiding Transylvania mere days after the signing. It's no wonder, then, that the burghers of Brașov, Sibiu, and Amlaș openly hosted two different pretenders to the throne, Dan and Vlad, respectively, after Hunyadi's eldest son Ladislaus wrote a letter about the Impaler's supposed crimes. After reading the letters, one might get the impression that Ladislaus was purposefully vague in his assessment of the Wallachian voivode, and one would be absolutely right. In the mind of Hunyadi's son, as well as the majority of Hungarian and Saxon nobility in major Transylvanian cities, Vlad was expendable, and they merely needed a good excuse to replace him with someone more submissive.

Of course, Vlad did not earn this treatment out of thin air. At some point between late 1456 and early 1457, the voivode had issued the production of new Wallachian coins. One such coin was the silver *ban*, which was similar to the golden ducats of Vladislav II insofar as it was made out of pure metal and weighed roughly 0.40 grams. Minting coins with their own heraldry and value might seem like a trivial matter, but we need to take into consideration that Hungary and Wallachia had been in a monetary union since 1424. In other words, the Wallachians were under obligation to use Hungarian coins, which made them, in no small part, financially reliant on the Buda court. With their own mint, the Wallachians gained a new level of autonomy, which would harm Hungarian interests. Moreover, the Hungarian coins were dangerously devalued at this time, as opposed to the new ones issued by Vlad III.

The other potential reason why Vlad was deemed an enemy by Ladislaus Hunyadi and the Transylvanians was the fact that he wanted to reclaim old territories that were no longer under direct Wallachian rule. Vlad would launch concentrated attacks on Braşov, Sibiu, and Beckendorf, a town that supposedly housed Dan III, one of the pretenders to the throne during Dracula's reign.

What's more interesting is that Dracula's sieges of Braşov and Sibiu were not entirely for his own benefit. Namely, despite Ladislaus's treatment of him, the voivode remained loyal to the Hunyadis, which would prove to be instrumental in the events to follow. After John Hunyadi's death in August 1456, his older son, along with his widow Elizabeth and his surviving brother-in-law Michael Szilágyi, created a rift in Hungarian court politics. Hunyadi's death came less than three weeks after the famous Siege of Belgrade, where he successfully crushed the Ottoman forces of Sultan Mehmed II, the same man who had crushed Constantinople and ended the Eastern Roman Empire a little over three years before the siege. One of the carryover disputes that had remained after Hunyadi's death was his rivalry with Ulrich of Celje; Ulrich would eventually be killed by Ladislaus Hunyadi on November 9th of the same year. Considering Ulrich's position as one of King Ladislaus V's regents, the young monarch had to swear to the House of Hunyadi that he would not pursue vengeance. However, his loyal barons, among whom were powerful figures such as Ladislaus Garai, Ladislaus Pálóci, and Nicholas Újlaki, strongly opposed this decision, and the country was flung into a de facto civil war. Garai and Pálóci were high-ranking court officials, with the former being a palatine (something akin to a viceroy or a regent) and the latter being a judge royal, which was the rank directly beneath the palatine. Újlaki, on the other hand, was a voivode of Transylvania, a position he shared with the now-late John Hunyadi, so his involvement in this matter would directly influence matters in Wallachia as well.

The aforementioned barons were merely three of the many supporters of Ladislaus the Posthumous. However, there was a growing sentiment that the House of Hunyadi should take the throne. The idea materialized when Ladislaus V imprisoned both Ladislaus Hunyadi and his younger brother Matthias, having the older brother executed in March of 1457. In retaliation, Elizabeth and Michael Szilágyi would form the so-called Szilágyi – Hunyadi Liga (League), a movement openly supporting the dethronement of Ladislaus and the elevation of young Matthias to the rank of king. Their troops began to raid the Hungarian regions east of the river Tisza, forcing the young king to flee to Vienna and take Matthias with him. While there, Ladislaus the Posthumous died unexpectedly on November 23rd, 1457. He had no issue, so a brief interregnum ensued. In order to avoid a proper civil war and to appease all parties, the Hungarian Diet (equivalent to a modern parliament) crowned Matthias king on January 24th, 1458. He married Anna, the widow of Matthias's late older brother and the daughter of Ladislaus Garai, sealing the treaty between the loyalists and the Liga. In addition, Michael Szilágyi became the regent of the new young king. Interestingly, though Nicholas Újlaki had been one of the biggest opponents of the Hunyadis, he would end up being one of King Matthias's most trusted supporters in later years, earning several important titles. Most of these titles were related to the territories in the West Balkans (he was dubbed the king of Bosnia, which had already been an Ottoman territory at the time, as well as the ban, a high-ranking noble akin to a prince, of Croatia, Slavonia, and Dalmatia, and, more importantly, a perpetual count of Teočak, an area in Bosnia near today's city of Tuzla). In other words, Újlaki had next to nothing to do with Transylvania long after Vlad III's deposition.

Michael Szilágyi was a key figure in Vlad's reign during 1457. As a loyal Hunyadi supporter, he launched a few campaigns against the Szeklers and the Saxons of Transylvania, focusing on Sibiu and Brașov. He did this in early 1457, around the same time that Vlad III issued his ultimatums to these cities. The Szilágyis and Vlad III took a decisive victory, forcing the local Saxon burghers and the people loyal to Ladislaus V to sign a treaty favoring the winning side. Vlad gained much from this treaty: the pretender Dan was expelled from the area, and the locals were under obligation to refuse any further aid to him. In addition, Vlad reopened trade with their merchants, which would see a boost in the local economy. Of course, the biggest win was the fact that Wallachian merchants finally had full freedom and safety to trade on Transylvanian soil, a feat no predecessor of Vlad's had managed to achieve despite years of failed attempts. In short, the Hungarian power struggle was the perfect opportunity for the Impaler to kill a few birds with one stone: first, to reclaim territories that he saw as his ancestral home (intriguingly, the treaty itself was signed in his native Sighișoara); next, to provide an easy economic boon for his country's merchants with minimal losses on his part; then, to secure a powerful outside ally in the form of Michael Szilágyi and to establish himself as a relevant political factor in the region; and finally, to establish himself as a dominant force in his native Wallachia and as a deterrent against any potential claimants to his throne. Vlad had been in power less than a year, and he had already accomplished this much simply by making prudent, strategic choices.

However, Vlad's good fortune would not last long. King Matthias would dismiss Garai as his palatine and later persuade Szilágyi to renounce his title as regent. In June of 1458, Szilágyi was appointed as the count of the district of Bistrița, one of several major seats of the Transylvanian Saxons. Though Szilágyi himself didn't resign as regent until the next year, young Matthias was effectively the sole ruler of the kingdom, and the two were immediately at odds. Because of the raven that was featured prominently on the House of Hunyadi's coat of arms, Matthias bore the nickname Corvinus, a sobriquet his issue would inherit.

Unlike some of his predecessors, Corvinus favored the Saxons over the Wallachians, hence why he didn't provide immediate support to Vlad III. In fact, while Szilágyi was plotting against the young king (and was arrested for his actions in Belgrade by the end of the year), Corvinus dispatched an envoy, the Polish noble known as the Benedict of Boythor, to Wallachia to have a delicate discussion with the voivode. According to legend (which we will cover in a later chapter), the ambassador didn't exactly feel welcome at the court in Târgoviște. In fact, he was downright terrified of the Wallachian ruler, and to be fair, if he hadn't approached the matter prudently, he would have most likely been killed on the spot. Benedict's mission was to convince Vlad III to stabilize his relations with the Transylvanian Saxons, who, in turn, would admit to wronging the voivode and his people in the past. Because of his history with the Saxons, Dracula wasn't too pleased with this task set before him by the young king. In fact, he would do the exact opposite in the coming months—not only would he issue a new silver ducat and have it minted in the new capital of Bucureşti, but he would reinstate the trading bans and high taxes to all Saxon merchants from Sibiu and Braşov. To be precise, he limited their capacities to three cities in total: Câmpulung, Târgşor, and Târgovişte. The Wallachians were, once again, exempt from these new laws, clearly letting the Saxons know where they were in the voivode's pecking order.

Vlad III was also asked to join the possible crusade against the Turks. The reasons for these were aplenty: Serbia, a notably weak country at that point, was going through political turmoil after the death of Despot Lazar Branković. His brother, known as Stephen the Blind, and Lazar's widow, Helena Palaiologina, held power and wanted to pledge their allegiance to the Hungarian court. However, an army commander known as Michael Angelović wanted to become a vassal of the Ottomans, largely due to the fact that his own brother, Mahmud Pasha, was the grand vizier and the sultan's main advisor at the time. Lazar's successors arrested Angelović, which prompted Sultan Mehmed II to send Mahmud Pasha with an army to Serbia and finish the conquest. At that point, only the city of Semendria (modern-day Smederevo) managed to withstand the Turkish advances.

The reason why Serbia's inevitable downfall was important to both King Matthias Corvinus and Vlad III is rather pragmatic. The remnants of the Serbian Despotate were literally the only thing that stood in the way between the Ottomans, on one side, and Wallachia and Hungary on the other. Without that buffer, both countries were exposed to potential lootings, attacks, incursions, and other dangers. Luckily, Mahmud Pasha didn't reach Semendria properly; according to some eyewitness accounts, which were written by an anonymous contemporary of these events, the Turkish commander entered Wallachia, claimed a fortress (more than likely the one at Turnu Severin, though this is yet to be confirmed), and, after attempting to cross the Danube with his soldiers and his prisoners, was brutally attacked by Dracula and his army of 5,000 people, which consisted of both Wallachians and Hungarians. If the historical account is to be believed, out of 18,000 Ottoman soldiers, less than 8,000 were able to retreat. The rest were either killed in battle or drowned in the river. The Serbian question would, of course, not be solved properly, as Matthias had agreed in a council with Holy Roman Emperor Frederick III to marry Despot Lazar's daughter to the current king of Bosnia, which was another failing state at the time. In 1459, Mehmed II would finally annex what was left of Serbia, leaving Hungary, Transylvania, and Wallachia exposed to further attacks.

Matthias Corvinus, due to Vlad's actions against the Saxons and the Szeklers, began to provide support to the pretenders to the Wallachian throne, not unlike how his father had handled things back in the day. Two of these pretenders were known as Basarab II and Dan III, the latter of which was presumably killed by Vlad himself in a particularly gruesome way. In addition to these actions, the young king had also allowed these pretenders to seek shelter among the Transylvanian Saxons, but more importantly, he prohibited any merchants from Brașov to trade arms with the Wallachians.

This animosity between the rulers would last at least up until 1460. However, as the years went by, the two men grew to understand one another, and their relations became somewhat normalized. In fact, in 1461, Matthias proposed that the Wallachian voivode marry a woman from his family, the noblewoman (and Vlad's future second wife) Jusztina Szilágyi. This bit of news greatly unnerved Sultan Mehmed II, who rightfully saw it as a way for Vlad to strengthen his alliances with the other Christian nations and possibly work on a way to fight off the Turks. In the final years of Vlad's second reign, this would spiral into war and deliver heavy losses to both sides.

Relief of King Matthias Corvinus, from Beatrice of Naples and Matthias Corvinus, *author unknown, circa 1485–1490 (this piece is a later copy from the 19th century)*

Vlad and the Turks

Initially, though not willingly, Vlad had been an ally to the Ottomans. For instance, he would not openly attack them during the early months of his reign, opting to stay, more or less, neutral with strengthening only some of the key relations with the Hungarians and the Moldavians. Interestingly, unlike most vassal states during the reigns of Murad II and Mehmed II, Wallachia had remained largely autonomous. Vlad, of course, had to pay an annual tribute to the Turks to prevent the wrath of the sultan's army. However, there were a few key elements that made him a more independent ruler than his contemporaries. For instance, none of Vlad's immediate family members were prisoners of the sultan other than his brother Radu. However, by this point, Radu had been staying at the Ottoman court willingly, having become somewhat of a favorite to the sultans. In fact, it might have even been Radu's insistence that brought Vlad III to the throne in the first place, which is made all the more plausible considering that the Impaler hadn't made any attacks on the Turks in his early reign.

Another important element to Wallachia's autonomy in 1456 was the fact that Vlad, even during the final days of his reign, never sent any young boys as a tribute. Sources from the time attest that he had to send at least 500 young boys to the sultan each year, but based on Vlad's personal correspondence with the rulers at the time (including his letter to King Matthias Corvinus), there didn't seem to be any mention of this demand on the side of the Ottomans. A reader might conclude that Vlad simply lied by omission that he didn't have to send any young boys as a tribute, but this is highly unlikely. After all, he clearly stated in his letters what he believed the Turks were planning and what dangers they posed to his country and countrymen. As someone seeking help against an aggressor, it would be illogical to leave out such a significant method of subjugation as the Devshirme.

We can find the third and final element that proves Vlad hadn't been a completely submissive vassal of the Ottomans within the legal documents from his time. While he was in power, Vlad had refused the Ottomans free passage through Wallachia for the purposes of raiding the Transylvanians. They were also not allowed to settle in Wallachia permanently, buy or own land, construct mosques, or attain any proper political power. In addition, Orthodox Christianity was freely practiced, and the prince, if not by means of primogeniture, could only be elected by the boyars and the clergy, not by the Ottomans directly.

Vlad III's Wars: Major Battles and Campaigns

The Danubian Campaign

Vlad's shaky relations with nearly everyone would soon bear bitter fruit. When Mehmed II learned of the voivode's planned marriage with the cousin of the Hungarian king in early 1462, he sent an envoy to try to convince Vlad to visit the Sublime Porte (the Ottoman's medieval court) and discuss future endeavors. The servant whom the sultan dispatched to finish this task was a Greek secretary known as Thomas Katabolenos, a skilled diplomat recommended by the ecumenical Christian patriarch himself. After the fall of Constantinople, the Greeks, who still considered themselves as Eastern Romans, were under the sultan's rule, but he did not exactly rule over them directly; instead, the patriarch and the Church took over most of the governing duties as proxies. Considering the status of the Eastern Roman Orthodox Church as ecumenical, i.e., the one above all others, the Orthodox Churches of both Wallachia and Moldavia were its direct underlings. Therefore, Mehmed II's move was quite prudent. A diplomat with the knowledge of Christian affairs would be able to convince Vlad more easily to visit the sultan than any Muslim diplomat would.

But Vlad was anything but ignorant of what this invitation meant. His own father had made the mistake of appearing at the sultan's court before, and the whole family ended up in disarray after that, to put it mildly. Therefore, the Impaler asked the sultan to send a local bey (a title meaning "chieftain of an area of land") to "guard the frontier and keep the country safe"; the reasoning Vlad used was, indeed, quite sound and surprisingly accurate, as he claimed that the country, which would be left to the local boyars, would fall apart since nobody was faithful to him. With that in mind, Mehmed II sent Hamza Bey, the governor of Nicopolis, to watch over the Danube River.

Cunningly, Dracula sent a letter to King Matthias Corvinus, warning him of the dangers that the Turks posed and, almost predictably, stating that his venture into Constantinople would mean his death and that Hamza Bey was more than willing to drag Dracula to the Ottoman's new capital, by force if necessary. So, Dracula acted quickly, capturing both Hamza Bey and Thomas Katabolenos and impaling them soon after. Around forty of their men were also impaled and mutilated, with their corpses lining the walls of Târgoviște.

Of course, that was merely the precursor to what we call Dracula's Danubian campaign. Not long after he had the two servants of the sultan dispatched, Vlad took his army across the frozen Danube and divided the men up into several squads. His plan was to cover all of the frontier lands next to the great river, from Chilia in the southeast to Rahova in the northwest, near the mouth of the Jiu River. It was a massive 800-kilometer (almost 500-mile) swath of land to cover, and they had to do this in the midst of a devastating winter, no less. But Vlad III did far more than simply succeed in his intended mission. In fact, he utterly crushed nearly everything next to the Danube River that wasn't Wallachian. In the process, he recaptured the important fortress of Giurgiu, reportedly ordering the locals to open the gates in fluent Turkish before having his men flood it and murder anything that moved.

Both Turks and local Bulgarians died in the constant raids, killed either on land or while on the river transporting goods. No women or children were spared during this horrific raid, and all of the people that didn't die by the sword would succumb to the flames of one of the hundreds of fires. By his own estimate, which might be exaggerated but is fascinating nonetheless, the voivode claims to have killed a grand total of 22,883 people. And, in his own words, those were just the ones whose heads were accounted for. He didn't count any of the people burned alive or killed in such a way that you couldn't separate the head from the body.

Aside from this mass murder, tantamount to genocide if not for the diverse nationalities that died under Wallachian swords, Vlad also ordered the destruction of material goods, transport vehicles like carts and rafts, houses, keeps, churches, and what few forts there were on the Danube on the Bulgarian side. His plan was to completely cripple the locals from funding and supplying the Ottoman troops in case the sultan felt like invading the voivode. But more importantly, Vlad wanted to show the Turks that he meant business, that even the best-prepared armies of the sultan could do no damage to his own warriors, and that he was both capable and willing to murder thousands of civilians to prove his point.

In a lengthy letter he sent to King Matthias Corvinus, Vlad lists off all of the cities, towns, villages, and forts that ended up burned, sacked, or damaged after he laid his siege. There is no real sympathy in the voivode's voice for all of the innocents that died; he merely lists them off and brushes them aside in the very next sentence. What's more disturbing, however, is the duplicity of some of Vlad's statements. He claims to have done what he did for the preservation of Christianity, the Catholic faith, and the crown of the Hungarian king, but every single one of those statements is patently hypocritical. Based on every source we have, Vlad only converted to Catholicism during his imprisonment, which took place sometime before his death. Up until that point, he was more than likely an Orthodox ruler, even if he wasn't practicing and despite his heinous acts while at court. Next, we know that he rarely put stock in Christianity as a moral goal, considering that he had refused to join a few potential crusades. Moreover, the Hungarian crown didn't exactly mean much to him, other than the fact that it was placed on the head of a powerful political ally (whose position at court was, at best, as shaky as his own in Wallachia). And lastly, Vlad had committed most of these atrocities against innocent Christian men and women of Bulgaria. No self-described fighter for Christianity would even think to condone the murder of civilians, let alone in the way that Vlad had done it.

The Night Attack

With the letter sent, it was Corvinus's time to act. Thanks to his efforts, this same letter reached other European rulers at the time, even finding its way to northern Italy. Though Matthias might have felt sympathetic to Vlad's cause (or at least saw an opportunity to crush the Ottomans), his royal budget and the state of his court would not allow him to waste any money on an anti-Turk campaign. He lobbied hard with various Italian nobles and the clergy for monetary assistance in this potential crusade, but it ultimately came to nothing. Alone, Corvinus could simply not risk a war with the sultan.

The defeat of the Ottomans was so crushing and devastating that it's not a stretch to call it their biggest defeat (up to that point) since Mehmed II came to power. Naturally, the Porte had to retaliate, so the sultan amassed what was possibly the biggest army since the Siege of Constantinople, which had taken place less than a decade prior. Two of the main regiments of his army consisted of ground troops, with himself at the helm. They headed directly for Dracula's old capital of Târgoviște. The fleet, however, was in Brăila, a port city close to another important inhabited area, the contested city of Chilia. Stephen the Great of Moldavia had always been an ally to the Wallachian voivode, but Chilia never stopped being a hot-button issue, one that the Moldavian ruler sought to fix. Brăila itself would be burned to the ground, but Chilia would not fall into Ottoman hands, nor would it go back to Prince Stephen that year. Though the Turks themselves saw this port as extremely important and placed great emphasis on capturing it, they wouldn't seize control of it until 1484.

Vlad had seen the sizable army of Mehmed II. On June 4th, 1462, the army crossed the Danube at Nicopolis (modern Nikopol in Bulgaria) and moved steadily toward Târgoviște. Once again showing his cunning nature, Vlad employed a scorched-earth policy; every time he retreated, his army would burn the crops and destroy all the dwellings, leaving nothing but ash to the conquerors.

The hot summer sun greatly helped Vlad in this endeavor. By the end of the campaign, the Turkish troops had suffered great heat exhaustion and strokes, with the losses on their side being significantly higher than those on the Wallachian side. However, Vlad's real moment of triumph, as well as potentially his biggest failure, would come on the night between June 17th and June 18th.

Several different historical accounts at the time spoke of this attack, and while there are some significant variations in terms of details, the basic course of events is the same. Upon reaching Târgoviște but before entering it, the Ottomans set up a base camp. Vlad saw this as a great opportunity for a task that was nowhere near easy but which could change the course of the war significantly. Taking anywhere between 7,000 and 10,000 men, the voivode divided them into two groups and attacked the camp at night, when the Ottomans least suspected it. His main goal was to kill Mehmed II and his chief viziers. The murders of these individuals would then act as a catalyst for the Turkish armies to fall into disarray. Had Vlad succeeded, there would have been a dynastic battle at the Porte, allowing the Christian nations of the Balkans to breathe a sigh of relief for a short while and reorganize their efforts. Sadly, Vlad did not harm the sultan (though, according to some sources, the voivode's army did wound Mehmed, albeit not fatally) and had to retreat into the thick Wallachian woodland. The Ottomans were, reportedly, terrified beyond belief, and after the confusion had settled, they somehow managed to capture a number of Wallachian soldiers and decapitate them in retaliation.

Vlad's final proper act of defiance was caused by his absence from Târgoviște when the Ottomans reached it by the end of June. Sources claim that the Muslim army had entered a deserted town, which was littered with impaled corpses of all ages, both male and female, and all nationalities. They even recognized some of the court dignitaries from Constantinople that had been dispatched earlier that year. The sultan himself stated that he could not deprive Wallachia of such a cruel yet competent ruler, so he left

the capital, with his men dumbfounded and confused as to what
had just happened.

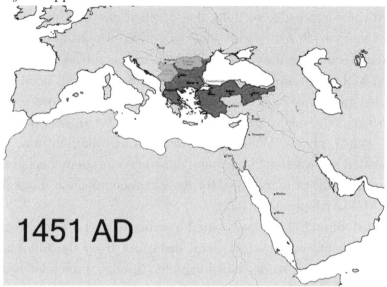

Map of the Ottoman Empire during the second reign of Mehmed II the
Conqueror; Wallachia and Serbia shown in light-green"

Final Battles of 1462 before the Dethroning

Upon his retreat, Mehmed began his movement toward Chilia,
which was now under attack from Stephen the Great. Some
documents from this time imply that the Moldavian prince had
begun raiding Vlad's borderlands earlier that year, even as early as
before Mehmed's campaign. Considering the friendship and
alliance between the two rulers (both before and after 1462), this
action on the part of Stephen might seem confusing at first until we
talk more about the city of Chilia.

As an important port, it had been in the hands of the
Wallachians (or rather the Hungarians through a Wallachian
proxy) since 1448. Stephen saw an opportunity to reclaim it in the
summer of 1462 when it was garrisoned by a mix of both
Hungarian and Wallachian troops. But in order to do that, he
needed to find the right moment, so he agitated Vlad in order to
split his attention between the Moldavian troops and the

approaching Turks. Once the Turks had returned from the Wallachian lands, the Moldavian prince laid siege to the city.

It's not impossible to think that Stephen managed to convince the Ottomans that they were allies due to his actions against Vlad, and even contemporary historians like Chalkokondyles and Tursun Bey, Mehmed's own secretary, claim that Stephen had been loyal to the sultan. However, the siege of this city was a failure for the attackers. Not only would the Ottomans suffer yet another defeat at the hands of the Wallachians, but Stephen himself was also wounded in his left ankle, an injury that never properly healed and which was the primary cause for the gangrene infection that killed the Moldavian prince in 1504.

Vlad himself had also started moving toward Chilia, leaving roughly 6,000 soldiers to defend the realm from the Ottomans, which they failed to do. Not long after, another pretender to the throne appeared in the Bărăgan Plain, a vast area extremely close to Târgoviște and a fertile land that housed some of Wallachia's biggest cities at the time. During his campaign, Mehmed II had taken with him a familiar servant who was his favorite in every way. Upon arriving in Wallachia, Radu the Handsome began to campaign hard in order to get as many boyars to accept him as the ruler and avoid more Ottoman attacks. Within months, the two brothers would clash in battle several times, and nearly all of those battles were won by Vlad. Nevertheless, more and more boyars began defecting to Radu, and the Ottoman forces did not stop advancing, leaving Vlad with barely any allies in his crucial moments.

Historians from mid-20th century Romania almost exclusively claimed that Vlad had done nothing but win against the Ottomans and that his exclusion from the throne was solely due to the traitors among the boyars. Of course, a more nuanced view suggests that there were a myriad of reasons. While it is absolutely true that there were boyars defecting to Radu, the number of potential traitors had greatly decreased while Vlad was in power, thanks in no small part to his brutal way of dealing with those who opposed him.

Dethroning and Capture of Vlad the Impaler

Stephen the Great's armies were now an enemy. The Ottomans did not slow their march. Towns and cities burned all over. Radu had become the voice of a significant number of traitorous boyars. All of those elements together were slowly but surely leading to Vlad's downfall in late 1462. An opportunist as always, Vlad retreated to the Carpathian Mountains, effectively dethroning himself and giving Radu all of the power. The voivode's plan was to meet up with Matthias Corvinus and, with the help of the Hungarians, reestablish his rule. But the situation kept getting grimmer by the day. Albert of Istenmező, a Szekler count at the time, declared that the Transylvanian Saxons were going to shift their allegiance to Radu and recognize him as the new voivode. In addition, the younger Dracul also struck up a deal with the Saxons of Brașov, promising them financial and economic benefits in exchange for their loyalty.

The young Hungarian king had, on the surface level, taken Vlad's pleas for help into consideration, seeing as he was in Transylvania in November 1462. Stephen the Great's stance on waging war against the Turks did not change from earlier that year, though—he simply did not have the manpower, nor the money, to finance the endeavor. The two rulers negotiated for weeks before the meeting, it would seem, but judging by what happened (and the documents that surfaced later), we can safely assume that Corvinus had absolutely zero intention of assisting Vlad. He ordered his mercenary commander, a Czech strategist called John Jiskra of Brandýs, to capture Vlad, which Jiskra did near the town of Rucăr. Some accounts state that it was Vlad's own companions who rebelled and captured him at the fortress of Piatra Craiului and then handed him over to Jiskra. Other sources state that Vlad was captured on his way back to Wallachia after the negotiations with the Hungarian king fell through.

Historians do not know the reason behind Corvinus's capture of Vlad in 1462. Even Corvinus's court historian, an Italian poet and famed humanist Antonio Bonfini, states that he did not know why the king captured the voivode. There are three important documents that relate directly to this event, and they were sent to both Pope Pious II in Rome and to the Venetians, who had actually sent some money to finance a potential crusade against the Ottomans during Vlad's military exploits. These documents are the supposed letters that Vlad himself had written. One of them was meant for Sultan Mehmed II, the other for his grand vizier Mahmud Pasha, and the third for Stephen the Great of Moldavia. Apparently, they all contain the same basic premise, with the voivode promising to invade Hungary if the Turks helped him stay in power.

After analyzing these letters, we can safely say that they are forgeries. Dating them reveals that they were most likely written during Vlad's captivity in the Hungarian town of Visegrád. More importantly, by analyzing the style and sentence structure, we can definitely conclude that none of Vlad's character, which emanates from letters that actually came from him, is present. These letters were, therefore, made to justify Vlad's imprisonment to King Matthias's Catholic allies from across the Adriatic, though we may never know why exactly the voivode was captured in the first place.

Chapter 3 – Final Years: A Decade and a Half of Captivity, Third Reign, Death

Vlad's Captivity in Hungary

In late 1462, Vlad was held at "Belgrade," though not the one that served as the former capital of medieval Serbia but rather a town in Wallachia (now named Alba Iulia). Soon after, however, he would be moved to Visegrád and would remain there for the better part of the next fourteen years

Very little is known about Vlad's captivity at Visegrád since there are no reliable records that tell us how he behaved or how he was treated, other than a few legends of him supposedly butchering a woman and exposing her womb simply to show that he did not impregnate her with his bastard child. However, based on what little information we do have on Dracula from the final few years of his life, we can piece together a possible chain of events.

Due to Jiskra's profession, it's not unlikely to think that the mercenary's own men were in charge of being Dracula's jailors. After his transfer from Alba Iulia to Visegrád, Vlad must have only been treated as a prisoner for a short while, long enough for the news of his capture and his cruel nature to reach the wider population of Europe. It's generally thought that the original incunabula (plural of incunabulum, meaning "book" but more specifically referring to pamphlets printed before 1501) that told the story of the voivode's brutalities were printed in Vienna in around 1463, possibly by an individual named Ulrich Han. And though the original text has been lost to time, at least four different copies have survived to this day, all kept at various locations in Austria, Switzerland, France, and the United Kingdom. The pamphlets about Vlad the Impaler must have been quite popular at the time, considering how many copies were made. Whether they reached the court at Buda is not known, though experts suggest that King Matthias Corvinus himself must have been at least aware of them. More importantly, whether or not Vlad himself saw the pamphlets is an unanswered question, but judging by his overall character, he would have probably not cared for their contents.

Historians debate whether Vlad remained at Visegrád or moved to Pest at some point. What we do know is that he owned a house in Pest, implying that even in captivity, he was able to own property within the borders of Corvinus's kingdom. If we apply this assumption on a larger scale, we realize that Vlad was not a mere prisoner. He was, in fact, probably treated more like a high-ranking noble and a "guest of honor," albeit obviously less pompous. He would also buy a house in Pécs, a home that is currently known as the *Drakula háza* ("the House of Dracula"). His widow, Jusztina Szilágyi, would end up inheriting this home after the voivode's death.

In the summer of 1475, after a long six months of beating back the Turks in the Battle of Vaslui and dethroning Radu the Handsome, but shortly after helping place the pretender Basarab Laiotă on the throne of Wallachia for the fourth time, Stephen the Great of Moldavia wrote to the Hungarian king, urging him to release Vlad and recognize him as the legitimate ruler over his native land. And while King Matthias did release Vlad that year (which was the same year Vlad would marry Jusztina and apparently convert to Catholicism), he did not provide the voivode with any troops against the invading Turks and the traitorous Basarab, who was, at the time, allied with Sultan Mehmed II against the Moldavian forces. It is this period, between the end of 1475 and the end of 1476, that we have the most information about the Impaler's exploits, which all took place before his third reign and eventual death.

Castle of Visegrád, a contemporary woodcut during the reign of Matthias Corvinus, 1480[ii]

Military Exploits in Bosnia

At some point in early 1476, possibly late January, King Matthias ordered some of his most reliable noblemen to take up arms against important forts in Bosnia and near its borders in order to expel the Ottomans. Both Vlad III and the Serbian noble Vuk Grgurević (a member of the House of Branković) set off to help with the siege of Šabac, now a modern-day city in Serbia but an important fort back then. The siege was long and drawn out, possibly lasting for a month and a half until the two expatriate nobles took a decisive victory with the Turks surrendering.

Having won this war, the two princes moved to besiege Srebrenica; however, they did so using entirely different tactics. They sent a total of 150 men disguised as Turks into the town so that they could intermingle. Vlad and Vuk, along with the bulk of the army, which was some 2,000 men strong, traveled at night so as not to be spotted. Within days, they seized control of the city, both from the outside and from within, looting and pillaging everything along the way.

Their next major campaign was at the town of Kušlat, which was again won by the Christian forces. The fourth and final victory, however, would come at a cost. While besieging Zvornik, Vuk Grgurević sustained a terrible foot injury during the battle. But the historians of the time paint a far more gruesome picture when talking about Dracula. In their words, he would grab the surrendered Ottomans with his bare hands and rip them apart, flesh, skin, and sinew. He would then proceed to do what he evidently did best, which was impaling them on stakes and leaving them out in the open for everyone to see. Much like in Târgoviște a decade prior, the arriving Ottomans would have been horrified beyond belief at the sight.

Moldavian-Turkish Conflicts of August 1476 and the Retaking of Wallachia

With this string of successes, it was only a matter of time before Vlad and Vuk Grgurević went on to help Stephen the Great flush the Ottomans out of his country. Apparently, they were also joined by a member of the Serbian House of Jakšić, though his name is unknown and is merely assumed to be Demetar. Stephen lost the crucial Battle of Valea Albă in July and was forced to retreat. However, this was a Pyrrhic victory for the Ottomans since they could not capture any of the important Moldavian strongholds, had suffered starvation, and were heavily exhausted by constant small-scale guerilla-style attacks by the local Moldavians. Moreover, there was an outbreak of the plague, which greatly hampered the progress of the Turks.

In August of 1476, Vlad III and the two Serbian nobles were deep within Transylvania, joining forces with the contemporary Transylvanian voivode Stephen V Báthory and his army of 30,000 men. The Christian forces managed to stop the Turkish siege of the fortress at Târgu Neamţ and force the Ottomans to flee. Not long after, the Hungarian king issued an order to the Transylvanian Saxons. They were to support Báthory's plan to invade Wallachia in September, which he did, liberating several key cities as he went about his campaign. A mere month later, Vlad the Impaler was in Braşov, reinstating the old trading privileges to the local merchants. Although the Braşov Saxons were still not entirely loyal to Vlad, they began openly supporting him over Basarab Laiotă as early as the first few skirmishes between Moldavia and Wallachia.

Third Reign and Death

November would prove to be the Impaler's glorious return to the throne. During his campaign, Báthory liberated Vlad's old capital, Târgovişte, around November 8th. Vlad himself was in that battle, reportedly defeating Laiotă and causing over 10,000 casualties during the siege. Eight days later, Laiotă's capital of Bucharest also fell, and the voivode, who had been dethroned for the fourth (yet not the final) time, fled to the Ottomans, seeking protection. Vlad and Stephen the Great ceremoniously entered the capital, possibly welcomed by the same disloyal boyars who had, at some point, been betraying nearly every ruler until Vlad's return.

With Vlad's victory, it was the right time to honor his word with the Saxons of Braşov, so the voivode sent the word about his victory to them, urging them to reenter Wallachia and resume their trade. Exactly ten days later, on November 26th, Vlad III Dracula was, yet again, crowned the voivode of Wallachia.

However, this dominion over his country wouldn't last past the end of the year. Prudently, Vlad asked Stephen to leave a contingent of loyal guards to safeguard him. The reason behind this decision was, as it normally tended to be in medieval Wallachia, the inherent distrust of the ruler toward his boyars. After all, those same boyars had, until recently, supported Basarab, and not long before him, they were answering to Vlad's own brother and Ottoman sympathizer Radu the Handsome. Stephen understood the situation well, leaving Dracula with 200 of his own guardsmen. In December, Laiotă would try to invade Wallachia yet again, this time with a sizable Turkish army backing him. Though accounts greatly differ on the details, we can say for sure that Dracula died fighting, causing heavy losses to the invading force but losing all 200 of his loyal guards in the process. After his death, he was decapitated, and his head was stuffed and sent to Mehmed II in Istanbul. Reportedly, it was paraded around the city for days in celebration of the voivode's final defeat. Stephen the Great received the news of his ally's demise in January of 1477, while the royal court of Matthias Corvinus learned of it a month later. Decades later, Tursun Bey would write about the death of the voivode, calling him *Kazıklı Voyvoda*, which quite literally translates to "impaler lord." The sobriquet was just descriptive and accurate enough to stick, to the point where even later Wallachian rulers would refer to Vlad with this new title. Therefore, Vlad III was never called "Impaler" during his lifetime.

Vlad III Dracula was definitely buried in a monastery, as was the custom of Eastern Orthodox Christian rulers in the Balkans. However, historians still debate as to where his final resting place might have been. The most likely candidate is the Monastery of Snagov since it is also thought to contain the remains of previous monarchs from the Drăculești line, including his own father and older brother. However, other experts claim that Dracula would more likely have been buried in the Comana Monastery since he had founded and built it. A headless corpse was found buried near the monastery, suggesting not only that these were Vlad's remains but also that he had breathed his final breath here during the battle.

Chapter 4 – Spreading the Story: Myths about Dracula and His Public Image, Portraits, and Depictions

Even during his lifetime, Vlad the Impaler had been a conversation starter in many European courts. Granted, he wouldn't get the sobriquet "Impaler" until after his death, but even though his name and title were not that ominous, his actions certainly were.

Since the very beginning of his rule, different legends had been popping up all over the medieval world. Considering his strained relations with some nations (and somewhat amicable relations with others), it's only fitting that the negative stereotypes usually associated with Vlad III almost exclusively originated from extremely biased sources. For instance, the Saxons who managed to flee from Transylvania and avoid Dracula's direct field of influence, often settling in other Germanic areas such as the Habsburg Monarchy (precursor to modern-day Austria), began printing various pamphlets retelling stories of the Wallachian ruler's supposed cruelties. On the other hand, Slavic and Wallachian sources present Vlad as a prudent, proactive ruler who took charge of the situation and did what needed to be done. Naturally, both of these sides were essentially printing propaganda that went one way or the other, and more often than not, it amounted to "popular literature." Indeed, a valid point can be made that the incunabula were reprinted by the Saxons in Vienna and other Germanic cities over and over again due to their popularity. After all, even the medieval man loved political scandals, and few can be as interesting as tales of a man who impales his prisoners and tortures them in the worst ways possible.

But how much truth is there to them? Well, oddly enough, even Slavic sources, like the famous *Skazanie o Drakule voivode* ("The Tale of Voivode Dracula"), which are generally more lenient toward the voivode, list off some of his cruel deeds. Of course, these sources, be it positive or negative propaganda, can be trusted wholly on face value. However, we can still look at the basic, bare-bones elements of each contemporary source and come up with some plausible theories.

Let's take impaling, for example. Nearly all propagandistic sources mention Vlad applying this type of punishment in practice. Some state that he did it with the bodies hanging upside down or right side up, others mention mass impalements, and others talk about the way the stake was inserted into the body (or the body rammed onto the stake), etc. Of course, we can't take the numbers of victims given by the ancient authors as gospel since, more often than not, even the most scholarly of medieval writers would exaggerate numbers. So, how do we go about this then? Well, since all sources mention him using impalement as a punishment, we can safely assume that he did so regularly. We also know for a fact that the Ottomans had been using this method of execution for centuries before invading the Balkans, and they were far from being the first to do so. Therefore, even if we reduce the number of victims and decide on the most prominent method, we can claim, without a doubt, that Vlad impaled his adversaries. With that knowledge, the sobriquet "Impaler" is still considered a historical fact, as well as a correct depiction of the man.

Next, we ought to discuss his appearance. We will cover the specific image(s) of Dracula in a little bit, but we do need to find some solid middle ground, just like in our assessment about his propensity for impaling. We know from some of the remaining paintings of the era what Dracula looked like. In other words, there's an actual realistic portrait of the man that we can point to and say, "That, there, is Vlad III." However, we can only be sure about our assessment completely when we look at the Saxon incunabula mentioned earlier. They contain stylized images of Dracula going about his day, and they are quite animated when it comes to movement and gestures. And based on what Vlad looked like in some of these incunabula, he definitely matches the aforementioned realistic portraits prominent in the Late Middle Ages and early Renaissance.

Dracula, like most historical figures of that era (and a huge number of other historical figures from entire millennia before Vlad's birth), is mentioned in very few contemporary documents in a way that gives us a glimpse of his character. That's why historians and researchers have delved deeper into the many legends and myths ascribed to the voivode. As we saw, these sources don't necessarily have to be 100 percent true, but they do give us some good insight into the general image of Vlad III. But the value of these myths goes beyond assessing historical accuracy. They are also splendid works of fiction, tales that have their own meanings and morals, and, in a way, they paint a good picture of what Wallachian (and Southern European) life must have been like when Vlad seized power.

Myths about Vlad III

Over the centuries, plenty of tales have emerged about Vlad's brutal behavior and his blood-sodden habits. Most Western readers have never heard of these legends, which is somewhat disappointing because they can pretty much rival Bram Stoker's novel when it comes to cruelty and gore. This chapter will provide some of these legends, retold in no particular order, chronological or otherwise. Most of them originate from contemporary amateur historians or Saxon booklets printed some years after Vlad's deposition and eventual death. It's also instructive to note that some of these tales have several variations depending on where they were recorded and by whom. Moreover, this is nowhere near an exhaustive list of legends and stories about Vlad III. For instance, no tale that came from rural Romanian folklore is on this list, as those are far too many and, in all likelihood, were crafted well after the voivode's death.

The Bloody Easter

It was March 25th, 1459, Easter Sunday. Matthias Corvinus had become more involved with his kingly duties, the Turks were restless, and there was a lot of commotion in and around Wallachia. Vlad had plenty of problems to deal with: the Saxons of Transylvania wanted to keep the lands of Amlaş and Făgăraş, the ancestral land of the Basarabs, and the young Hungarian king wanted the Wallachians to make peace with the Saxon folk. Of course, Vlad knew what happens when the Hungarian king doesn't support your side and advocates for the benefit of your enemies. He knew it well, considering how many princes and voivodes came before him.

It was on this fateful Easter that he summoned all of his boyars and other members of the nobility for a meal. Nearly 500 of them appeared. Some were as old as oak trees, others barely fifteen of age. Three were boyars he recognized, though a lot more were surely unknown to him. There were even some boyars he wished he didn't know at all. But they were all there, and they ate dinner in reverence of Christ's resurrection.

Soon enough, the meal was done, stomachs were full. The boyars were enjoying a bit of respite from the meal. Ever vigilant, Vlad turned to one of the oldest lords in the keep. "Tell me," he asked the old man, "how many lords and voivodes do you remember who ruled this land before me?" The lord gave his answer. Then Vlad turned to a younger lord and asked the same question. And the young boyar gave his answer. Again, Vlad turned to the next lord, and his answer followed. One by one, Vlad asked them all the same question, and the responses varied greatly. Some lords said, "About thirty, my lord." Others replied with, "I think twelve, my liege." Some of them would say ten or twelve or twenty, while others would go as high as thirty, forty, and even fifty. Not a single one of the young lords uttered a number smaller than seven.

Satisfied with his answers, Vlad got up from his seat and gave an order to his royal guard. Within minutes, hundreds of screams filled the room as the guards began dragging the boyars out. One by one, the lords and nobles that had dined at Dracula's table were now dying, impaled onto stakes and bleeding profusely to death. It was not unlike a canopy of corpses in front of the royal palace. Many died that day, but many more learned that Vlad didn't think highly of the frequent changes of the voivodes. Indeed, he intended to keep his seat as long as possible, via any means.

The Death of Dan III

Dan III was a pretender to Dracula's throne. He was living in Braşov and enjoying the hospitality of the local Saxon burghers, establishing himself as the anti-voivode to the Impaler. 1459 was coming to a close, and Vlad had already attained the reputation of being a ruthless yet effective ruler. But Dan wasn't afraid. He had the backing of the Hungarian Diet and the king himself. And so, he went about ruling Braşov, issuing a charter here, an edict there. Although he was self-stylized as the lord of Amlaş and Făgăraş, his ambitions went higher. He wanted to be yet another in the long line of revolving princes that occupied the throne of Wallachia. And in order to do that, he would have to go through Vlad.

It was winter, and Dan III had successfully rallied the Saxons. But then again, they didn't need much rallying. Not long ago, their merchants had been forbidden from trading in most of the territory of Wallachia, and the taxes coming from the voivode were dreadful. In addition, information regarding his legendary brutal behavior had reached them mere months prior. Dan knew this information well, and more importantly, he knew how to use it. After all, who would the Saxons support? A man neither loyal to the Crown of Hungary nor the Sultan over at Constantinople? Or the man who openly stood against this tyrant and, more importantly, treated the Saxons with admiration and respect? The local boyars were of one mind—Vlad had to go.

But Vlad didn't budge. The pretender's army crossed the frontier during Easter Week on April 13th, 1460, and went to war with Vlad, a war that Dan lost in the most humiliating way possible. All of Dan's soldiers were captured and executed by April 22nd of the same year, a mere nine days after the incursion had started. Some even reported that Vlad had ordered Saxon women and other women sympathetic to Dan III's cause to be impaled upon stakes as well. Horrifyingly, the babies and infants of these women were also killed and sewn to the dead women's breasts. A truly dreadful sight, to be sure.

But by far, the biggest humiliation came to Dan himself. After he was captured and imprisoned, he was then taken out of his dungeon and brought before the executioners. Vlad himself was there, as were the priests and some of the loyal boyars. But most disturbingly, there lay a gravesite. A gravesite with a tombstone. And it bore Dan's own name on it. The pretender was swiftly placed next to the grave, on his knees, probably too stunned to move. Vlad ordered the priests to read a funeral service for the "late" pretender voivode while some freemen dug a man-sized hole in front of the monument. The only respite Dan could have had was his lack of knowledge of Church Slavonic, the language which the priests were using when reciting their morbid lines. But Dan didn't have to wait long. After the service ended and the priests uttered their last few lines, Vlad had Dan killed on the spot, via decapitation. Whether he did it himself or not, we do not know. But he did deal Dan and all other future pretenders to the throne a crushing blow with a clear message: anyone who tried to take his throne through less than reputable means would find themselves dead.

The Golden Cup

Târgoviște, Vlad's first capital, was quite large, boasting close to 60,000 souls. It had been unruly during the reigns of the previous Wallachian rulers, including Vlad's namesake father and older brother Mircea. The restless and fickle boyars were one reason, but the common folk were no better. Thievery and muggings were common in the capital, as it had an astounding number of poor inhabitants who had to steal to survive, but there were also opportunistic thieves who managed to get away one too many times. But when Vlad came to power, nearly all the criminals in the land started receiving brutal punishments for their deeds. People wouldn't believe some of the stories that merchants and travelers would tell after passing through the voivode's land. Two tales, in particular, stood out.

According to the first tale, a traveler or a merchant had entered Târgoviște and needed a room at an inn to spend the night. However, he was carrying with him large sums of money, which he understandably wanted to deposit somewhere safe. However, the innkeeper and the locals simply told him to keep the money outside with his horse, out in the open. The traveler was stunned, and against his better judgment, he listened to the people and left the bags with his horse. The next morning, expecting to wake up penniless, the traveler was stunned to see the bags intact, with not a single coin missing.

The other tale concerns a certain golden cup. This magnificent dish was placed by Vlad in the middle of Târgoviște's town square. According to his decree, everyone could drink water from this valuable cup. However, if a person was to try and take the cup with them, they would face severe punishment. Vlad ruled Wallachia for six years, and during those six years, not a single soul in his capital city of 60,000 people took the cup.

So, be it the gold of a stranger or a drinking cup for the masses, it was safe on Vlad's streets. People would remember the early days of his rule when thieves still robbed the weak and the powerless. But thanks to Vlad's unusual and disturbing practice of impalement, thieves thought better than to harass people with potentially deep pockets.

A Hearty Meal

Vlad's reputation had already begun to precede him. The king of Hungary knew of his repute, so he sent a total of 55 ambassadors to Dracula's court. The voivode received them well enough, giving them lodgings for the night, as well as food and entertainment. However, he had ordered that stakes be placed, erect, in front of the rooms of each individual ambassador. They were naturally afraid of this development, so they asked the monarch why he did this. He merely stated that it was for his own safety, that he was afraid of treachery. While they were staying at his court, the voivode invaded the Bârsa region. He would proceed to destroy everything—village huts, forts, fields full of wheat and rye, stored grain, it all went up in flames. His men captured the people of the Saxon town of Braşov, which allowed the dreaded prince to reach into the city as far as the chapel of St. Jakob. Before he arrived, he issued orders to have the town's suburbs burned to a crisp, which his men did, allowing the smoke and ash to welcome the ruler into the city.

But the Wallachian monarch didn't rest. The very next morning, he ordered the prisoners to be taken outside. Each and every prisoner was lined up at the foot of the mountain where the church of St. Jakob rested. The prisoners were many and varied: old men and women alike, youths not older than five, men and women of all statures and standings—all of them were now his prisoners. Of course, as was his wont, Vlad ordered a mass execution by impalement. Every single prisoner found their way to the stake, and soon they were all dead, lining the foot of the mountain and surrounding the chapel. Pleased with this grim state of events, Dracula approached a set table, filled with food. He sat down, pulled up a plate, and enjoyed every bite with the grizzly sight sitting before him.

But not even this satisfied the voivode. On St. Bartholomew's Day, he gave an order to burn two churches, including St. Bartholomew in the village of Codlea. His captain was sent to perform this task, but the locals rebelled and resisted the burning. The captain, with his tail tucked between his legs, returned to Vlad and told him that he had failed. The voivode, not one to tolerate failure well, had the captain impaled on the spot.

"The Forest of Corpses," a Saxon woodcut depicting Dracula having a meal while observing the torture and impalement of his enemies, from the title page of the incunabulum published by Markus Ayrer, Nuremberg, 1499[iii]

Discussing the Stakes

Benedict of Boythor was a Polish ambassador in the service of Matthias Corvinus, the king of Hungary. He was dispatched to Wallachia to discuss the matter of settling past aggressions with the Saxons of Transylvania with the current voivode. The king needed his important subjects to get along, which was not an easy task, considering that the Saxons and the Wallachians had been in disputes for years, if not decades. The ambassador reached Dracula's fort, and the two sat to eat dinner. At one point, Vlad ordered that the ambassador stay seated while the voivode's servant ran off to bring something. The corpses strewn across the room had already greatly unnerved the Polish man, but he remained calm enough. Moments later, the servant placed a huge, gelded stake on the table, right next to a serious, unflinching Dracula.

"Tell me, ambassador," the son of Dracul finally spoke, "why do you think I placed this stake on the table right now?"

Deathly afraid but still maintaining his composure, the ambassador replied, "It seems to me, your grace, that a man of some nobility had committed a great crime in your eyes. As such, you want to punish him with a death more honorable than any commoner might deserve."

Still as stern as a rock, the Wallachian autocrat continued, "Indeed, you are correct. You are a royal ambassador to a great and powerful king. Thus, I have made this stake for you."

Wiser than most, Benedict replied, "My lord, if you deem me as someone who has committed a great crime against you, do what you feel is just. You are an impartial judge, and should I die, you will not be the one to blame. The blame is on me and me alone."

A moment or two of silence passed. Soon enough, Vlad burst out laughing, slowly removing the stake. Almost immediately, he ordered that the Polish servant of King Matthias be showered with gifts, riches, and other fineries. "Had you not used those words, my good lord," Dracula said, "you'd have ended up dead upon this stake. You are indeed fit to be an ambassador of great rulers, for you have honed the art of speaking to great rulers. However, other ambassadors should not even dare to do this, not until they've learned the art of speaking to royalty like you."

A Captive of Ill Repute

Upon his fall from power, Vlad, the son of Dracul, had been a prisoner of the Hungarian Crown. But even though he was a prisoner, he was treated like more of an honored guest, someone who could freely walk about the estate, who could converse with barons and lords, and who could taste the finer things in life. But with men of ill repute, rumors tend to rise. Some people claimed that the former voivode had violated a girl and had left her with child. Vlad himself did not like this rumor, so he set about proving his accusers wrong in the most direct way possible. Using a dagger, he cut the poor girl open before the eyes of spectators, moments later showing her open womb and declaring that there was, clearly, no child inside.

Building a Castle

Shortly after reclaiming power in 1456, Vlad wanted to exact revenge on the boyars who had allegedly participated in the expulsion and murder of his father and his older brother. He invited these lords and ladies, as well as their extended family, to dinner one night, possibly on Easter Sunday. After the guests had their fill, Vlad ordered their swift capture. But he didn't immediately have them executed. Instead, he had them march many miles until they reached the almost ruined Poenari Castle. Vlad saw the strategic importance of this fort, so he had every prisoner toil day and night until they fully repaired it. Everyone, from the oldest man to the youngest babe, from the healthiest man to the frailest woman, had to work on rebuilding Poenari, and many of them died trying.

The Turbans

At one point, a delegation from the sultan came to visit Vlad. For years, Vlad had been preventing the Turks from capturing his land and turning it into an Ottoman province. He paid them tribute but refused them other commodities, such as young men and boys for their army. The delegation that arrived wanted to pay their respects to the Wallachian voivode, but Vlad was curious as to why they didn't take off their turbans. The Muslim soldiers replied that it was their custom that the turban always stayed on one's head. In fact, they did not even remove them for the sultan himself. Vlad saw fit to make the Turks keep their word, so he had his soldiers nail the turbans to the Turks' heads.

Vlad and the Priests

Though a religious man, Vlad had no tolerance for priests who did not see eye to eye with him. Two tales speak of his dealings with the men of the cloth.

Once, two priests came from a distant land. The son of Dracul invited them over, willing to have a talk with them. He asked a simple question to the first priest: "What do the people say about me?"

Scared for his life, the first priest mumbled that the people had nothing but words of grace for the voivode. "They think that he is noble and just," the priest said, adding that he was also saying the same things about the monarch. Vlad let him go, but he did not let the priest stray too far. He then asked the same question to the other priest.

"We all have to die someday," the other priest started, "so I'll tell the truth. The people despise you. To them, you are the worst tyrant to have walked the earth, and you've committed countless atrocities that I can't even recount. I know this to be true, for I have spoken with the people about you, and they told me no lies."

Dracula freed this priest, for he was telling the truth. When the other priest was asked the same question again, he simply repeated what the released priest had just said. Vlad had the monk impaled for having lied to him in the beginning.

Another time, a few priests from Gornji Grad (a Catholic convent in modern-day Slovenia) sought refuge in Târgovişte. They were well apprised of Vlad's dealings, but only one priest, Brother Hans, had the courage to confront the voivode. "You tyrant, you murderer, you absolute despot!" the priest cried. "How vile are you to kill innocents? What did the pregnant women do to deserve to be maimed and impaled like that? Or what about the children? Some were only three years old. Others were not even three hours old! Yet you impale them all, healthy and ill alike, young and old alike, both guilty and innocent. Tell me, why kill those who committed no crimes? Why women and children?"

Dracula, of course, had a ready response. "If you need to clean your soil for plowing, you should do it properly and thoroughly. You shouldn't only get rid of the stems of weeds and thorns but also the roots. For, you see, if the roots are left behind, then another dangerous weed will grow, stronger than before. For that reason, I have to weed out my adversaries before they even grow up. These children are those adversaries."

In order to "honor" Brother Hans for his insult, Vlad impaled him personally. Moreover, he didn't use the tried and true method of inserting the stake through the anal cavity. Instead, he forced the sharp stake directly into Brother Hans's forehead. His head was now at the bottom, with his feet in the air, and he thus hung on that stake upside-down, terrifying the other monks so much that a few of them fled, barely surviving to tell the tale.

Sacking Bulgarian Lands

Vlad moved with his army to Nicopolis in 1462. The voivode made short work of the local Jews, Christians, and pagans, slaughtering over 5,000 people, not counting those who burned in the fires. Some of his soldiers spared dozens of maidens and beautiful women, asking the voivode if they could marry them. But Vlad would have none of it. He ordered that all of the soldiers and their women be chopped into pieces with swords and spears, much akin to slicing cabbage.

As a tributary state to the Ottomans, Vlad had to pay a yearly sum of money. He claimed to the Turkish emissaries that he would bring the tribute personally. The Turks, overwhelmed, welcomed him into Bulgaria, arriving on horseback in small groups. Once most of them were there, Vlad enacted his plan and had them all slaughtered. This was an easy task since none of the Ottomans came bearing arms. Shortly after, the Wallachian voivode would burn Bulgaria to the ground, taking 25,000 lives that day, at the very least.

Portraits and Artistic Depictions of Vlad III

Vlad the Impaler had been somewhat of a celebrity in late medieval Europe. Even during his own life, minstrels and bards would travel the countryside and sing of his exploits at various royal courts. As such, certain rulers became interested in what this monstrous man looked like, so much so that they would pay good money to have his portrait hung on the wall of their castle.

Quite a few portraits of Dracula exist from medieval times, but before we can assess whether or not they match his historical appearance, we need to find out if there was an eyewitness description of the voivode from when he was alive. As luck would have it, there was one person with both the capabilities and proximity to the Impaler who provided a physical description of him.

During Vlad's reign, Hungary, as well as other Catholic Balkan countries, was in frequent correspondence with the pope, usually on the matters of foreign affairs and dealings with heathens. Since the pope operated from Rome, he would send formal legates to various European courts, and these legates would serve as the Catholic representatives of the Holy See. One such legate was a Croatian bishop called Nicholas of Modruš. Nicholas was a learned man who was well-versed in the Glagolitic script and the matters of faith, and he was a papal legate at several European courts, most notably that of the Bosnian king Stephen Tomašević and of the Hungarian king Matthias Corvinus. Considering that Nicholas lived until 1480 and that he had been a court staple throughout his service to Corvinus, he had to have met Dracula at some point in his life.

Upon meeting the voivode for the first time, Nicholas was as fascinated as most people would be. "He was not very tall," begins the legate, "but had indeed been quite stocky and strong, bearing a terrible, cold appearance. He had a strong, aquiline nose, wide nostrils, a reddish, thin face upon which the exceptionally long eyelashes framed his large, wide-open green eyes; those eyes were made threatening with his thick, bushy black eyebrows. Both his face and chin were clean-shaven, except for his notable moustache. The swollen temples appeared to be increasing the bulk of his head. A neck thick as a bull's connected with his head, and from his head hung thick, black, curly locks of hair, falling on his wide-shouldered back."

From this image, we can see that Dracula must have been quite imposing, despite the fact that some of his traits were not those characteristic of a stern, harsh ruler. Usually, medieval nobles like the Serbian emperor Stefan Dušan the Great and the Hungarian general John Hunyadi were described as tall, gallant men. Dracula being described as "not very tall" and "stocky" invokes an image of an everyman rather than a ruler, and his facial characteristics (bushy unkempt brows, thick dark hair, mustache, sunken features) only support that image. However, Nicholas saw it fit not only to describe Vlad in detail but also to provide the pope with some of the earliest stories recorded about him and his cruelty in Wallachia (Nicholas did so as early as 1462, the same year Vlad was imprisoned by King Matthias).

Even though Nicholas didn't capture every single detail about the voivode (like his garb, his posture, etc.), we still have a basic description to go off of when we delve into the many portraits of Vlad. Indeed, almost a dozen portraits of the Impaler have survived from the Middle Ages, which is more than any other Wallachian ruler. But before we discuss those, we need to cover the extraordinary circumstances that led to their creation.

As the stories of the voivode spread throughout Europe, they caught the ear of Ferdinand II, Archduke of Further Austria. Though he had come to power in 1564, which was almost a century after Vlad's death, the archduke had a keen eye for the arts, as was the case with a great number of European nobles during the Renaissance era. An avid collector, Ferdinand moved into Ambras Castle at Innsbruck, using it as his place of residence in 1567. Within the castle walls, he began collecting a wide variety of items such as armor and weaponry, musical instruments, scientific apparatuses, and precious items, as well as various paintings from different artists, well-known and anonymous alike. The castle still stands today, though a great portion of the collection had to be moved to the Kunsthistorisches Museum in Vienna.

Ferdinand II wanted his collection to be as varied and intriguing as possible, which is why we find, among other things, portraits with unusual and morbid undertones, somewhat akin to showcasing circus freaks on canvas. Four portraits, in particular, stand out from the collection. The first is that of Petrus Gonsalvus, or rather Pedro González, a Spanish man with a rare condition known as hypertrichosis. González had an excess of hair growing on his face and all over his body, making him look like a werewolf. He had been a staple of several European courts, most notably that of Parma, Italy, where he had married and become a member of the nobility. Because the portrait's first appearance was at Ambras Castle, the condition we know as hypertrichosis also bears the name "Ambras syndrome"; as an aside, this condition still occurs today, affecting no more than fifty people worldwide.

The next notable portrait is associated with Gregor Baci (though not explicitly so), a Hungarian nobleman who had survived a fatal injury to the head. The portrait itself depicts a man with a lance rammed through his head, more specifically through his right eye socket, with the left eye bulging out unnaturally and bleeding and a small scar on the left side of his shaven scalp. Legend has it that Baci survived a joust and had lived with the spear in his socket for about one year before ultimately succumbing to his injury.

The third in the list of portraits is that of a man with an evident disability. As far as portraits go, this one has an incredibly bizarre composition, showing a man prostrate on the floor, almost naked save for a neckpiece and a hat, both of which look expensive and made for the higher classes. He is looking directly at the viewer, which makes the painting all the more unsettling. When an onlooker analyzes the man's body, they can ascertain that his arms and legs are withered and bent unnaturally to the point of being useless. Initially, the painting contained a red piece of paper covering the body, forcing the viewer to remove the paper and get shocked by the revelation underneath. According to some art critics and historians, the painting probably depicts a court jester since it was not uncommon for people with physical disabilities to entertain monarchs.

However, it is the fourth portrait that we ought to focus on, for it is the most famous artistic depiction of none other than Vlad the Impaler himself. Looking into the middle distance and dressed in a mix of Wallachian and Ottoman garb, the voivode looks every bit as menacing as Nicholas of Modruš described him. There are some discrepancies, such as Vlad being depicted with somewhat fair hair (it's not as dark as Nicholas described it) and with well-groomed eyebrows, but everything else is right there, from the hawkish nose to the wide-open eyes and thick mustache. Notably, the Ambras portrait also shows Dracula with an oversized lower lip, which seems to have been a staple of his portraits at the time.

We should note that the Ambras portrait was painted in the 16th century, well after the Impaler had passed away. However, art historians believe that the portrait is based off on an older painting with only a few stylistic changes. The portrait at Ambras was meant to show the voivode as a "psychogram of evil" rather than just a ruler. And considering the impression it left next to the other three portraits described above, this portrait, made decades after the Impaler's death, is a testament to just how infamous and fascinating he was to the medieval man.

Medieval and Renaissance paintings saw the voivode as a spectacular leitmotif in artwork that featured some sort of grim scene, usually from the Bible. The first known depictions assumed to be those of the Impaler, as seen in the Ambras portrait, were found as early as 1460 when Vlad was still in power at Târgovişte. One such painting is the Calvary of Christ, a fresco in the Maria am Gestade church in Vienna. A man bearing a striking resemblance to Dracula, right down to his robes and headgear, is seen conversing with another person. Another painting, called *Pilate Judging Jesus Christ*, depicts Pilate as the Wallachian voivode, again right down to the robes and headgear. This painting was made in 1463, a year into Vlad's imprisonment at Visegrád. But perhaps the most famous example can be found in the Österreichische Galerie Belvedere museum in Vienna in a painting called *The Martyrdom of Saint Andrew*. Curiously, Dracula is depicted as one of the onlookers, observing Saint Andrew as he is being tortured by three other men. Not only does the appearance of this enigmatic onlooker match that of Dracula, but his apparent enjoyment of the brutal scene was well in line with how the Saxons of Transylvania depicted him to the Viennese people.

And speaking of the Saxons, we have to include the earliest known portraits that actually depicted Dracula in person and didn't use him as a motif in an artistic rendering of a biblical event. These portraits all come from the incunabula printed in the late 15th century, with the earliest surviving copies dating back to 1488 and 1491. On both of these pamphlets, we see the portrait of Dracula, once again looking into the middle distance, with an ornate headdress and elaborate garb. But more importantly, we can see the facial features of the man that terrified so many Saxons back in his day, and once again, we see that everything Nicholas of Modruš said about the voivode (save for a few notable details) fits the description perfectly. This Vlad is just as long-haired, mustachioed, and bug-eyed as the portrait at Ambras depicts him, but we also see the sunken face, the pronounced lower lip, and the thick bushy eyebrows. Even in this stylized form, Dracula shows an imposing, dreadful presence to the viewer, so much so that an average Saxon would gladly read any shred of info on the man.

One of the last known depictions of Vlad during the Renaissance era is from the 17th century, and to date, it is the only Renaissance painting that shows the voivode's full body. Currently on display in the Gallery of Ancestors of the Hungarian House of Esterházy, located in Forchtenstein Castle in Austria, this full-sized portrait shows Vlad as a gaunt, somewhat emaciated man wearing royal garb, with a saber at his hip and a mace in his hand. Though not as detailed as some of the other depictions of the voivode, it certainly follows the trend of showing him as a man of action and morbid mystery, keeping the same bulging eyes and the same aquiline nose.

Of course, not all contemporary depictions of Dracula were consistent. For instance, within the Saxon incunabula, there were depictions of scenes with the Impaler dining in a forest of impaled corpses. While we do see some elements that match the other portraits, such as the mustache, the bulging eyes, and even the headgear to an extent, we also see that the voivode is sporting an unkempt beard. Naturally, having a beard was not uncommon among medieval rulers, Christian and Muslim alike, but Nicholas himself clearly stated the voivode had a clean-shaven appearance and a groomed mustache. We can speculate that the Saxons who departed Transylvania did so at a period where Vlad might have had a beard, but the more likely scenario is that the artist simply did this rendition of the Impaler with a bushy, messy beard to give him more of an insane look. There are even a few woodcuts that show Vlad with short hair and a turban, which is more reminiscent of a Turkish bey or a janissary than a Wallachian lord; even more noteworthy is the absence of that morbid insanity and cruel, calculated stare that came to dominate most Dracula artwork. Instead, here we see a rather content man gazing blissfully forward.

Artistic depictions of Vlad III, both oral and on canvas, were not kind to him. They would almost exclusively come from Germanic sources, so there would always be an air of monstrosity to them that practically dehumanized the voivode. However, the artists who depicted him visually knew to give him that aristocratic gravitas, from the earliest portraits all the way until the Renaissance. Despite his unimpressive description given to us by Bishop Nicholas, we can definitely see an important trait that only someone like Vlad would emanate—that of a man who, despite his appearances, made a dent in human history to the point where he terrified people even centuries after being dead.

Saxon woodcut depicting the portrait of Vlad the Impaler, Nuremberg, 1488

Chapter 5 – The Character of Dracula: Personality Traits, Motivations

Dracula has always been one of those historical figures that fascinate mankind on multiple levels. It's not that much of a stretch to compare him to other popular figures like Hitler, Stalin, Rasputin, Napoleon, Caligula, Gandhi, Alexander the Great, William the Conqueror, Joan of Arc, Einstein, or Ivan the Terrible. As we saw earlier, the public image of the Impaler had been a conversation starter many decades after his death, to the point where some of the biggest European elites were fascinated by him and, arguably, even dreaded him. Moreover, the rekindled interest for the voivode after Bram Stoker published his novel only helped to show that the people of the late 19th century had the same type of passion and fascination that those of the 15th century did, as do the people living today. And that passion has everything to do with how a controversial person acted and, more importantly, why they acted that way.

It's incredibly difficult to discern personality traits of someone who has long been gone. Most of the time, when historians try to give a character profile of a historical figure, they have to piece it together from any number of relevant sources, which is not always easy to do. For example, we can't really say what type of person Aristotle was like since none of his original writings survived, nor are there any written works that describe him in detail. Moreover, we don't have any of his correspondence (like letters and such), so we can't ascertain what kind of views he had and how he acted upon them. On the other hand, we have people like H. P. Lovecraft who wrote tens of thousands of letters, detailing their life and opinions prominently. That's why we know more about Lovecraft, who lived in the early 20th century, than we do about Aristotle, and we still don't know everything about the horror author.

How do these examples relate to Vlad III, however? Well, before we can discern what type of person he was, we need to go over everything we know about his character from the limited information gathered about him. Very few documents issued by or written by Dracula survive, and those that do offer scant clues into his character. Quite literally, more than 90 percent of the sources that mention Dracula are outside of Wallachia, and they often contradict themselves. More importantly, they weren't always written by people who had his best interests in mind. The courtiers at Buda or Catholic monks would frequently refer to the voivode as someone beneath them, while the Saxons would portray him as an outright monster. On the other hand, the Kievan Russians and some of the local Balkan populace would hail him as a hero and a man of virtue. And then there were ancient historians who would merely mention the Impaler in passing, not really providing an opinion one way or the other.

So, in order to make heads or tails of what Dracula was like, we need to provide a few caveats, and they are as follows:

> • There is not enough information about this ruler; before any deeper analysis can be conducted, we need to find more contemporary sources that look into Vlad III on a personal level

- Not all of the sources we have on him are reliable; depending on who wrote them, they can differ wildly from the actual person that lived in and ruled over Wallachia in the 15th century

- Aside from the sources, we also need to take into account where Dracula was born, where he lived, the events that shaped his life, the acts he performed during his life, the company he kept, and the legacy he left behind; in other words, we have to let his actions speak for him.

Obviously, the first thing we need to address is the Impaler's supposed extreme cruelty. It's undeniable that the voivode committed numerous acts during his three reigns that people in the 21st century would deem inhumane. Aside from impaling, there were also decapitations, public executions, mutilations, potential genocides, unfair taxation, and open xenophobia, among others. Considering how often these acts occurred during his time on the throne, and how frequently both people sympathetic to his cause and his fiercest detractors spoke of them, a reader would not be judged too harshly if they thought that Vlad III was one of the cruelest people in Europe at the time. But therein lies the misconception. Vlad's cruelty, as heinous as it might have been, was the norm for the time. Both his frequent allies (the Moldavians, Hungarians, Bulgarians) and his enemies (the Ottoman Empire, Wallachian claimants to the throne, Transylvanian upstarts) employed similar, if not the same, methods of punishment. In that sense, we can say that Vlad's cruelty was calculated and very much warranted for the time.

This brings us to a specific personality trait that we can definitely ascribe to the infamous voivode. Namely, Vlad III was possibly one of the shrewdest politicians in the Balkans at the time, more or less on the same level as Skanderbeg, John Hunyadi, Đurađ Branković, Mehmed the Conqueror, and Matthias Corvinus. During his short time in office, Vlad knew exactly what types of measures he needed to employ to keep his realm safe and in one piece. Oftentimes, he would solve disputes and issues with brute force, such as punishing the traitorous boyars who claimed loyalty to any voivode before him if they found it beneficial. Other times, he would settle for lesser forms of punishment, such as banishing his adversaries or issuing edicts that banned trade. But Vlad also exhibited examples of positive behavior. During his reign, the native Wallachians of Transylvania, as well as Wallachia proper, enjoyed a period of relative stability. Laws were enforced, and the average villager felt secure that they wouldn't be mugged or killed out in the open. Dracula also donated vast amounts of wealth to monasteries and, despite his later conversion to Roman Catholicism, was a patron of the Wallachian Orthodox Church. For instance, he gave tax exemptions to the monasteries of Cozia and Tismana, probably expanded the Monastery of Snagov, founded the Comana Monastery as well as a church in the city of Târgşor, and donated graciously to the monasteries at Mount Athos, located in modern-day Greece. In addition, he was most likely instrumental in enabling the Wallachian Orthodox Church to elect its own metropolitan; in his time, metropolitans were elected from the clergy at Constantinople, so his promotion of the abbot of Cozia to the position of a metropolitan singlehandedly gave the Wallachian Church its independence from the Ecumenical Church in the Eastern Roman capital.

We should note that the positive aspects of Vlad's reign, just like the negatives, were not a reflection of him as either a "morally good" or a "morally evil" person. In fact, all of them show just how prudent he was as a ruler. Donating to the churches and monasteries in medieval times was almost a requirement for a ruler. It didn't make matters any easier if you were a child from a religiously mixed marriage (and those were a dime a dozen in an area laden with both Orthodox and Catholic Christian rulers, as well as rulers who belonged to other minor sects of Christianity and Islam). Moreover, if you were a bastard child born out of wedlock or out of infidelity, the Church had the power to sway public opinion against you. And let's not forget that Vlad's father was an illegitimate son of a previous ruler and was, in the eyes of many Wallachians even during the Impaler's reign, an illegitimate successor of the great Basarab name. And to top it all off, Vlad had been in the sultan's court as a child, so fears of him becoming a Turkish vassal and subjugating the Christian majority to Islamic rule were very much warranted. Vlad becoming a patron of the Orthodox Christians was not merely a shrewd decision on his part; realistically speaking, he more or less had no other choice.

However, his intellect was just as notable in foreign affairs. The voivode became an ally of several key players early in his political career. He knew that he had to secure an alliance with the Hungarians and the Moldavians and that he had to pacify the Transylvanian Saxon and Szekler communities. With Moldavia, he didn't have too many issues, considering how long the two realms had collaborated with one another. Vlad knew how to capitalize on these relations; had it not been for his one border disagreement with Stephen the Great, he would have remained in power a lot longer than he did. The Hungarians, on the other hand, were not exactly friends to the Wallachian throne, and Vlad knew that very well. His alliance with the court at Buda was purely out of political interest, considering he needed strong allies against the Turks. At the time, few Balkan-based realms could stand up to the sultan, so Hungary appeared as the logical solution.

And it's his very relationship with the Turks that brings up a key aspect of Vlad III that we can safely say was an important part of his personality—vengefulness. Again, this trait was common with medieval rulers, but knowing what we do about the voivode, we can definitely say that his whole raison d'être was to take vengeance upon the Ottomans. Being taken in as a young boy on the cusp of adolescence by the sultan's forces must have triggered a massive sense of xenophobia in Vlad, a kind obviously not found with his brother Radu. But then again, the two were treated somewhat differently, insofar as Radu was clearly the meek, submissive favorite, and the older Vlad was the upstart who didn't know his place. Gradually, Dracula's outbursts at Edirne would subside, but his hatred for the Ottomans only grew from there. So, when he finally reached power in a more tangible sense, i.e., when he became voivode for a second time, he took a more aggressive stance toward his former captors. Not only did he defy the Ottoman court often, but he would also exact severe punishments upon his captives. Even in his losing battles, Vlad would prove to be a ruthless warrior whom even some of the sternest of Turkish warriors feared.

Of course, his vengeful nature also showed in his dealings with traitors and non-Wallachians. He treated the Transylvanian Saxons in a similar manner as the sultan would with his disloyal subjects, by subjecting them to everything from torture to impalement. And while the stories published by the Saxons decades later definitely have a lot of exaggeration to them, there was a grain of truth to Dracula's supposed cruel treatment of their people while he was in charge. Let's not forget that, even if there is a possibility that he wasn't born there, Vlad certainly did grow up in Transylvania during a period where the Saxons, as subjects, didn't have a lot of love for any Wallachian overlord, and that the ethnic relations were, to put it lightly, tense. In other words, the reason behind Vlad's cruel treatment of the Saxons is the possibility that the Saxons treated him just as badly when he was a youth.

Judging by the contemporary views of the Wallachians, Vlad was harsh but never to the point where he wasn't respected or even admired. Indeed, most contemporary Wallachian, Moldavian, and Slavic sources claim that Vlad was counted among the greatest rulers that his land had ever seen. Not only did he donate graciously to a multitude of monasteries, but his punishments also didn't seem as frequent or as severe when they were directed at his own native folk. Of course, the punishments were still far from being mild or even warranted, but when comparing the treatment of the Wallachians in Vlad's land to that of the Saxons, we can definitely say that his own people were somewhat better off. With that in mind, we can ascertain that Vlad III was, in a medieval sense of the word, a great patriot and loyal to his people. Thanks to his reputation, even the people outside of Wallachia, including members of royalty, feared him and saw him as a force to be reckoned with. Local boyars and noblemen could no longer exploit the system, and interestingly, the lowest classes saw some improvement when it came to their daily lives. Local legends suggest that thanks to Vlad's brutal penalties, thievery had gone down so much that you could leave a chest full of gold outside, and nobody would dare to take it. And while this is most certainly hyperbole, considering it's a rumor from his time, it's not too much of a stretch to claim that his methods worked in favor of the people.

One other key piece of circumstantial evidence to the theory of Vlad being patriotic is the reactions of the common folk. As the years went by, rebellions (the ones not instigated by foreign powers or local pretenders to the throne) were greatly reduced, and Dracula enjoyed a fair amount of loyalty coming from his native Wallachian common folk. It had been a while since they could rally behind a leader who was as consistent and rational as Vlad, despite his bloody habits. In fact, even people today who live in the rural area where Vlad spent most of his life revere him as a national hero, and most of the legends surrounding him there have a positive spin to them. So, without a doubt, we can say that Vlad's dealings with outsiders such as the Saxons and the Turks were partly inspired by his love of the common folk and the desire to do right by them.

Remains of Vlad III's Princely Court, Târgovişte

Chapter 6 – Dracula's Successors: Descendants of the Impaler

The story of the Impaler is fascinating enough on its own, but historians (as well as lay readers and researchers) often focus on the more prominent aspects of his life, i.e., his imprisonment by the Turks, his bloody reign, his military exploits, his death, and, most notably, his methods of executing law and justice. However, few tend to focus on Vlad's immediate family, as well as his offspring and successors.

As a ruler and a member of the royal family, Vlad had a family history every bit as complicated as that of the most noteworthy monarchs in Europe. He was married at least twice and, as was customary (though not legal or moral by any standard), probably had more than a few mistresses. And while he did die with the reputation of a monster and a tyrant, he did not die without issue. The Drăculeşti line would continue through three major branches, and all three of those were started by the surviving sons of Vlad II Dracul. So, before we move onto discussing Vlad's own progeny, we should quickly cover those of his brothers.

By far the most prominent descendant of Dracul, other than Vlad himself, was his younger brother Radu. A favorite of Mehmed II's court, Radu quickly rose in the Ottoman ranks and became a skilled military commander with a learned background. Some sources even speculate that he had a prominent part in the Siege of Constantinople in 1453, though these are unconfirmed.

Unlike Vlad, Radu was a prominent supporter of the sultan, and when Mehmed's army began invading Wallachia in the early 1600s, he was one of the generals at the forefront. When Vlad was captured and taken to Hungary, the sultan installed Radu as the bey of Wallachia, legitimizing him as the successor of the Impaler. Interestingly, Wallachia had not become a pashaluk (a province governed by a pasha, i.e., a high-ranking Ottoman noble, as an integral part of the empire) but had retained its independence, merely paying the yearly tributes despite the fact that the ruler was possibly the most staunch Ottoman supporter at the time. One notable consequence of Radu's reign is the fact that the *Sipahi* ("cavalrymen") of the Turkish army increased their activity in southern Wallachia, settling there.

Radu would come to clash with Stephen the Great of Moldavia on multiple occasions, with their first battle being at the Soci River for the city of Chilia in 1471. Bizarrely, Stephen would dethrone Radu a grand total of four times, always replacing him with Basarab Laiotă; even more bizarrely, Radu ruled Wallachia on four separate occasions, meaning he was dethroned and replaced by the same man due to the actions of Stephen the Great. But the bizarreness doesn't end there. Radu's only daughter, Maria Voichiţa, ended up marrying Stephen the Great in 1478, barely a few years after Radu's death. Through her line, Radu's descendants would come to rule over Moldavia, on and off, until the country's subjugation by the Russians. The last recorded descendant of this line died in 1704.

The other brother that had ruled over Wallachia in the Impaler's time was Vlad IV, known as Vlad the Monk. Some sources state that he was either a legitimate or an illegitimate son of Vlad II Dracul, but there is no definitive proof to either claim. Unlike his brothers, Vlad IV would not openly vie for the throne until the 1480s, when both Vlad III and Radu had long been dead. He would end up ruling longer than both of them, a little over thirteen years in total.

His own sobriquet, "the Monk," doesn't have a definite source. He was either an incredibly pious ruler, which was not uncommon at the time, or he simply dressed in priestly garb to avoid being killed for political purposes during Vlad's and Radu's turbulent reigns. He himself would dethrone (and be dethroned once by) Basarab IV Țepeluș ("the Little Impaler"), a descendant of the House of Dănești, but Vlad IV would ultimately be succeeded by his son, known to history as Radu IV the Great. Vlad IV's descendants would come to rule both Wallachia and Moldavia, as well as Transylvania, at certain points in history. His own line of the House of Drăculești would see thirteen voivodes succeed him:

- Radu IV the Great
- Vlad V the Younger (also known as *Vladuț*)
- Radu of Afumați
- Radu Bădica
- Vlad VI Înecatul ("The Drowned")
- Vlad Vintilă de la Slatina
- Radu VII Paisie
- Mircea Ciobanul ("The Shepherd")
- Pătrașcu the Good
- Petru the Younger
- Vintilă, son of Pătrașcu
- Petru II Cercel
- Mihai Viteazul ("The Brave")

Naturally, Vlad III's successors didn't stand idly by during the post-Dracula years of Wallachia's history. The Impaler had two wives, with his second wife being Jusztina Szilágyi and the first still unknown to historians. Some speculate that she had been an illegitimate daughter of John Hunyadi, which would make Vlad's descendants with her potential candidates to the Hungarian throne. Other experts claim that Vlad probably never married the noblewoman in question. Whatever the case may be, these two marriages produced three sons. Vlad's second son's name doesn't appear in any official records, and the boy died at some point before 1486. The youngest son, also called Vlad, had been a minor noble in the court of the Hungarian king Vladislaus II, a member of the Jagiellonian dynasty and the direct successor to Matthias Corvinus. At some point in 1495, while stationed in southern Transylvania, Vlad began raiding the lands and became a contender for the throne held by Radu the Great. King Vladislaus ordered Vlad to cease all activities and move to the Banat region. Vlad acquiesced, and after his departure of Wallachia, he lived and died as a minor noble. However, the younger Vlad did manage to establish a new house within Hungary, known as the House of Sinteşti. Some of his descendants include Ludovicus Drakulya, his own two sons called Ladislaus (or Vlad) and John, and Ladislaus's son John Dracula de Band. John was the last known male descendant of Vlad's Sinteşti line, though the female descendants who bore the Dracula name survived well into the 18ᵗʰ century.

Another interesting case of a potential descendant of Dracula was a certain Russian priest called Vasian. Apparently, he had been a descendant of the families who fled from Wallachia (or Moldavia) to Russia and had styled himself with the signature of "Vasian, surnamed Dracula" while copying a 1512 chronicle in 1538. It's unclear whether he was really a descendant of Dracula, but if we were to assume that he was, he would have likely been a bastard child born out of wedlock.

By far the most prominent descendants of Vlad the Impaler came through his eldest son, Mihnea cel Rău ("The Evil"). As a staunch opponent of the Turks, Mihnea was incredibly similar to his father in terms of cruelty toward the disloyal boyars. Reports unfavorable to Mihnea state that he confiscated boyar property frequently, slept with their wives, worked the men to the bone, cut off the noses and lips of those who opposed him, and either hung or drowned the rest. Most of these stories come from the Craiovești boyars, who were his open adversaries, so they ought to be taken with a grain of salt. However, even if they are taken at their word, that would still make Mihnea not as infamous or as bloodthirsty as his late father.

Mihnea only ruled between 1508 and 1510, having fled Wallachia when the boyars revolted. His son, Mircea III, briefly ruled the land before being deposed by Vlad the Younger, while his other son, Miloş, had no prominent role in courtly affairs at the time. Mihnea's only daughter, Ruxandra, married the Moldavian prince Bogdan III cel Orb ("The One-Eyed"). After fleeing Wallachia, Mihnea settled in Sibiu, in his father's old home, and soon converted to Catholicism. One morning, he was leaving the Dominican Holy Cross church after a mass and was cornered by a group of 33 hired assassins. He was killed on the spot by Dimitrije Jakšić, a Serbian noble whose daughter Mihnea had raped while in power. Both Jakšić and the other 32 men were of the Craiovești boyar faction.

Mircea III, Dracula's grandson, might not have ruled for long, but he did have several noteworthy descendants. They were Alexander, Peter, and Miloş. Of the three, Miloş would be the only one who did not become a ruler. Since he was born with a withered arm, he spent his days as a professor in the patriarchal school of Constantinople and enjoyed great prestige among the Greek intellectual elites. He was also credited as the founder of the monastery of Nea Mone on Chios in 1573.

Peter, known as Peter the Lame due to a physical deformity, would become the prince of Moldavia without initially even knowing of his Wallachian origins, having been raised by the Turks his whole life. Since Peter was a weak ruler, he would be dethroned twice, but he left it willingly the third time after falling in love with a

Romani woman named Irina. The two moved to Bolzano, a city in the present-day Italian province of Tyrol, where Peter fell in love with another woman, a Circassian lady-in-waiting called Maria. She would give him an heir, Ștefăniță, who never ascended the throne. Peter died of syphilis in 1594 and was buried in Bolzano.

Alexander II Mircea was, therefore, the most prominent of Vlad III's great-grandchildren to ascend to the Wallachian throne, which Alexander did in 1568 (and then again in 1574). Soon after his coronation, he showed the same tendencies his ancestor had, decapitating over 200 boyars the very next month after his coronation. Several other massacres followed throughout his reign, and Alexander would, eventually, die in 1577, possibly due to poisoning by unsatisfied boyars. Aside from his massacres, Alexander was also known for imposing a ridiculous tax on unfertile sheep, as well as founding several stunning monasteries near Bucharest and Craiova.

Alexander's son, Mihnea II, would ascend the throne at twelve years of age, with his mother acting as a regent. They ruled until 1583, and they are remembered as extremely unpopular rulers, as they increased taxes constantly and continued the cruel policies of Alexander II. Mihnea was deposed in favor of Petru II Cercel and was held captive by the Ottomans, but his mother managed to buy favor with the sultan to have Mihnea reclaim the throne. During his next rule, from 1585 to 1591, Mihnea became even more infamous to the local Wallachians, so the Ottomans deposed him, this time in favor of Ștefan Surdul, a supposed harness maker and leather cutter. Humiliated, Mihnea tried vying for the Moldavian throne with no success and even went so far as to convert himself and his eldest son to Islam, taking the name Mehmed Bey. This political move earned him the sobriquet Turcitul ("The Islamized"), as well as the governorship of the sanjak ("district") of Nicopolis in Bulgaria. Despite these measures, he would die without reclaiming the Wallachian throne in 1601, buried in an unmarked grave.

Interestingly, Mihnea II's oldest son did not succeed him to the throne of Wallachia. That honor went to his youngest son, Radu Mihnea, and more importantly, the young voivode achieved this feat in 1601, the same year Mihnea died unceremoniously. Radu was possibly the most beloved ruler to descend from Dracula, having been an educated man of culture, a lover of the arts, and a great unifier who would come to rule both Wallachia and Moldavia, as well as Transylvania, a feat that was achieved only by one ruler before him, Voivode Mihai the Brave.

Radu Mihnea was instrumental during the peace of Hotin in 1621, which was concluded between the Ottomans (of whom Radu was the vassal) and the Poles. Both sides praised the ruler's prowess and ingenuity and were grateful for his mediation of the treaty. Aside from his diplomatic skills, Radu was also a great friend of the Orthodox Church, having gifted numerous monasteries, including the ones he was educated in. He died from gout in 1626 when he was 42 years old.

The last two descendants of Dracula who held any power in Wallachia were Alexandru Coconul ("The Child") and Mihnea III. Little is known of either, other than the fact that Alexandru ruled between 1623 and 1627 as a voivode of Wallachia and between 1629 and 1630 as a prince of Moldavia, while Mihnea III ruled Wallachia between 1658 and 1659, thus making him the last official ruler of the land who came directly from Dracula's male line.

Of course, the story of Dracula's descendants doesn't necessarily end there. At some point in Romania in the 1950s, a news article stated that the final descendant of the male line of Dracula had passed away a day earlier. However, people claiming to be the direct descendants of Vlad the Impaler were not a new phenomenon in Romania. In fact, some Romanian historians even claim to be descended from Vlad's bloodline. However, it might be possible that his successors through the female line still live to this very day.

Radu Mihnea, descendant of Vlad III, image over his tombstone, from Radu Voda Monastery, Bucharest[a]

Chapter 7 – Legacy of Dracula: Historical Importance, Bram Stoker's Novel, Popular View Today

The Historical Importance of Vlad the Impaler

Students of history will know how to recognize the importance of an event or a sequence of events not just out of emotional reasons (i.e., because they happen to like a certain individual) but out of an overall sense of historical cause and effect. As an example, let's take the fall of the Western Roman Empire in 476. To us, it marked the end of an era, a shift from the classical period to medieval times, with drastically different outlooks on life, customs, daily affairs, etc. Now, these differences are not so drastic when you actually live through them; to the average Roman citizen, the fall of Rome was a tragic event, but they didn't suddenly stop being Roman just because they lost their independence to a barbarian king. Indeed, to them, as brutal as it was, the fall of the empire was simply another day. The same goes for all events we deem historic and groundbreaking. However, that doesn't diminish their historical importance in the grand scheme of things, no matter how small their contribution seems to be.

When you study the medieval Balkans, you understand just how important this region is for the entire history of Europe, all thanks to individuals and events that occurred on this small peninsula. The Fall of Constantinople, for example, was an event that still echoes worldwide, as it represented the end of an era and resulted in a huge Muslim expansion in the East. That same expansion was greatly reduced by some important events happening before (the Battle of Kosovo in 1389) and after the fall (Skanderbeg's wars against the Turks, John Hunyadi's campaigns). Had it not been for these minor Balkan countries, the Ottoman expansion would definitely have come more rapidly, and the geopolitical map of Europe as we know it today would look drastically different.

In that sense, Vlad III was possibly one of the most important figures of his age. His shrewdness and cruelty aside, he was one of the few rulers at the time who could stand up to the Ottomans in an effective, meaningful way and manage to protect the smallfolk in the process. Though he didn't reign for more than six years, a figure which includes all three of his reigns, he definitely made an impact on the people at the time. His enemies grew to fear his tenacity and his propensity to do everything in his power to win. It's rare to see a minor noble like Vlad (for, in the grand scheme of things and looking at it objectively, he was a minor noble) stir up so much fear in the sultan of what was becoming the biggest empire in medieval times, the same sultan who had sacked a holy city not long ago (Constantinople's fall was still within living memory when Dracula came to power).

However, it's also rare to see just how much of an impact a supposed tyrant had on the common folk. Yes, they definitely feared him, much more than his successors (some of whom committed acts arguably just as cruel), but there was a trend growing among the Wallachian non-gentry, a trend that saw a rehabilitation of sorts of the Impaler. Villagers soon began to weave tales of their own concerning the voivode, and villages around the areas where he either dwelled or passed away started getting renamed, bearing either his own name or his sobriquet. To this very day, Romanian folklore in these areas is heavy with Dracula's spirit weighing it down, and the rural folks of Romania still fear him as if he had never died.

Folklore, like official historical documents, books, and letters, is incredibly important to modern historians. Dismissing folk tales about Dracula, or any historical figure, as simple fiction is by no means the right thing to do when studying history. Naturally, you need to take into account that there will be heavy distortions and changes, considering most of the folklore is passed down through oral tradition, and nothing from contemporary folklore should be believed at face value. But folklore, in and of itself, can serve as a good starting point in finding historical facts and even figuring out the potential thought processes and attitudes of the people living several hundred years ago. Some of the greatest discoveries (the city of Ur, the labyrinth at Knossos, the city of Troy) were made thanks to the archeologists and researchers taking written and oral legends into account. The same goes for Vlad III; though the legends about him may exaggerate numbers and get more than a few names wrong, some of the basic questions about his life and times can be answered by analyzing these folk myths to find scraps of useful, logical information.

Artistic Influence; Bram Stoker and His Novel

Even when Vlad was alive, the tales of his cruel acts had reached the ears of many prominent artists. Painters such as the German Renaissance artist Matthias Grünewald and the Swiss painter Niklaus Manuel Deutsch prominently depicted death and gory scenes in their work, with Deutsch even portraying a brutal group impaling in his painting *The Martyrdom of the Ten Thousand*. It became quite an evident trend among the Germanic Renaissance authors, these depictions of gruesome deaths and graphic imagery, and it's not that far-fetched to claim that these painters, among others, had read the incunabula containing the stories of Vlad the Impaler since they were very much in print during the artists' lifetimes.

Other artists of later centuries also tried their hands at depicting gruesome scenes, though when it came to Dracula himself, he underwent a slight shift from a tyrant to a pragmatic yet cruel leader fighting for independence. The interest for the Wallachian voivode would have died down had it not been for a novel by an Irish writer that, unwittingly, put the old monarch back into the limelight, though not in the best of ways.

Bram Stoker published his novel, *Dracula*, in 1897. The novel was not an immediate hit, though Victorian readers did receive it positively, embracing it as a good adventure story. However, Stoker almost unwittingly spearheaded a new "school of thought" on Vlad the Impaler, ascribing to him a number of misattributions that sometimes went completely contrary to historical facts. As Stoker himself stated, he knew next to nothing on the voivode, and what limited knowledge he had on Wallachia, he based on a somewhat obsolete source, a book published in 1820 with the title *Account of the Principalities of Wallachia and Moldavia with Political Observations Relative to Them* by William Wilkinson. Stoker's interest was simply to write a good novel featuring vampires after being inspired by an article about Transylvanian vampiric activity that had been published two years prior. In fact, the main villain of the piece wasn't even called "Dracula" in his early drafts and instead bore the name *Count Wampyr*.

There are quite a few misconceptions about Vlad III that were a direct result of Stoker's novel becoming more and more popular over the years, so much so that actual historians took them at face value. Some of the more egregious ones are the following:

- In the novel, Dracula is a count; there is no title of "count" when it comes to either Wallachian or Transylvanian rulers. Vlad was a voivode (the roughest equivalent to that is "prince" or "duke").

- In the novel, Dracula is of Szekler origin; Vlad was actually Wallachian, from a long and established list of Wallachian rulers.

- In the novel, Dracula rules over Transylvania; while Vlad was born in Transylvania and did have both political and personal investment in the region, he was the ruler of Wallachia.

- In the novel, Dracula is portrayed as a bloodthirsty vampire, which his subjects are aware of it; vampirism is a widespread phenomenon throughout the Balkans even today, but no contemporary source actually references vampirism when talking about Vlad III.

Of course, readers (and even contemporary historians) can't be too harsh on Stoker; he was merely writing a novel with fantastical elements, and he decided to borrow the name of an infamous ruler from a distant land that would hopefully entice readers and pique their interest. Notably, Stoker did include a few passing references about Vlad's life in the novel, which were somewhat factually accurate. For instance, his characters discuss Dracula's victory over the Turks at a river that formed a natural border between the two nations. Considering Vlad's extensive warfare on the Danube, this nugget of information on Stoker's part is not false. The same goes for Stoker retelling parts of Dracula's life story, where he had been betrayed by his own brother who was loyal to the Turks. Once again, knowing what we know about Radu the Handsome and the final years of Vlad's second reign, we can commend Stoker for including that bit within the novel.

Ultimately, while Stoker's novel did cause harm to the historical research into Vlad the Impaler (to the point where his sobriquet, "Dracula," wasn't even used by official history books until after the novel had become popular), it also had a positive effect. More and more people became interested in the history of both Romania and Transylvania, which spearheaded the efforts of some scholars of Romanian studies to delve deeper into the House of Drăculeşti. As of today, the field of Romanian history has greatly expanded, and new discoveries about Dracula's time are being made almost every year, and it's in no small part thanks to Stoker sparking interest through his fiction.

Bram Stoker, circa 1906[ii]

Dracula Today: A View of the Impaler in Modern Times

Views of the Wallachian voivode fluctuated quite a bit in the 19th century, ranging from seeing him as a murderer and a sadist (a view no doubt inspired by the original Saxon texts) or as a benevolent leader who had to commit cruel acts (inspired by Wallachian folklore and the Slavic texts).

Interestingly, Communist Romania would elevate Vlad as a national hero but only doing so within the service of the Party and with heavy historical inaccuracies. Books, studies, papers, and treatises were written exalting the voivode and extolling his many virtues, painting him as the perfect Romanian national hero and, astonishingly, even justifying some of his brutal acts. Nicolae Ceaușescu himself, the president of the Socialist Republic of Romania and the country's most notorious dictator, saw Vlad as the perfect role model that a ruler should aspire to be, frequently saying so publicly. However, this view of the Impaler dealt a powerful blow to Romanian historiography at the time; lots of scholarly written material was censored or outright banned because it portrayed Vlad "in a negative light," i.e., it spoke both of his accomplishments and his atrocities. The situation regarding these historical revisions would not end until the regime change in 1989, and even then, it was a gradual climb back to regain some semblance of objectivity and historicity.

The 21st-century view of Vlad the Impaler is, therefore, one of pure scholarly fascination. Some political groups label his acts as hate crimes and genocides, but these are viewed through the lens of modern politics, and such opinions are not to be taken into consideration when discussing historical validity to any claims about the voivode. The interest in Vlad the Impaler has not waned among Romanian historians and researchers, and the relevant field of studies on the subject is constantly growing, especially since the Romanian intellectual elite has gained access to some of the latest research methods, as well as connections with professional historical institutes from across the globe, all in the interest of learning everything there is to know about the son of Dracul and his turbulent life.

Vlad the Impaler and the Turkish Envoys, *painted by Theodor Aman, oil on canvas, from National Museum of Romania, 1886*[xiii]

Conclusion

Fans of the fictional Dracula, now a staple of modern horror and a pop culture icon, may find it difficult to reconcile that image with the wide-eyed, stern, and haunting visage of the historical Vlad III the Impaler. In many ways, the Wallachian monarch is far more intriguing than the vampire count, with his life constantly ebbing and flowing, remaining full of thrills and excitement until the very end. But then again, truth, as they say, is stranger than fiction.

And indeed, a brief overview of Vlad's life does seem strange and unlikely, especially for a medieval minor noble. How many rulers can attest to being captured as a child by the Ottomans, raised there, then taking the throne for themselves, losing it once, retaking it again, murdering hundreds of thousands of people and successfully repelling the same captors that held him prisoner years ago (captors whose country was almost ten times the size of his), losing the throne again, being captured by a former ally's son, being released by that same person (and marrying his cousin, no less), winning war after war in reclaiming his country, retaking the throne again, and losing it for the final time in the heat of battle? How many rulers can say that they had so many stories written, spoken, and sung about him, or paintings painted of him that ended up in some of Europe's wealthiest castles, that it ended up terrifying some of Europe's most powerful rulers? And most importantly, how many rulers can attest that they had, in a sense, become the ruler of the people despite enacting some of the most monstrous punishments in human history?

Dracula was, more or less, a product of his time. With all of the nuances and context, we can see that he merely exaggerated his deeds, something other rulers before (and even after) him had done. The short period of his reign is almost disproportionate to the number of acts he committed, wars he fought, people he killed, people he protected, and locations he either visited or dwelled in. The mere fact that he still survives in Romanian folklore is more than enough to tell you just how much of an impact he has had on human history. He was a man who could impale hundreds of people in a single day just because they irked him a little bit, or cut down a trusted general or a staunch supporter for simply making an honest mistake. But he was also a man who could provide troops to protect his people, pass laws that would make it easier for his fellow Wallachians to trade without unfair competition, and both build and gift numerous monasteries to the same Church that probably didn't take too kindly to him. Ironically enough, Vlad was also a monarch who quite literally used underhanded means and barbaric acts to weed out corruption at the very top, and he did so effectively. And thanks to his prudent nature, he would take his long-overdue vengeance on the Ottomans over and over again, beating and humiliating them to the point of desperation.

Of course, we shouldn't romanticize Vlad the Impaler. In the end, he was a human being who committed horrible deeds for both personal and political reasons, which makes him comparatively less of a monster than, for example, some of the 20th-century's worst dictators. But we shouldn't exclude him from the history books either. Even modern rulers can learn a thing or two from Vlad's example (obviously avoiding all of the slaughter) and, in doing so, manage to run a country in a way that makes the little guy feel safer.

Here's another book by Captivating History that you might like

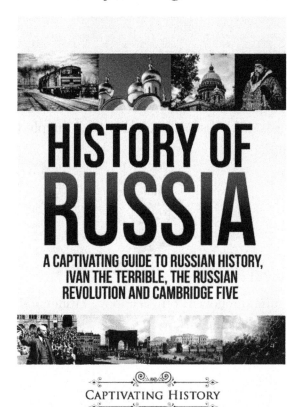

Free Bonus from Captivating History (Available for a Limited time)

Hi History Lovers!

Now you have a chance to join our exclusive history list so you can get your first history ebook for free as well as discounts and a potential to get more history books for free! Simply visit the link below to join.

Captivatinghistory.com/ebook

Also, make sure to follow us on Facebook, Twitter and Youtube by searching for Captivating History.

References

Abraham, F. (2017). *Romania since the Second World War: A Political, Social and Economic History.* London: Bloomsbury Academic, an imprint of Bloomsbury Publishing Plc.

Andreescu, S. (1998). *Vlad Tepes: (Dracula): Intre legenda si adevar istoric.* Bucureşti: Editura Enciclopedica.

Bărbulescu, M., Deletant, D., & Hitchins, K. (2014). *Istoria României.* Bucureşti: Corint Educaţional.

Comunismul în România: 1945-1989. (2007). Bucureşti: Muzeul Naţional de Istorie a României.

Cosma, E. (2005). *Revoluţia de la 1848: Un catalog de documente şi regeste (Fondul Institutului de Istorie din Cluj).* Cluj-Napoca: Editura Argonaut.

Giurescu, D. C. (2000). *Romania in the Second World War: 1939-1945.* Boulder: East European Monographs.

Hitchins, K. (2009). *The Identity of Romania.* Bucharest: The Encyclopaedic Publishing House.

Ioniţă, G. I., Cârţână, I., Scurtu, I., & Petric, A. (1981). *Istoria României: Intre anii 1918-1981: Manual universitar.* Bucureşti: Editura Didactică şi Pedagogică.

Nedelea, M. (1994). *Istoria României: Compendiu de curente si personalităti politice.* București: Niculescu.

Petrescu-Dîmbovița, M., & Daicoviciu, H. (1995). *Istoria României: De la începuturi până în secolul al VIII-lea.* București: Editura Didactică și Pedagogică.

Platon, G. (1980). *Geneza revoluției române de la 1848: Introducere în istoria modernă a României.* Iași: "Junimea".

Romalo, M. (2001). *România în al doilea război mondial 1941-1945.* București: Editura Vestala.

Scorpan, C. (1997). *Istoria României: Enciclopedie.* București: Nemira.

Torrey, G. E. (1999). *Romania and World War I: A collection of Studies.* Iași, Romania: Center for Romanian Studies.

Akeroyd, J. (2009): The Historical Dracula: Monster or Machiavellian Prince?, In *History Ireland* Vol. 17, No. 2, (pp. 299-315). Dublin, IE: Wordwell Ltd.

Babinger, F. (1992): *Mehmed the Conqueror and His Time.* Princeton, NJ, USA: Princeton University Press

Cazacu, M. (2011): *Dracula.* Leiden, NL & Boston, MA, USA: Brill

Encyclopedia Britannica (1981), Retrieved on May 21ˢᵗ 2020, from https://www.britannica.com

McNally, R. T. & Florescu, R. (1989): *Dracula, Prince of Many Faces: His Life and His Times.* New York, NY, USA: Hachette Book Group

McNally, R. T. & Florescu, R. (1994): *In Search of Dracula: The History of Dracula and Vampires.* Boston, MA, USA: Mariner Books

Mihajlović, K. (2010): *Memoirs of a Janissary.* Princeton, NJ, USA: Markus Wiener Publishers

Perić, Z. et al. (2013): From Wallachian Duke to the Prince of Darkness, In *Researches Review of the Department of Geography, Tourism and Hotel Management* No. 42, (pp. 139-151). Novi Sad,

RS: University of Novi Sad, Faculty of Sciences, Department of Geography, Tourism and Hotel Management

Nandriş, G. (1959): A Philological Analysis of "Dracula" and Rumanian Place-Names and Masculine Personal Names in –a/-ea, In *The Slavonic and East European Review,* Vol. 37, No. 89, (pp. 371-377). London, UK: University of London, School of Slavonic and East European Studies

Nandriş, G. (1966): The Historical Dracula: The Theme of His Legend in the Western and in the Eastern Literatures of Europe, In *Comparative Literature Studies* Vol. 3, No. 4, (pp. 367-396). University Park, PA, USA: Penn State University Press

Radin, A. (1998): History, Legend, Literature: Prince Vlad Tepes alias Count Dracula, In *BALCANICA - Annual of the Institute for Balkan Studies* Vol. 29, (pp. 237-258). Belgrade, RS: Serbian Academy of Sciences and Arts, Institute for Balkan Studies

Treptow, K. W. (Ed.) (2018): *Dracula: Essays on the Life and Times of Vlad the Impaler.* Las Vegas, NV, USA: Histria Books

Wikipedia (January 15, 2001), Retrieved on May 21st 2020, from www.wikipedia.org/

Notes on Images

[1] Original image uploaded by Hohum on 31 December 2016. Retrieved from https://commons.wikimedia.org/ on May 2020 under the following license: *Public Domain.* This item is in the public domain, and can be used, copied, and modified.

[1] Original image uploaded by Qbotcenko on 9 November 2008. Retrieved from https://commons.wikimedia.org/ on May 2020 under the following license: Creative Commons Attribution-ShareAlike 3.0 Unported. This license lets others remix, tweak, and build upon your work even for commercial reasons, as long as they credit you and license their new creations under the identical terms.

[1] Original image uploaded by Osmanh98 on 15 September 2013. Retrieved from https://commons.wikimedia.org/ on May 2020 under the following license: *Public Domain.* This item is in the public domain, and can be used, copied, and modified.

[1] Original image uploaded by Herbythyme on 26 October 2007. Retrieved from https://commons.wikimedia.org/ on May 2020 under the following license: Creative Commons Attribution-ShareAlike 3.0 Unported. This license lets others remix, tweak, and build upon your work even for commercial reasons, as long as they credit you and license their new creations under the identical terms.

[1] Original image uploaded by Nagualdesign on 1 August 2014. Retrieved from https://commons.wikimedia.org/ on May 2020 under the following license: Creative Commons Attribution-ShareAlike 3.0 Unported. This license lets others remix, tweak, and build upon your work even for commercial reasons, as long as they credit you and license their new creations under the identical terms.

[1] Original image uploaded by Maxpushka on 27 January 2019. Retrieved from https://commons.wikimedia.org/ on May 2020 under the following license:

Creative Commons Attribution-ShareAlike 4.0 International. This license lets others remix, tweak, and build upon your work even for commercial reasons, as long as they credit you and license their new creations under the identical terms.

ii Original image uploaded by Qbotcenko on 9 November 2008. Retrieved from https://commons.wikimedia.org/ on May 2020 under the following license: Creative Commons Attribution-ShareAlike 3.0 Unported. This license lets others remix, tweak, and build upon your work even for commercial reasons, as long as they credit you and license their new creations under the identical terms.

iii Original image uploaded by Osmanh98 on 15 September 2013. Retrieved from https://commons.wikimedia.org/ on May 2020 under the following license: *Public Domain*. This item is in the public domain, and can be used, copied, and modified.

iv Original image uploaded by Herbythyme on 26 October 2007. Retrieved from https://commons.wikimedia.org/ on May 2020 under the following license: Creative Commons Attribution-ShareAlike 3.0 Unported. This license lets others remix, tweak, and build upon your work even for commercial reasons, as long as they credit you and license their new creations under the identical terms.

v Original image uploaded by Nagualdesign on 1 August 2014. Retrieved from https://commons.wikimedia.org/ on May 2020 under the following license: Creative Commons Attribution-ShareAlike 3.0 Unported. This license lets others remix, tweak, and build upon your work even for commercial reasons, as long as they credit you and license their new creations under the identical terms.

vi Original image uploaded by Maxpushka on 27 January 2019. Retrieved from https://commons.wikimedia.org/ on May 2020 under the following license: Creative Commons Attribution-ShareAlike 4.0 International. This license lets others remix, tweak, and build upon your work even for commercial reasons, as long as they credit you and license their new creations under the identical terms.

vii Original image uploaded by CoolKoon on 17 April 2012. Retrieved from https://commons.wikimedia.org/ on May 2020 under the following license: *Public Domain*. This item is in the public domain, and can be used, copied, and modified.

viii Original image uploaded by Dbachmann on 11 September 2011. Retrieved from https://commons.wikimedia.org/ May 2020 under the following license: *Public Domain*. This item is in the public domain, and can be used, copied, and modified.

ix Original image uploaded by Unibond on 31 December 2016. Retrieved from https://commons.wikimedia.org/ on May 2020 under the following license: *Public Domain*. This item is in the public domain, and can be used, copied, and modified.

x Original image uploaded by CristianChirita on 23 September 2011. Retrieved from https://commons.wikimedia.org/ on May 2020 under the following license: Creative Commons Attribution-ShareAlike 3.0 Romania. This license lets others remix, tweak, and build upon your work even for commercial reasons, as long as they credit you and license their new creations under the identical terms.

[xi] Original image uploaded by Alex:D on 20 June 2007. Retrieved from https://commons.wikimedia.org/ on May 2020 under the following license: *Public Domain*. This item is in the public domain, and can be used, copied, and modified.

[xii] Original image uploaded by Alexis Jazz on 19 July 2018. Retrieved from https://commons.wikimedia.org/ on May 2020 under the following license: *Public Domain*. This item is in the public domain, and can be used, copied, and modified.

[xiii] Original image uploaded by Bogdan on 31 July 2006. Retrieved from https://commons.wikimedia.org/ on May 2020 under the following license: *Public Domain*. This item is in the public domain, and can be used, copied, and modified.

Made in the USA
Las Vegas, NV
30 January 2022

42634840R00174